THE
MEETING *of* CIVILIZATIONS

To

Professor Herbert Kelman

Steven Bloomfield

David Salomon

In appreciation for your vision and support

THE
MEETING *of*
CIVILIZATIONS

MUSLIM, CHRISTIAN, AND JEWISH

Edited by
MOSHE MA'OZ

sussex
ACADEMIC
PRESS
Brighton • Portland • Toronto

Copyright © Sussex Academic Press 2009; editorial organization of this
volume copyright © Moshe Ma'oz, 2009

The right of Moshe Ma'oz to be identified as Editor of this work has been asserted
in accordance with the Copyright, Designs and Patents Act 1988.

2 4 6 8 10 9 7 5 3 1

First published 2009 in Great Britain by
SUSSEX ACADEMIC PRESS
PO Box 139
Eastbourne BN24 9BP

and in the United States of America by
SUSSEX ACADEMIC PRESS
920 NE 58th Ave   Suite 300
Portland, Oregon 97213-3786

British Library Cataloguing in Publication Data
A CIP catalogue record for this book is available from the British Library.

Library of Congress Cataloging-in-Publication Data
The meeting of civilizations : Muslim, Christian, and Jewish / edited by
Moshe Ma'oz.
p. cm.
Includes bibliographical references and index.
ISBN 978-1-84519-287-7 (h/c : alk. paper)
1. Judaism—Relations—Christianity—History. 2. Christianity and other
religions—Judaism—History. 3. Judaism—Relations—Islam—History.
4. Islam—Relations—Judaism—History. 5. Jews—Election, Doctrine of.
6. Jerusalem—History. 7. Religious education. I. Ma'oz, Moshe.
BM535.M395 2009
201'.5—dc22

2008018038

Mixed Sources
Product group from well-managed
forests and other controlled sources
www.fsc.org Cert no. SGS-COC-2482
© 1996 Forest Stewardship Council

Typeset & Designed by SAP, Brighton & Eastbourne.
Printed by TJ International, Padstow, Cornwall.
This book is printed on acid-free paper.

Contents

Part III *Education and Textbooks*

Part IV *Contemporary Relations and Challenges*

Preface

Two critical and related developments have occurred during the last decades: On the one hand, the emergence of militant Islamic groups committing many acts of anti-Western and anti-Jewish terrorism as well as verbal castigation. On the other hand, these phenomena have been depicted by many Christians and Jews as a "clash of civilizations," namely an Islamic onslaught on the Judeo-Christian civilization. Non-Muslim political and religious leaders, and even scholars, have characterized Islam in general – not militant Muslims – as a "violent," "wicked," and "anti-Semitic" civilization. For example, in his book *The Clash of Civilizations and the Remaking of World Order*, Prof. Samuel P. Huntington alleged in 1996 that "two-thirds to three-quarters of intercivilizational wars (in the early 1990s) were between Muslims and non-Muslims. Islam's borders are bloody and so are its innards."[1] Around the same time, Prof. Jean Kilpatrick, former US Ambassador to the UN, in a public lecture in New York, indicated that "Islam is a civilization that breeds violence." In September 2006, Pope Benedict XVI quoted a 14th century Byzantine Christian emperor Manuel II Paleologus: "Show me just what Muhammad brought that was new, and there you will find things only *evil and inhuman* (editor's emphasis), such as his command to spread by the sword the faith he preached" – a view probably based on the concept "the religion of Muhammad must spread by the sword" (*Din Muhammad bi'lsayf*) and perhaps also based on the notion of *Dar al-Islam* and *Dar al-Harb* (The Domain of Islam and the Domain of War).

Benedict also briefly considered the Islamic concept of *jihad*, which he defined as "holy war," and said that violence in the name of religion was contrary to God-s nature and reason."[2] In August 2006, President Bush declared that America is at war with "Islamic fascism." Earlier, he had referred to "Islamo-fascists" and described the war on (Islamic) terrorism as a "crusade."[3] Several Israeli-Jewish politicians and scholars went even further, equating Islam with Nazism, terrorism and suicide bombing.[4]

There is no doubt whatsoever that these horrific acts of terrorism committed by Muslim militants, notably the 9/11 suicide acts in the US as well as the vicious anti-Jewish expressions, are evil, inhuman and despicable. They must be eradicated by Muslims and non-Muslims alike in order to preempt an emergence of a comprehensive clash between Muslims, on the one hand, and Christians and Jews on the other. Indeed, these violent acts by Muslim extremists claimed the lives of many innocent people in the United States, Europe and Israel, including also innocent Muslims. Their acts have greatly contributed to the distortion of genuine and positive tenets of Islam, or Islam's mainstream, in the eyes of a growing number of Christians and Jews.

Unfortunately, the negative characterization of Islam by Western, Christian and Jewish leaders has in turn induced not a few Muslims to develop defensive and/or hostile attitudes toward the West and Israel. Many other Muslims have developed such attitudes owing to the US occupation of Iraq and Afghanistan, and the Israeli occupation of Palestinian territories, including East Jerusalem (1967), which has also nourished the newly emerged Muslim anti-Semitism.

This vicious cycle of antagonism, fear and alienation between Muslims and non-Muslims has been articulated in several international public surveys. For example, according to a Gallup poll prepared for the Davos Global Economic Forum in January 2008, most Muslims and Westerners believe that the rift between the two civilizations has aggravated and the chances for a dialogue between Islam and the West are slim. Similarly, a 2006 survey of the "Pew Global Affiliates Project" found that most Muslims and Westerners consider their mutual relations as bad, while blaming each other to be violent and intolerant.[5] This survey also indicated that anti-Jewish hostility in Muslim countries "is astonishing" with 98 percent in Jordan and 97 percent in Egypt (the only two Arab countries that have signed peace agreements with Israel).

By contrast, it should be stressed that prominent Muslims, including senior religious and political leaders, have in recent years advocated inter-civilizational dialogue and strongly denounced terrorist acts, suicide bombing as well as anti-Western and anti-Semitic expressions by Muslim extremists. And this, on the plea that these extremists do not represent the genuine tenets of Islam, or mainstream Islam. Thus, for example, in October 2007, 138 Muslim scholars and religious leaders issued an open letter to the Christian world entitled "A Common Word Between Us and You." Reportedly it represented "a part of a growing movement to strengthen mainstream Islam against violent extremism and to promote interfaith dialogue." Aref Ali Nayed, one of the Muslim signatories, stated *inter alia:* "Some minority voices, because of their extreme and violent nature, managed to capture media attention. This has resulted in a very skewed and distorted picture of Islam."

This unique Muslim message stressed the following notions: "The future of the world depends on peace between Muslims and Christians. The basis for this peace and understanding already exist. It is part of the very foundational principles of both factions: love of One God and love of the neighbour . . . So let our differences not cause hatred and strife between us . . . Let us respect each other, be fair, just and kind to another and live in sincere peace, harmony and good will."[6] Dozens of Christian theologians, scholars and leaders published a response open letter endorsing and applauding the Muslim public message and stressing that "peaceful relations between Muslims and Christians stand as one of the central challenges of this century."

Unfortunately in both open letters, representing a unique public Muslim–Christian dialogue, there was no direct appeal to Jews and Judaism.

Nevertheless, both letters briefly refer to the Jewish faith and to the Bible, namely: "some core common ground between Christianity and Islam which lies at the heart of our respective faiths as well as at the heart of the most ancient Abrahamic faith, Judaism." Also, for the first time representatives of the British Muslim community participated, in early 2008, in the Holocaust memorial service.[7] Around the same time a group of Muslim leaders and scholars called for a Muslim–Jewish dialogue, with no connection to the Arab–Israeli problem. On earlier occasions prominent Muslim leaders, such as Abd al Rahman Wahid, former president of Indonesia, and Muhammad Khatemi, former president of Iran, advocated dialogue of civilizations. Prince Hassan Bin Talal of Jordan, while highlighting the common heritage of the three faiths, indicated that "violence and faith are contradictions; hatred in Judaism and Islam, and violence justified by a mistaken interpretation of a faith is obviously the greatest threat to peace in our region and the world."[8]

Along similar lines, many interfaith societies and groups, mostly Christian–Muslim and also Abrahamic (including Jewish) have been active in the US, Europe and in the Middle East (mostly in Israel), working for dialogue or trialogue and peaceful co-existence.[9]

But despite these important initiatives and peaceful messages by religious leaders, many if not most Christians and Jews are still deeply concerned about the alleged Islamic threat to Judeo-Christian civilization. They tend to ignore the crucial differences between the dangerous radical Muslim groups and the mainstream of peaceful, moderate Muslims. Many Jews and Christians are also unaware of the great historical contribution of the Islamic civilization as well as its common values with the Jewish and Christian civilizations. Thus, vis-à-vis the populist concept of clash of civilizations, this book seeks to present the multiple, complex relations among the three Abrahamic-monotheistic faiths and civilizations, their commonalities and divergences, cooperation and conflicts, both in medieval and modern times. Obviously, it is beyond the scope of this volume to discuss in full these prolonged and intricate relations during the last two millennia, or even since the rise of Islam. Thus, in addition to a broad outline of Muslim–Christian–Jewish interconnections, mostly under Islamic rule, the contributors examine relevant and significant cases and issues in the fields of religion, culture, education and politics, including the problem of Jerusalem. A recurring theme throughout is the contemporary relations between Muslims on the one hand, and Christians and Jews on the other, and the obstacles and challenges all faiths and parties have to face.

The contributors to this volume are scholars and religious leaders – Christian, Jewish and Muslim – from North America, the Middle East, and South East Asia. They discussed these issues at Harvard University in late October 2007, at an international conference entitled "Children of Abraham: Trialogue of Civilizations." The conference was sponsored by Harvard's Weatherhead Center for International Affairs and Harvard Divinity School, and was generously supported by Mr. David Salomon, chairman, FATTOC and by Madison Tyler, Los Angeles. My deep gratitude and appreciation go to the sponsors. I am also grateful to Mrs. Esther Porath for her efficient work in preparing this manuscript.

Notes

1   (New York, Simon and Schuster, 1996), p. 258. For a critical article, see M. Steven Fish, "Islam and Authoritarianism," *World Politics*, 55 (October 2002), pp. 4–37.
2   Ian Fisher, *New York Times*, September 19, 2006.
3   Ori Nir, in *Forward*, August 18, 2006.
4   Robert S. Wistrich, *Muslim Anti-Semitism: A Clear and Present Danger* (American Jewish Committee, 2002). Raphael Israeli, *Islamikaze Manifestations of Islamic Martyrology* (London, Frank Cass, 2003).
5   See respectively *Ha'aretz*, January 22, 2008 and June 25, 2006. See also *The Economist*, June 24, 2006, pp. 29–33.
6   See respectively Guy Dinmore, *Financial Times*, December 22, 2007; <www.acommonword.com>, December 2007. See also Neil MacFaquhar, *New York Times*, October 12, 2007.
7   See respectively, *New York Times*, November 18, 2007; *Ha'aretz*, January 27, 2008; <www.islamonline>, February 26, 2008.
8   *Ha'aretz*, October 18, 2007.
9   See, for example, *Newsletter, Centre for the Study of Islam and Christian–Muslim Relations*: 34th Conference of Jews, Christians and Muslims, No. 57, Summer 2007.

THE
MEETING *of*
CIVILIZATIONS

MUSLIM, CHRISTIAN, AND JEWISH

Introduction

MOSHE MA'OZ

Among the three civilizations – Muslim, Christian and Jewish, – there have been throughout history a range of commonalities and divergences, as well as periods of cooperation and conflict. The main intercivilizational relations have obviously included Christianity and Islam, the two global communities. But the small ethnic Jewish communities were significantly involved in this interplay, not only because they have resided amongst or alongside Christians and Muslims. As the original monotheistic faith, Judaism had been both a point of reference and an ideological rival for both Christianity and Islam.

Judaism, Christianity and Islam, as we know, profess common divine and human values in different priorities: a belief in one God, his commandments, and the scriptures; social equality, justice and compassion. All three civilizations also consider in various degrees Abraham as their grand patriarch, and the Old City of Jerusalem as their holy center.

Yet each of these three religions over long periods claimed exclusivity and chosenness, as Prof. Reuven Firestone writes in Chapter 1, "A Phenomenology of Chosenness": "All three Scriptures convey a sense that there can be only one truly chosen and that being chosen necessarily excludes the other religious communities from the equation. In the language of game theory, chosenness in Scripture is often expressed as a 'zero-sum' situation. There can be only one chosen at any time." This has certainly been the position of Jews, the first "and only religious community of believers that truly understands and acts out the will of that universal God." Consequently not a few Jews have disavowed the revelations of Christianity and Islam. By comparison, both Christians and Muslims, although accepting that Jews had been the chosen people at one time, claim that they sinned and lost this unique standing to the new revelations.

Indeed, for almost two millennia most Christians believed that Christianity had displaced Judaism. But during the last decades the Catholic Church and most Protestants have discarded this belief. In contrast, many Muslims still believe that Judaism and Christianity had represented the first two phases of the Abrahamic religion, while Moses and Jesus had each a partial revelation of God. But Muhammad was bestowed the final and full revelation, making Islam the true and complete religion, the religion of Abraham. Accordingly, Abraham (Ibrahim) was the first monotheist (*hanif*) and the first Muslim (*Awwal al-Muslimin*), who also built, with his son Ishmael (Ismail) the Ka'ba in Mecca and subsequently the Aqsa Mosque in Jerusalem. Jews and Christians do not accept this Islamic narrative and adhere to the Biblical story.

Yet Christians believe that God's covenant with Abraham was rendered again to Jesus, the Messiah, a descendant of Abraham. Jews, by contrast, consider Abraham as their first patriarch and leader of the Hebrew nation. Nevertheless, they have acknowledged that Abraham was also the father of Ishmael, the patriarch of the Arab peoples (most of whom later became Muslims); although Ishmael was allegedly excluded from God's covenant. But apart from this initial "family connection," Jews and Muslims share Abraham's pure monotheism and a strong rebuff of Christian Trinity, and the divine nature of Jesus, the "son of God."

Other manifestations of commonalities and divergences among Jews, Christians and Muslims are their attitudes to the Jewish Bible. Part I – Religious and Historical themes – continues with Prof. Benjamin Braude's "Interdependence of Scripture" in Chapter 2: "The commonalities and divergences are particularly noteworthy with regard to Scripture. Christians, Jews and Muslims do and do not 'read' the same sacred text . . . Two share more Scripture with each other than they do with the third, but the sacred words of Jews are not exactly the same as the sacred words of Christians . . . Each sectarian tradition must be understood as part of a hermeneutic enterprise that is greater than any text alone. The interconnectedness of the three demonstrates that despite their many differences, Judaism, Christianity and Islam share the same sacred textual space. In that sense the three do read the same sacred text."

In addition to the notions of One God, Patriarch Abraham and the Holy Scripture, the Old City of Jerusalem is also sacred to Jews, Christians and Muslims alike, and these issues are addressed in Part II – Jerusalem A Center for the Three Civilizations. But for long periods of time each community claimed exclusivity, refusing to share it with the others. For Jews, Jerusalem has been for more than 3,000 years the only unique center of Judaism and the Jewish people; whereas Christianity and Islam, which appeared later in history, have their own religious centers: Rome and Constantinople, Mecca and Medina, respectively. And although the Jewish Temple was destroyed twice (in 586 BC and AD 70) and Jews were exiled, they have never disengaged from Jerusalem or forgotten it. They would occasionally vow, "If I forget thee, O Jerusalem, may my right arm wither." Over the last centuries, Jews have returned to Jerusalem from the Diaspora and since the early 20th century, they have outnumbered both Muslims and Christians in Jerusalem. In 1949 West Jerusalem became the capital of the newly-established Jewish state, Israel. And after the June 1967 war, Israel annexed East Jerusalem, including the Old City, and proclaimed the unified city as the eternal capital of Israel and the Jewish people.

Most Muslims and Christians strongly protested, although their religious freedom has not been curtailed, notably the Christians. Unlike Judaism and Islam, Christianity was born in Jerusalem through events related to the life and death of Jesus. The destruction of the second Jewish Temple was considered as a victory of Christianity over Judaism. Under the first Christian emperor, Byzantium (AD 326–614, 624–58), Jews were not permitted to reside in Jerusalem, but were admitted once a year, on the Ninth of Av, to mourn at the Western Wall of the destroyed Temple. Prof. Harvey Cox, in Chapter 5, "Making Jerusalem a 'Holy' City for Three Faiths," explains: "The Christian authorities of Jerusalem wanted the Jews to play an unintended role in a cruel theological drama. As the Jews wailed, the Christians watched and were told that their sorrow was a result of God's punishment on them for refusing the recognize their messiah. By the 600s . . . Christians now viewed it [Jerusalem] as the holiest of cities, and the tomb of Christ as the navel of the cosmos and the very source of salvation."

When the Christian Crusaders occupied Jerusalem (AD 1099–1187, 1229–1244), they initially massacred many Jews and Muslims and even Greek Orthodox Christians who had defended the city alongside Muslims and Jews. Jews and Muslims were prohibited by the Crusaders to reside in Jerusalem until it was occupied by the Muslim leader, Salah a-Din (Saladin) in AD 1187; 730 years later, in December 1917, the city was occupied by the British General Allenby and, according to Prof. Cox, British newspapers announced that he had completed the work of the Crusaders and that the Holy City was now a "Christmas present" and "back in Christian hands . . . " "But Allenby promised that he would protect the holy places and preserve religious freedom for all three faiths."

His promise was kept during the British Mandate (1920–1948) and after Israel was created in 1948, the Vatican and most Christian churches gradually changed their position on the status of Jerusalem: from favoring Christian control to an international regime, and to advocating negotiations among Jews, Christians and Muslims for a compromise solution for Jerusalem. At the same time, the Vatican also changed its traditional anti-Jewish stance – blaming the Jewish people for murdering Jesus, and retracted this accusation in 1965; later, in 1993 the Vatican concluded diplomatic relations with Israel. Yet over the years the Vatican and other Christian churches, certainly the Eastern churches, sought to establish good relations with Muslim countries and institutions. Many Christians have also backed the Muslim-Palestinian opposition to the Israeli annexation of East Jerusalem, as well as the Islamic claim to the Temple Mount (*Al-Haram Al-Sharif*).

Indeed, contrary to the Jewish position, many Muslims consider Al-Aqsa Mosque on the Temple Mount as holy as the *Al-Haram* Mosque in Mecca. As Prof. Mustafa Abu Sway writes in Chapter 6, "The Holy Land, Jerusalem and Al-Aqsa Mosque in the Qu'ran, Sunnah and other Islamic Literary Sources": "Since the miraculous night journey of Prophet Muhammad (peace be upon him) *al-Isra' wa'al-Miraj* took place more than fourteen centuries ago, Muslims have established a sublime and perpetual relation with Al-Aqsa

Mosque. The Prophet was taken from Al-Masjid Al-Haram in Mecca to Al-Masjid al-Aqsa in Jerusalem."

In addition, Jerusalem has been sacred to Muslims because the Prophet Muhammad initially requested his followers, including Jews, to pray in the direction (*qibla*) of Jerusalem (*Awla al-qiblalayn* – the first of the two *qiblas*), but subsequently to Mecca, after the Jews rejected his request. Also, many Muslims have adhered to an Islamic tradition that no Jewish Temple was ever built in Jerusalem. Nevertheless, for long periods of time, Jews were permitted by Muslim rulers to pray at the Western Wall.

Since the Israeli occupation of the West Bank, including East Jerusalem and the Old City (1967), a growing number of Palestinians and other Arab and Muslim leaders have called for a holy war (*jihad*) to liberate Jerusalem and the Palestinian lands from Israeli occupation. Jerusalem has thus become a grave point of friction between Muslims and Jews; and between the Muslim and Arab world against Israel. But, as Prof. Cox argues: "The conflicting 'holinesses' that have been the city's affliction for centuries could be also a source of healing." He suggests *inter alia* that the Jerusalem issue should be placed first on the agenda in the negotiation for an Israeli–Palestinian settlement. Such settlement would comprise a two-state solution, two capitals – in West and East Jerusalem respectively – placing the Old City, or at least the Temple Mount, "under the sovereignty of God," sharing it among Jews, Muslims and Christians.

Prof. Moshe Ma'oz articulates similar ideas after examining the historic narratives of Jews, Christians and Muslims regarding Jerusalem (Chapter 7: "Jerusalem: From Conflict to Compromise?"). Prof. Diane E. Davis concurs with such an approach in Chapter 8: "Divergent Epistemologies in the Search for Co-Existence: The Jerusalem 2050 Project." Tackling the question of Jerusalem from a disciplinary perspective of urbanism, she writes: "In the case of longstanding and virulent conflicts among Muslims, Christians and Jews, it is not difficult to see how the theoretical and normative path of urbanism could lead directly to the gates of Jerusalem, an important spiritual center for all. Jerusalem is not only a city where the question of boundaries remains politically and socially contested, and where claims of cultural or religious 'ownership' have led to conflict; it is also a city whose historical diversity, tolerance and cosmopolitanism are as famous as its more recent division and persistent instances of intolerance. In this sense, it may be the single most important key to peace among the 'children of Abraham,' not to mention the larger region as a whole . . . "

Indeed, in order to foster peaceful co-existence among the children of Abraham – Jews, Christians and Muslims – at present and in the future, in Jerusalem and elsewhere, lessons must be drawn from past history, namely: that alongside periods of religious fanaticism that brought about violence and death there were also long periods of religious tolerance and inter-civilizational co-existence and cooperation; and that alongside religious motives, there were political, cultural, socio-economic and psychological factors that greatly contributed to shaping interrelations among Muslims, Christians and Jews throughout history.

Confining our survey to the Islamic period, we should point out that Islam was a great historical civilization with extraordinary richness prior to the Christian-European civilization. For centuries Islam was more tolerant than Christianity toward Jews. Islam had been initially influenced by, and has shared common tenets with, Christianity and particularly Judaism. For example, Islam adopted monotheism in its pure – Jewish – form, acknowledged the revelations of Moses and Jesus, parts of the Bible and the New Testament, and the holiness of Jerusalem. The tenets of Islamic *fiqh* (law), prayer, fasting and social equality were also impacted by Judaism.

Yet, under Islamic rule, Jews and Christians did not enjoy the same political and judicial status as Muslims, the only full members of the Muslim political community. Jews and Christians were considered inferior subjects, were not allowed to carry arms, and had to pay a special poll tax, *jizya*, as a symbol of their contemptibility but also as a fee for their protection (*dhimma*) by the state. As the people of the Book (*Ahl al-Kitab*), Jews and Christians were allowed to worship their religions, but for long periods not to build new synagogues and churches or to renovate old ones. Periodically they had to wear clothing in certain colors – yellow for Jews and red for Christians – to distinguish them from Muslims. Occasionally Jews and Christians were humiliated, maltreated and oppressed by Muslim rulers and commoners. Still, during long periods of time individual Jews and Christians rose to prominent administrative, financial and professional positions, while their communities flourished economically and culturally. Jews were certainly better off under Islam than under Christendom during medieval times; likewise under Byzantium, the Reconquista in Spain and the Crusaders.

Thus, for example, during the era of the first Arab-Muslim empire, the Umayyad state (AD 661–750), with its capital in Damascus, Christians and Jews were treated fairly well and many were employed in various public quarters, including in the royal court of Khalif Mu'awiyya (who also married a Christian Jacobite woman, Maysun). In addition, Christian theology influenced at that time the emerging Islamic *Kalam* (philosophical theology) while Arab language, philology, poetry and prose flourished at that period. During the long era of the Abbasid Muslim empire (nominally more than 500 years, AD 750–1250, and centered in Baghdad), a similar pattern of relations among Muslims, Christians and Jews continued albeit with some exceptions. These relations were accompanied with great cultural blooming and economic prosperity for Muslims and non-Muslims alike. This was also the case in other parts of the Muslim world, notably Islamic Spain (from mid-10th to mid-12th centuries).

Prof. Mark Cohen, in Chapter 3, "The 'Convivencia' of Jews and Muslims in the High Middle Ages," examines Muslim–Jewish relations, but his analysis can also be applied to Muslim–Christian relations. He writes as follows: "The convivencia of Jews and Muslims in Muslim Spain and elsewhere in the medieval Islamic world was real, but its harmony had limits. It was marked by a legally prescribed regime of discrimination and even witnessed periodic outbursts of violence. Nonetheless, the cultural achievement of Arabic-speaking Jewry; the political influence that some Jews attained in Muslim courts and in Muslim intellectual circles; and the substantial security Jews experienced living among Muslims cannot be denied. Moreover, notwith-standing attempts in recent years to prove the contrary, anti-Semitism . . . simply did not exist in the Islam of the Middle Ages . . . we need also to under-stand why the Jews of Islam, in stark contrast with their brethren in Christian lands who constructed their history as a long chain of suffering, preserved very little collective memory of Muslims acts of violence, or of being victims of anti-Semitism. The answer to these questions does not lie in a simple contrast between tolerance (Islamic) and intolerance (Christian). It entails fundamental religious, political, economic and social realities of the Islamic world – realities that contrast with those of northern Europe and, by compar-ison, explains more completely the symbiosis of Judeo-Arabic civilization."

To be sure, not only Jews but also Christians in Europe and in the Middle East were influenced by and participated in the Islamic cultural prosperity in the fields of philosophy, astronomy, medicine, mathematics and alchemy. But in the political domains Jews and Christians continued to be discriminated against under Islamic rule. Thus, similar to the situation in the Umayyad and Abbasid periods, Jews and Christians under the Fatimid-Shi'i-Ismaili (AD 969–1171) and the Ayyubid-Sunni-Kurdish (AD 1171–1250) dynasties – in Egypt and Syria – experienced dual conditions. On the one hand, they were treated as inferior subjects and occasionally maltreated, even oppressed. But, on the other hand, not a few of them held senior administrative, economic and some medical positions, while their communities periodically enjoyed religious-cultural freedom.

As Prof. Mohamed Hawary explains, in Chapter 4, "Muslim–Jewish Relations in Ayyubid Egypt, 1171–1250)": "The Fatimids and their succes-sors, the Ayyubids, employed *ahl-al-dimma* [Jews and Christians] in their administrations far beyond their proportion in the general population . . . The Jewish and Christian populations were allowed to go on living under the same laws . . . " Prof. Hawary quotes *inter alia* a contemporary Egyptian [Muslim] poet who wrote, with some exaggeration, the following lines: "The Jews of our time have attained the goal of their aspirations: the honors are theirs and so are the riches. Counselors and kings are taken from their midst . . . Egyptians! I advise you, become Jews, for Heaven itself has turned Jewish."

By contrast, whereas Jews and Christians lived tolerably in medieval Islam and participated in its cultural and scientific developments, the conditions of Jews in Christian Europe continued to be very grim. Just emerging from its barbarian Dark Ages, Christian Europe produced the fanatic Crusaders (1096) who massacred Jews along the Rhine valley as well as Jews and Muslims in Jerusalem (1099) where Jews were also prohibited to reside. The Crusaders' conquest of Jerusalem induced many Muslims to develop the concept of *jihad* (holy war) against these Christian religious foes. And in 1187 the Muslim Ayyubid leader, Salah al-Din [Saladin], defeated the Crusaders, occupied Jerusalem, and permitted Jews to return there. But on the western side of the Mediterranean, the Christian Reconquista pushed the borders of Islamic Spain since the 13th century, spreading European anti-Semitism there. In 1492 Jews and (later) Muslims were deported from the Iberian peninsula; many of them were admitted, even welcomed, in the Ottoman-Muslim Empire.

Dealing a final blow to Byzantium with the occupation of Constantinople in 1453, the Ottoman-Muslims dominated large territories in Asia Minor, the Balkans, the Middle East and nominally also North Africa. Two other Muslim empires also emerged during the 15th and 16th centuries – the Moghul empire in India and the Safavid-Shi'i empire in Iran. Like former Islamic states, the Moghuls and Ottomans (but not the Safavids) exhibited for long periods significant tolerance toward their non-Muslim subjects. But each Muslim dynasty adopted its own version of tolerance. The Moghuls, for a long time, particularly under Emperor Akbar, highly respected Hindus and cooperated with them in inter-religious associations. By comparison, "the Ottoman Empire was tolerant of other religions, in accordance with Islamic law and tradition, and its Christian and Jews subjects lived, on the whole, in peace and security. But they were strictly segregated from the Muslims in their own separate communities. Never were they able to mix freely in Muslim society, as they had once done in Baghdad and Cairo – nor to make any contribution worth to mention to the intellectual life of the Ottomans. There are no Ottoman equivalents to Christian poets and Jewish scientists of the Arabic Golden Age."[1]

Yet, Christians and Jews held important positions in Ottoman financial administration and diplomacy as well as in commerce and banking. As in previous Muslim empires, they also enjoyed significant communal autonomy within the Ottoman *millet* (religious community)[2] system in matters of religious worship, education and certain legal issues. But they were not permitted to carry arms and rise to positions of decision-making in the government. They continued to pay the *jizya* (poll tax for males from the age of 15, officially abolished in 1855) and by and large were held in contempt. Occasionally, Christians and Jews were humiliated, maltreated, even oppressed, by Ottoman rulers and Muslim neighbors alike. And on a few occasions many Christians were massacred by Muslims – notoriously in 1860 in Syria and in 1915 in Turkey (the Armenian massacres).

The reasons for these horrendous, but rare, anti-Christian massacres were not solely religious-Islamic, but were substantially interwoven with political psychological and economic factors. To illustrate this point, it is worth comparing briefly Muslim-Christian interplay with Muslim–Jewish relations in Turkey and Syria, in the mid-19th century. This was a period of the Ottoman Tanzimat reforms that *inter alia* officially placed Christians and Jews on an equal footing with Muslims. Unlike Jews who continued to behave as a modest religious community with no political ambitions, Christians did not waste time to demonstrate their new privileges, thus provoking many Muslims. As a Christian Turk wrote in 1840: "This tranquility [of Jews] under Ottoman rule so opposite to the agitations and convulsions of other *raiahs* [non-Muslim subjects] . . . is explained partly by the peaceable habits and disposition of the Jews, which cause no umbrage to the *porte* [the Ottoman government] . . . patient, industrious and resigned to their fate, they were without apparent sense of humiliation the coloured *benish* [*jehoudane*] which the ancient sumptuary laws of the empire enjoined as a mark to distinguish them from the Mussulman."[3]

Christians, by contrast, demonstrated their new religious rights, for example, by ringing church bells and carrying crosses in public processions for the first time in centuries. In addition, Christians in Syrian towns manifested their new richness by building new, large houses and churches, as well as opening new wineshops. They also exhibited their contacts with, and reliance on, foreign consuls and missionaries. And, in Damascus, Christians also refused to pay the compulsory *badal* (or *bedel* in Turkish), an exemption fee for military service. To be sure, many Muslims did not feel empathy with these Christians' acts of emancipation and sights of richness, particularly when many Muslims had been impoverished by the growing impact of cheaper European goods that seriously damaged local Muslim industry and trade. Furthermore, many Muslims were concerned, even afraid of, the association of their Christian neighbors with the European powers. Indeed, a British consul cited in 1842 a common belief among Muslims namely: that "the European powers are hostile to the Turkish authority in Syria and . . . in union with the Christians they wish to overset it."[4]

The deep concern of Ottoman Muslims regarding the Christian-European threat to their Muslim state and to their own political and economic interests was not new. Already since the 17th century, Ottoman Muslim power and military conquests had been receding; Christian Europe, on the other hand, had made strident advances since the 15th century, surpassing the Islamic world in many fields, including military and economic power as well as science and technology. Nevertheless, the Ottoman governments had established good working relations with several European powers, notably France and Britain, in the areas of economy, military, diplomacy, printing presses, science and even life style. Aiming at modernizing their army and other institutions, the Ottomans worked towards the imitation and adoption of certain selected elements from the civilization of western Europe.[5] These elements also included, since the late 18th century, ideas of the French Revolution that were adjusted to Muslim concepts and influenced the Ottoman reforms, largely through young French-speaking Ottoman officers and diplomats.

But whereas France and Britain rendered the Ottomans western ideas and helped modernize Ottoman institutions, Russia and Austria waged several wars against the Ottoman empire, capturing large territories, weakening its strategic posture and draining its economic resources. Even France and

Britain, allies of the Ottoman Empire for long periods, occupied nominally-ruled Ottoman-Muslim lands. For example: Egypt was occupied in 1799 by Napoleon's troops and, in 1882, by the British army; Algeria was seized in 1831 and Morocco in 1912, by France; Britain occupied India with its large Muslim population in the late 18th century; and during World War I Britain and France occupied the Arab East and divided and dominated it for a quarter of a century.

These colonial powers and many other Europeans continued to look with contempt at Muslims as inferior people and at Islam as a backward civilization. Muslims reacted in diverse ways: radical Muslims and nationalist Arabs felt humiliated and frustrated by Western (Christian) military occupation, political control, economic exploitation and cultural religious condescension. Consequently, in various places and periods there occurred violent anti-European rebellions or riots. For example: In the late 19th century by the Islamic Mahdi movement against the British-backed Egyptian occupation of Sudan; in early 20th century by the Islamic Sanussi movement against Italian occupation of Libya; in 1919 by Egyptian nationalists against British control; in 1920 by Muslim and nationalist groups against British occupation of Iraq; in 1925–7 the nationalist/Druze rebellion against the French Mandate in Syria; and during 1936–1939, the nationalist-Islamic revolt in Palestine against the British Mandate and the Zionist-Jewish enterprise.

To be sure, the Zionist enterprise in Palestine, the creation of Israel (1948) and Israeli occupation of East Jerusalem in 1967 have greatly radicalized many Muslims and Arabs. They have blamed the West, particularly the United States, for supporting Israeli policies vis-à-vis the Arab nations, notably the Palestinians. Moreover, these Israeli policies, especially the prolonged occupation of the Muslim holy places in Jerusalem, and of Palestinian lands, caused militant Muslim groups to develop for the first time anti-Jewish, anti-Semitic positions and messages. Although Islamic ideology and tradition had been devoid of anti-Semitism, these militant Muslims have used extreme, perhaps distorted, interpretations of Koranic verses, as well as borrowed Christian anti-Semitic notions, in their new fanatic theology.

It should be noted that the targets of these Muslim fanatics – particularly Iran's Islamic regime and the *al-Qaida* organization – are not only "Zionists" (Israel) and "Crusaders" (the USA), but also many moderate Muslim regimes in the world that apparently represent the major current of Islamic civilization. Most of these regimes, as well as religious and secular elites, have conducted long-term dialogues and working relations with the West (and not a few, also with Israel) in the areas of politics, economics, science and culture. Among these Muslim countries are Indonesia (the largest Muslim nation), Pakistan, Turkey, Central Asia states, Azerbayjan, Egypt, Morocco and Jordan. A substantial number of Muslim political, religious and intellectual leaders have called for a "dialogue of civilizations" with the West. Muslim leaders also criticized terrorism, anti-Semitism and suicide bombing by Muslims as anti-Islamic actions.[6] Still, not a few of them have hesitated to speak out bluntly against Muslim fanaticism for fear of their personal security. Equally crucial, many moderate-pragmatic Muslim regimes have failed to address some of the deep causes for the development of extreme positions among their Muslim populations, namely, poverty, unemployment, social inequality, as well as ignorance and narrow Islamic education. Other factors that have contributed to radicalize many Muslims are the modern means of communication as well as the continued American occupation of Iraq, and the Israeli control over East Jerusalem and Palestinian lands.

Several of these issues and problems are discussed by Prof. Muhammad Shafiq in Chapter 9: "Teaching Interfaith Initiatives (Jews and Christians) in Muslim Educational Institutions", the first contribution to Part III – Education and Textbooks. In his view: "The Qur'anic stance on interfaith dialogue, appreciation of pluralistic society and freedom of religious belief and expression has become questionable today. Muslims are divided over the interpretation of some of its verses. There are some who have taken an extreme view of interpretation and there are many who listen to them. Listening to pro-al Qaeda tapes, many in the West today believe that Islam is not a religion of *Salam* [peace] . . . the Iraq war and the continuing Israel–Palestine conflict have fueled the anger . . . The curriculum in each of these different [Islamic] schools of thought [in Pakistan] have little to do with interfaith relations, especially about Judaism and Christianity. More disturbing are the facts that other Muslim countries, even the pro-Western Kingdom of Jordan, which has peaceful relations with Israel, 'encourages hatred toward Jews in its schools . . . [and] attacks Western cultural intrusions', for example: according to Jordanian textbooks, Christians and Jews refused to listen to not only Muhammad but their own prophets as well . . . The verses [of the Qu'ran] make clear that animosity between the bands of the People of the Book will continue until the day of judgement . . . The West aims to exploit and plunder the Arab world, seeking to humiliate the Arabs and to devastate their culture and religion."[7] Reportedly in a Saudi Islamic school in London, textbooks depicted Jews as monkeys and Christians as pigs.[8]

True, some Muslim nations, like Egyptians and Palestinians, have reduced in recent years their anti-Israeli/anti-Jewish and anti-Western expressions, while other Muslim nations have developed more modern and pluralist textbooks in certain school systems, including Islamic *madrasas*.[9] But many, if not most school textbooks in Muslim countries still contain bias or ignorant materials regarding Judaism and Christianity, while many Muslims at large are deeply antagonistic to the West, particularly Israel and the United States. By comparison, most school textbooks in the West, including the USA and Israel, have articulated by and large an accurate approach to Islamic religion and civilization. Thus, for instance Israeli textbooks have undergone significant improvement according to Prof. Elie Podeh. In Chapter 10, "Teaching Islam and Christianity in the Jewish Education System in Israel, 1948–2007," Podeh writes: "The current Israeli history textbooks belong, according to my findings, to the third generation of books. The first two generations contained many biases, distortions and omissions . . . ; these were largely eliminated in the third generation . . . Overall, the textbooks for the Jewish school system do not make use of stigmatic terminology or present Islam and Christianity stereotypically. They generally present these religions in a reasonably accurate and balanced fashion." But textbooks in religious schools in Israel still reflect ignorance and bias concerning Islam.

Similarly, in the United States, except for certain Christian evangelist schools, the teaching of Islam in many textbooks is fairly balanced, although not always sufficiently informative. In addition, in the USA, Europe and Israel there are numerous associations, programs, colleges and schools that promote interfaith understanding and dialogues. One of them is the noted interfaith training program for Jews, Christians and Muslims called "Building Abrahamic Partnership (BAP)" at Hartford Seminary. Rabbi Yehezkel Landau, a Hartford Faculty Associate, describes this program in Chapter 12: "Lessons from the *Building Abrahamic Partnerships* Program at Hartford Seminary." Among the program's goals, he cites: "educating participants about the beliefs and practices of the three Abrahamic traditions . . . It [the program] seeks to heal the historic wounds that have traumatized us and left us, as Abrahamic siblings, estranged from one another. It has a vision of inter-religious reconciliation and cooperation."

A similar approach is broadly expressed by Prof. Abdul Aziz Said in Chapter 11, "Educating for Global Citizenship. Perspectives from the Abrahamic Traditions": "We need to find a way to synthesize the traditional and the modern to create new educational processes and institutions that will give individuals the material, intellectual, moral and emotional skills necessary to transcend the crisis of our world. One such source of traditional wisdom rests with the Abrahamic faiths . . . The world needs a model of education that is capable of conceiving a global model for citizenship."

Part IV – Contemporary Relations and Challenges, the concluding section, discusses the obstacles, challenges and prospects for mutual appreciation, dialogue, cooperation and peace, among the three civilizations. Denying the recently propagated concept of "clash of civilizations," and analyzing the causes for friction and violence, the writers highlight the common legacy, values and interests among Christians, Muslims and Jews as a basis for peaceful co-existence.

Professors Nathan C. Funk and Meana Sharify-Funk, in Chapter 13, "Peacemaking among the Religions of Abraham: Overcoming Obstacles to Co-existence," argue *inter alia*: "Destructive encounters can bring out the worst among adherents of the Abrahamic religious traditions, but carefully constructed positive approaches can significantly aid efforts to rediscover resources for peace. Sincere dialogue among Jews, Christians and Muslims has become one of the most vital tasks for ensuring that religious expression remains life-affirming and life-enhancing in our present global era . . . It is not an exaggeration to state that most of the religious values held by Muslims,

Christians and Jews are shared . . . Through formal dialogue as well as through informal habits of 'living in relationship' with one another, Christian, Muslim and Jewish peacemakers have an opportunity to embrace their interdependence and to acknowledge those aspects of their spiritual and cultural heritages that are shared."

These spiritual and cultural heritages are discussed in Chapter 14, "Trialogue of Abrahamic Faiths: Towards an Alliance of Civilizations," by Professor Azyumardi Azra: "the fact is that besides of intellectual and cultural cross-enrichment and cross-fertilization, the history of the Children of Abraham had also been colored by tension, conflicts and wars that were destructive not only for human life, but also for the human civilization as a whole. That is why now it is the duty for all of us to recreate a new narrative of an alliance of civilizations both among the Children of Abraham and the rest of humanity . . . it is now increasingly recognized by the historian of human civilizations that Western civilization owed its origin not only to the Greek, but also to the Judeo-Christian–Muslim traditions that had mutually interacted through centuries. That is why it is not really appropriate to talk about the 'clash of civilizations,' particularly among the Children of Abraham."[10]

Prof. Azra argues also that "the continued Israeli–Palestinian conflict is a major factor in the widening rift between the Muslim and Judeo-Christian world . . . Therefore, it is necessary to resolve the conflict by achieving a just and sustainable solution . . . The progress in this front rests on the recognition of both Palestinian and Jewish aspirations and on the establishment of two fully sovereign and independent states living side by side in peace and security."

Indeed, it is possible that the prolonged Israeli–Palestinian conflict has constituted one of the main causes for anti-Western sentiments among Muslims and for the emergence of a new Islamic anti-Semitism. Thus, according to Muslim leaders and Middle East pundits, a fair and acceptable solution to the Israeli–Palestinian problem, and to the Muslim Holy sites in Jerusalem, will significantly improve Muslim–Jewish relations, as well as greatly diminish Muslim and Christian anti-Semitism.

Whether or not Rabbi David Saperstein shares this evaluation, he discusses and compares Muslim and Christian anti-Semitism in Chapter 15, "The Children of Abraham at a Time of Crisis: Challenges and Opportunities": "Across the globe, the resurgence of anti-Semitism in forms Jews thought we would never see again, has sent shock waves through my community. And we are witnessing the rise of anti-Semitism in the Muslim world in many forms never witnessed before in history – including, ironically, those heretofore associated only with Christian and other forms of Western anti-Semitism . . . assertions of the blood libel, the widespread popularizing of conspiracy theories such as the Elders of Zion and the arrogation and adaptation of Nazi images . . . the success and appeal of Islamists worldwide is because they are brimming with energy and ideas and have vast and easily mobilized grassroots networks through charitable organizations and mosques. Moderate voices therefore need to not only speak out with their voices, but with their hands as well; they must replicate the model used by Islamists worldwide . . . "

Rabbi Saperstein discusses also the mutual changes in Christian–Jewish relations over the last decades, which have significantly improved, although "irrational [Christian] anti-Semitic canards that underlie much of the hatred continue."

Finally, it is necessary to point out that within the scope of this book it was not possible to include more references to Christian-Jewish relations. Similarly, other issues and periods concerning the meeting of civilizations have not been fully reviewed, such as the Ottoman and contemporary eras, as well as the interplay among the three civilizations in the areas of economics, philosophy, mysticism, poetry, medicine and science. These matters will hopefully be tackled in a subsequent book.

Still, as an illustration of the importance of these issues in inter-civilizational relations, the final chapter of this book, Chapter 16 by Dr. Richard J. Deckelbaum, deals with "Health and Science: Win–Win Modalities towards Brotherhood." As he pertinently points out, "scholars from Islam, Judaism and Christianity have long interacted closely and favorably in improving human health, mutual understanding and advancement of society." During medieval times, Galen's "contributions influenced the rise and spread of Islamic medicine in the Arab Empire, so did the Muslim contributions mingle with those of the Jewish physicians, philosophers and scientists, which in turn impacted the later developments in western, or Christian, medicine and science. In recent times, Arab scientists and physicians have collaborated with Israeli counterparts closely over the last two decades . . . These programs led to health interventions, which improved the status of the populations . . . "

Indeed, physicians, scientists, philosophers and scholars, as well as religious and intellectual leaders – Muslim, Christian and Jewish – now face crucial challenges: to overcome the psychological barriers among the three Abrahamic civilizations, caused by traumatic experiences throughout history; by fanatic interpretations of religious texts; as well as by negative polemics and acts of violence and terrorism. These scholars and leaders must cooperate and coordinate efforts to foster deeper appreciation and mutual knowledge and understanding of each other's traditions, as well as to highlight their common religious and human values, without overlooking the diversities among the three great civilizations. Alongside these long-term endeavors, political leaders should be induced to improve socio-economic conditions and educational programs, and to cooperate in settling critical international conflicts, notably in Iraq and Palestine. Indeed, a fair and acceptable solution for the Israeli–Palestinian dispute and for the Jerusalem problem will significantly improve relations among the Children of Abraham and hopefully set in motion a new dynamics of peaceful co-existence.

Jerusalem, March 2008

Notes

1   Bernard Lewis, *The Emergence of Modern Turkey* (London, Oxford University Press, 1962), pp. 14–15.
2   See Benjamin Braude and Bernard Lewis (eds.), *Christians and Jews in the Ottoman Empire* (New York, Holmes and Meier, 1982), vol. I, chapters 3, 8, 10, 12, 13.
3   M. A. Ubicini, *Letters on Turkey* (London, 1856), vol. 2, p. 346.
4   Quoted in Moshe Ma'oz, *Ottoman Reform in Syria and Palestine, 1840–1861* (Oxford, The Clarendon Press, 1968), p. 210.
5   Lewis, *The Emergence of Modern Turkey*, p. 45.
6   See MacFarquhar, *New York Times*, October 12, 2007; Guy Ornmore, *Financial Times*, December 22, 2007.
7   Betty Anderson, "Jordan: Prescription for Obedience and Conformity," *Teaching Islam: Textbooks and Religion in the Middle East*, edited by Eleanor Abdella Doumato and Gregory Starrat (Boulder, Lynne Reinner, 2007), pp. 81, 84, 86. See also *The War Curriculum in Iranian Schoolbooks*, Researched, translated and edited by Arnon Groiss and Nethanel (Navid) Toobian, American Jewish Committee, 2007.
8   *Yediot Ahronot*, February 8, 2007.
9   See for example: Doumato, p. 130 and *passim*; see also *Schooling Islam: The Culture and Politics of Modern Muslim Education*, edited by Robert W. Hefner and Muhammad Qasim Zaman (Princeton, Princeton University Press, 2007), p. 3.
10   Cf. Striving for Global Co-Existence – A Message from HRH Prince Hassan bin Talal, Copenhagen, October 31, 2006.

PART

I

Religious and Historical Themes

1

A Phenomenolgy of Choseness

REUVEN FIRESTONE

In other forums I have theorized an origin for the concept of chosenness that appears to be deeply imbedded in all expressions of monotheism.[1] I am interested here in considering how theological notions of chosenness work themselves out in terms of policies of relationship with non-believers in the three great monotheistic families of religion. We begin by citing some of the classic scriptural texts upon which Jews, Christians and Muslims have relied in order to support a position of being elected or chosen by God to be in a unique and exclusive relationship.

The chosenness texts that follow have been limited to those that are quite explicit in their language of divine selection. Were texts added that argue over the closely related notion of divine covenant, the number would increase exponentially in all three scriptures.

The Hebrew Bible

The Hebrew Bible is riddled with chosenness texts, and only a few need be cited here. They begin to appear at the very commencement of the biblical history of Israel.[2] Abraham is mysteriously chosen by God to engage in a physical and spiritual journey to and with the one great God. *The Lord said to Abram, "Go forth from your native land and from your father's house to the land that I will show you. I will make of you a great nation, and I will bless you. I will make your name great, and you shall be a blessing. I will bless those who bless you and curse him that curses you, and all the families of the earth shall be blessed through you . . . ."* (Gen. 12:1–3). As the community expands from a nuclear family to a clan, a tribe, and then a fellowship of many tribes, God reaffirms the unique relationship when giving the Torah to Israel at Mt. Sinai. *"Moses went up to God. The Lord called to him from the mountain, saying: "Thus shall you say to the house of Jacob and declare to the children* of Israel: *⁴'You have seen what I did to the Egyptians, how I bore you on eagles' wings and brought you to Me.'"*

That unique relationship is reaffirmed repeatedly in the Hebrew Bible. *I, the Lord, am your God who has set you apart from other peoples* (Lev. 20:24). *For you are a people consecrated to the Lord your God: of all the peoples of the earth the Lord your God chose you to be His treasured people* (Deut. 7:6). *The Lord your God chose you from among all other peoples on earth to be His treasured people* (Deut. 14:2). *Hear now, O Jacob My servant, Israel whom I have chosen!* (Isaiah 44:1). *You alone have I singled out [known] of all the families of the earth* (Amos 3:2). *Happy is the nation whose God is the Lord, the people He has chosen to be His own* (Ps. 33:12).

The sense and significance of chosenness represented by these passages are not all alike. Their meanings are shaped by the historical (including political, social, religious) contexts out of which the texts emerged. Although the nuances of meaning and contextual background are important for understanding the history and development of the notion, this is not the goal here, so we will observe simply that the concept is well-developed in the Hebrew Bible and serves as a kind of identifying factor for the religion of Israel.

The religion of Israel is the foundational expression of monotheism. It is the first and, until Christianity, the only sustained expression of monotheism that we know of.[3] Religion in the ancient Near East seems to have been defined and organized more along ethnic lines than according to theological ideas. Distinct religious communities were distinct ethnically, and most of the peoples in the region had unique, even "chosen" relationships with their national Gods who would protect and sustain their particular ethnic communities in exchange for proper worship. The Moabites had their particular national God named Kemosh (1 Kings 11:33, Jer. 48:46), the Ammonites had a national God called Milkom (1 Kings 11:33), the Philistine national God was Dagon (1 Sam. 5:1–7), the deity of Tyre was Ashtoret (2 Kings 23:13), and so forth. Like the others, Israel had its own national God whose name is no longer pronounced in Jewish circles.[4] Because religious identity in the ancient Near East was expressed and organized ethnically, one worshipped according to one's ethnic or national identity. Each national group was in a unique relationship with its God. The relationship could be defined as one of mutual chosenness.

For reasons that we are not able to reconstruct at this time, the religious community of Israel made a conceptual transition in its perception of deity that scholars now date to the late monarchy or exilic period.[5] This was the profound shift from henotheism or monolatry to true monotheism. Israel nevertheless retained its organic sense of ethnic religion and ethnic relationship with its God, a God that had come to be perceived of as the God of all creation.

The God of Israel thus became also the God of the universe. Israel was the first religious community to arrive at this two-fold understanding of ethnic plus universal God, and Judaism today, along with all subsequent forms of monotheism, seems to retain some aspect of this unique perspective. On the one hand, God is universal and the sovereign creator-God for all things and all peoples. On the other, that universal God has a particular, unique and even exclusive relationship with the one and only religious community of believers that truly understands and acts out the will of that universal God.

The New Testament

Because all scriptures reflect the particular historical (including political, linguistic, cultural, religious, social and technological) contexts in which they were revealed, the New Testament tends to express the notion of chosenness in a different manner and with a different discourse than the Hebrew Bible. Nevertheless, being chosen by God is no less important. The chosenness of Christianity begins with the unique chosen quality of God's own and only son. *As these two were moving away from Jesus, Peter said to him, 'Master, it is good that we are here. Shall we make three shelters, one for you, one for Moses, and one for Elijah?' but he spoke without knowing what he was saying. As he spoke there came a cloud which cast its shadow over them; they were afraid as they entered the cloud, and from it a voice spoke: 'This is my son, my Chosen; listen to him'* (Luke 9:33–35).

Chosenness in the New Testament tends to be removed from a single national group (such as Israel) and applied to both the divine incarnation and to the religious system that emerged from it. That is, chosenness is identified less with a people than with a trans-ethnic or trans-national community of believers. It is the Church (Gr., *ekklesia*, 'the chosen'), the spiritual rather than tribal community of believers that defines the chosen of God. This change is articulated famously through the parable of Jesus as shepherd in the Gospel of John, who gathers the chosen among all the nations. Anyone may enter the fold. Jesus is the door to the sheepfold and the source of entry to God the Father. *In very truth I tell you, the man who does not enter the sheepfold by the door, but climbs in some other way, is nothing but a thief and a robber. He who enters by the door is the shepherd in charge of the sheep. The door-keeper admits him, and the sheep hear his voice; he calls his own sheep by name, and leads them out. When he has brought them all out, he goes ahead of them and the sheep follow, because they know his voice. They will not follow a stranger; they will run away from him, because they do not recognize the voice of strangers. This was a parable that Jesus told them, but they did not understand what he meant by it. So Jesus spoke again: 'In very truth I tell you, I am the door of the sheepfold. The sheep paid no heed to any who came before me, for they were all thieves and robbers. I am the door;* anyone *who comes into the fold through me will be safe. He will go in and out and find pasture. . . . I am the good shepherd; I know my own and my own knows me, as the Father knows me and I know the Father. . . .* (John 10:1–15).

There remains, however, at least in some layers represented by New Testament scripture, an articulation of concern for the chosenness of a Christian religious peoplehood, even if not a tribal or ethnic religious peoplehood as the Hebrew Bible defines Israel. *Tell me now, you who are so anxious to be under the law, will you not listen to what the Law says? It is written there that Abraham had two sons, one by his slave and the other by his free-born wife. The slave-woman's son was born in the course of nature, the free woman's through God's promise. This is an allegory. The two women stand for two covenants. The one bearing children into slavery is the covenant that comes from Mt. Sinai: that is Hagar. Sinai is a mountain in Arabia and it represents the Jerusalem of today, for she and her children are in slavery. But the heavenly Jerusalem is the free woman; she is our mother! . . . Now you, my friends, like Isaac, are children of God's promise, but just as in those days the natural-born son persecuted the spiritual son, so it is today. Yet what does scripture say? 'Drive out the slave and her son, for the son of the slave shall not share the inheritance with the son of the free woman.'* [Cf. Gen.21:10] *You see, then, my friends, we are no slave's children; our mother is the free woman. It is for freedom that Christ set us free. Stand firm, therefore, and refuse to submit again to the yoke of slavery* (Gal. 4:21–31).[6]

This sentiment is even stronger in 1 Peter 2:9–10: *But you are a chosen race, a royal priesthood, a dedicated nation, a people claimed by God for his own, to proclaim the glorious deeds of him who has called you out of darkness into his marvelous light. Once you were not a people at all; but now you are God's people. Once you were outside his mercy; but now you are outside no longer.*[7]

The Qur'an

The Qur'an also finds meaning in divine chosenness. As in prior scripture, it expresses the particularity of its historical context. *You are the best community that has been brought forth for humanity, commanding the reputable and forbidding the repugnant, and you believe in God. If the People of the Book believed, it would surely be best for them. Some of them are believers, but most are deviants* (Q. 3:110). Only the true believers merit a future of eternal bliss. *Round up those who did wrong and their spouses, and what they used to worship Aside from God, and guide them to the path of Hell [lit. "the hot place"] . . . . This is what We do to the sinners. For when it was said to them, "There is no god but God, they made as if they were too great, saying, "We should abandon our Gods because of a mad poet?" . . . . You receive your recompense [punishment] only for what you do except for the loyal/pure servants of God. These receive well-known reward, fruits, being well-honored in gardens of delight . . .* (Q. 37:22–43).

...oyal or pure servan...
...nter (38), the term ...
...bhyar which convey...
...l entrance into Para...
...n". And remember o...
...ability and vision. We puri-...
...e Home [of paradise?] They...
...w. And remember Ishmael and...
...he best. This is a reminder; for the...
...ardens of Eden, whose doors are open...

...eater effort is necessary to identify the notion ...it is not articulated as often or as centrally as it ...d New Testament. It is nevertheless an important ...ggested (as a compliment) to a university audience in ...ss is not as important a concept for Islam as it is for ...stianity, the reaction was hostile. At issue was whether the ...e the best community that has been brought forth for humanity ... be conditional on the second part of the sentence: *commanding ...table and condemning the repugnant.* The overwhelming sentiment ...ssed to me in this anecdotal experience was that the chosen nature of the ...uslim community is unconditional. One additional verse is also of interest in this regard: *"God has promised those of you who believe and do good works that He will make them successors on earth, just as He made those before them successors. He will surely establish their religion for them that He has approved[8] for them, exchanging security for them in place of fear"* (Q. 24:55).

The reader will note that in the Christian and Islamic scriptures, the notion of chosenness is expressed in a manner that is no less polemical than in the Hebrew Bible. All three scriptures convey a sense that there can be only one truly chosen and that being chosen necessarily excludes the other religious communities from the equation. The latter two scriptures seem to agree that the chosenness of the Israelites expressed in the Hebrew Bible was certainly accurate at one time, but that for reasons that cannot be explored here, they lost that standing as those who responded to the new revelations assumed the extraordinary status once held by them. In the language of game theory, chosenness in scripture is often expressed as a "zero-sum" situation. There can be only one chosen at any time.

The zero-sum nature of chosenness that is often (though not always) expressed in monotheistic religion is probably influenced by a number of human or social-psychological factors, including the natural association of choosing with hierarchy (the one chosen takes a higher position than those that have not been chosen), the structural manner in which humans have conceived of the divine–human relationship, and with the polemical environments in which new religious movements emerge in history.[9] The remainder

...reats how chosenness seems to affect poli...
...ers in the three families of monotheistic...
...ual nature of scriptural discourse in general, thi...
...lationship must also take into consideration hist...
...ntexts.

Before entering that discussion, however, we must first ...
order to clarify what three monotheistic systems are being trea...
three are Judaism, Christianity and Islam, all three of which ar...
what I will refer to here as Biblical Religion.[10] This reality is ...
persistent erroneous notion among many non-Jews and Jews ali...
Judaism practiced today, especially among the most traditional Jew...
ally the same religion as that of the Bible. The differences between...
and Biblical Religion are many and significant, ranging from matters ...
worship ritual to theology to the articulation of religious commitment i...
tice (*halakhah* and custom), concepts of the endtime and afterlife, and s...
There certainly is a profound continuity between Biblical Religion...
Rabbinic Judaism in all of the fields just mentioned, but so can it be argu...
that there is a profound continuity between Biblical Religion and Christiani...
and even Islam (I use the term "even" in reference to Islam only because...
Muslims tend not to rely on the same quality of association with the Hebrew...
Bible that Jews and Christians claim).

What makes Judaism particularly different from Biblical Religion is the virtual extension of scripture into Rabbinic literature, which includes the Talmud but is not limited to the Talmud. I lump all the relevant Rabbinic literature together for the purposes of this discussion and call it "Talmud" for reasons of simplicity, and I use the term "virtual extension" because the Talmud is simultaneously a self-acknowledged extension of scripture and an interpretation of scripture. It is referred to consistently by rabbinic Jews as the "Oral Torah," a profound statement about its quality as scripture.[11] On the other hand, the very discourse articulated by the sages who appear and speak within the Talmud acknowledges that it is also a complex interpretive enterprise whose goal is to make sense of tradition in its relationship to the scripture of the Hebrew Bible.

This of course complicates the discussion, but it also allows for a kind of symmetry. The Hebrew Bible/Old Testament no longer represents any single religion, but rather serves as a kind of "Ur-scripture" for all three post-biblical monotheistic systems. It has a primary place in the scriptural canon of both Judaism and Christianity, even though it serves more as an authority that authenticates the next level of scripture in the New Testament and the Talmud than a scripture in its own right. It is referenced as divine in origin also by Islam, but is not relied upon to authenticate the Qur'an aside from its role as early revelation that became corrupted by human manipulation, thereby opening the way for a third and final revelation in the Qur'an.

Chosenness and Policies of Relationship with
Those not Chosen

We focus here on two closely related subjects: how the monotheistic systems have understood the chosen bond with God in terms of relations with other peoples or religions, and how this sense of relationship was played out historically in policy and action.[12] Clearly, a sense of elitism is deeply imbedded in the relationship between the chosen and the non-chosen Other. This elitism is not without its critics, even within the scriptures that overwhelmingly preach the special quality and nature of the chosen.[13] Nevertheless, elitism seems to be a sine qua non of chosenness. That superiority can and has been articulated differently in various scriptural verses. It may be triumphant or patronizing, arrogant and jubilant, or aloof and even tolerant, but it is an essential part of having been chosen by the divine power that governs the universe. What follows represents some preliminary observations and thoughts about how various communities' sense of chosenness has been acted out in relations with other, non-chosen communities.

In Ancient Israel

In the Hebrew Bible the hierarchy is most clear: "Of all the peoples on earth the Lord your God chose you to be his treasured people" (Deut. 7:6–8, cf. 14:2). "You shall be holy to Me, for I the Lord am holy, and I have set you apart from other peoples to be Mine" (Lev. 20:26).[14] This is elitism combined with separatism, and it reflects the historical context of the ancient Near East where all religions were ethnically organized and defined. Similar to their neighboring religious communities, when Israel's God was conceived simply as the "God of Israel," it was natural and logical to consider the bond with God unique and exclusive.[15] But as biblical scholars now tend to agree, the God of Israel transformed in the eyes of the Israelites to become the God of the entire universe sometime roughly around the time of the destruction of the First Temple and the period of the exilic prophets (6th century, BCE). The notion of divine chosenness of a single ethnic group that would be so natural in the particularist setting of ethnic polytheism, seems to have become problematic to some in the universal setting of monotheism, and some biblical texts reflect that ambivalence (Ex. 19:5, Amos 3:2, 9:7–8).

Because people worshipped according to their ethnic or national identity in the ancient Near East, the notion of religious conversion seems not to have been a conceptual possibility at the time. It emerged only in the Hellenistic period, probably under the influence of the philosophic schools that one could study and determine which among them best accounted for the workings of the universe.[16] Because the history represented by the Hebrew Bible was pre-Hellenistic, the notion of religious conversion and therefore, proselytism, simply cannot be found there. The relationship of Israel to other nations, therefore, was never one of mission, and one finds no clear reference to proselytizing in the Hebrew Bible. Compare, for example, with the Christian New Testament or Jewish Rabbinic literature, both of which clearly acknowledge the notions and activity of conversion and proselytism.[17]

The lack of reference to mission in the Hebrew Bible may have also been related to the lack of a developed notion of reward and punishment in an afterlife. Modern Westerners tend to presume that such a notion was "always" operative, but the notion of divine salvation seems to have emerged only in the period of Late Antiquity following the biblical period.[18] Without such a notion, it would have been a conceptual impossibility to "save souls" through a program of mission. Political, economic and military motives are also bound up in the bundle of incentives to encourage mission, to be sure, but while these certainly impact the outcome of campaigns for conversion, they tend not to be clearly articulated as have religious motivations.

In earlier layers of the Bible that seem to reflect a period in which a sense of nascent monotheism was only emerging, neighboring peoples and their Gods were treated as a fact of life, and interaction between early biblical heroes and non-Israelites and their Gods was normative.[19] As the developing sense of monotheism became increasingly central among Israel, however, it became ever more important to separate from the religious practices of neighboring peoples who worshipped limited Gods and powers. It is likely that some social practices that emerged in the Bible did so, at least in part, in order to separate Israelites from social intercourse with other peoples. This represents quite a different situation from what would have obtained had the Hebrew Bible been interested in mission.

In the ancient Near East, the only way to leave one's ancestral religion was to assimilate into another ethnic group or nation. If one's social and ritual practice required activities that discouraged social interaction with other peoples, one would be less likely to become attracted to them and their practices. Intermarriage was always a threat to the unity and survival of the small community of Israel. Even those groups such as the Egyptians and Ammonites, among whom the Israelites were permitted by biblical scripture to intermarry, exogamous relations were sanctioned only after three generations of the foreigners' assimilation into the Israelite cultural and religious system (Deut. 23:8–9).

These kinds of rules and behavioral expectations do not reflect political power. As David Biale has so aptly written, "For most of the time from the beginning of the Israelite settlement in the land of Canaan to the fall of the Second Temple, the Jewish people lived in the shadow of great empires, rarely enjoying what would today be called full national sovereignty."[20] The elitism of Israelite monotheism with its sense of chosenness remained the trait of a small and often embattled community. In one instance, however, the religion of Israel was forcibly imposed upon another community. This was the case of the conversion of the Idumeans under the Judean ruler, John Hyrcanus, in the

2nd century BCE. Such an act became a possibility only because of a confluence of factors: the influence of Hellenism, the temporary vacuum of political
power caused by the collapse of the Hellenistic Seleucid Empire in the 2nd
century, and the acquisition of the reigns of political and military power by
Jews under the Hasmonean kingdom. In any case, the episode represents the
first known case where monotheism was imposed on non-believers en masse.
We know little about the program or the process, but the Idumeans seem to
have integrated fairly well into the Hasmonean Kingdom (a phenomenon that
would find subsequent historical parallels with mass conversions of polythe-
ists to other forms of monotheism), with many upper class Idumeans moving
into key social and governmental positions.[21]

In Rabbinic Judaism

Rabbinic Judaism began to emerge during the late Second Temple period after
the notions of conversion, mission and salvation in a world to come had
entered into the conceptual repertoire of the Hellenistic world. Rabbinic
Judaism emerged into history during an extended period of Jewish political
powerlessness. With the destruction of the Second Temple in 70 CE, Jewish
communities lived in political exile, even within the Land of Israel, among
polities governed by non-Jews. There were two important stages in this period
of emergent Rabbinic Judaism.

In the first, the Roman Empire was pagan, and many Greco-Romans were
in search of a religious system that was more meaningful than that of their
increasingly irrelevant traditional religious options. A variety of new religious
movements in addition to Rabbinic Judaism and Christianity were emerging
at this time that are sometimes called "mystery cults," such as Eleusinian
Mysteries, Mithraic Mysteries (or "Mithraism) and the Orphic Mysteries.
During this period, many religiously disaffected Greco-Romans began
engaging in Judaizing practices that brought them into the orbit of Judaism.
These included at least partial observance of Jewish dietary laws, ritual practices, study, and even circumcision among men, and it had become possible
by that time to enter into the community of Israel as converts.[22] So many
Greco-Romans entered into emerging Rabbinic Judaism that historians esti-
mate that some 10 percent of the Roman Empire, and 20 percent of the area
in the Eastern Mediterranean, were composed of Jews by the 1st century CE.[23]
There developed a sense of mission among some Jews during this period, or
at least a willingness to accept proselytes. This was certainly influenced by the
early Christian claim that Christianity had replaced the old religion of the
Bible as the "true Israel" (*verus Israel*), a newly chosen people who had chosen
Christ.

Rabbinic Jews, who represented the monotheistic religious establishment
at the time, felt threatened by the emerging competition and the Christian
claims to exclusivity, which threatened their own exclusivist claims. The New

Testament records that some Jews engaged in overt and covert acts to prevent the success of the Jesus movement.[24] Both Jews and Christians were living under the rule of a pagan Roman Empire that had little institutional love for either system. Mobilization by either side to gain influence and new members thus occurred under conditions under which political or military power could not be independently employed. Such influence was only possible by appropriating the power of Rome, which neither was able to do except in extraordinary and limited, temporary circumstances.

In the second stage of emerging Rabbinic Judaism, the Roman Empire had Christianized, with the result that Christianity absorbed and took on the power and influence of the empire. When the establishment religion of Rome became Christian, Judaism continued in its status as a tolerated minority tradition that it enjoyed during the pagan period, but that tolerated status began shortly to be eroded. In crude terms, Christianity had won the competition for the prize of the Empire. Judaism had lost. In this environment, the elitism of chosenness among Jews tended to become internalized, partly as a consolation for lack of outward religious and political success.[25]

Mission by Jews was no longer possible under Byzantine law, as it became a capital crime.[26] As a result of these developments, Rabbinic Judaism separated itself increasingly from non-Jews, but this does not represent a withdrawal from intellectual engagement with non-Jews. In fact, as Christian writers from this period convey, a nagging articulation of Jewish superiority continued to plague many Christian thinkers.[27] That sense of Jewish religious elitism, however, could not be applied to political, social or military policy. The reason for this is probably as simple as it was structural. Rabbinic Judaism was never a religion of an independent polity that could apply its sense of chosenness elitism to public policy. Jewish proselytizing was suppressed in the Christian world, and when it became a capital crime also in the Muslim world it became virtually impossible anywhere. As a result, perhaps, those energies associated with chosenness elitism became sublimated and applied to other pursuits.

In Christianity and Islam

As observed above, Christianity emerged in the same general environment of political powerlessness under Roman rule as Rabbinic Judaism. In fact, Christians held less power and were held with far more disdain by Rome than Jews for most of the period from the emergence of Christianity until to the Christianization of the empire; certainly by the middle of the 2nd century they were persecuted far more as well. But Christianity was more successful in making inroads among Greco-Romans seeking a religion that would provide more meaning than the other religious options of the Greco-Roman world.

By the middle of the 4th century, Christians found themselves the dominant and then ruling religion of the Empire. For the first time in human history, monotheists controlled a world empire with all of its institutions of power: political rule, administrative bureaucracies, tax collection, control of the media and education, and the military. This was the first opportunity for applying the religious ideology of monotheist elitism into imperial law, and it began to be done early on. Before the end of the century, pagan practices were outlawed, and monotheistic practices that were not in line with those in power were prohibited or restricted.[28]

The conceptual notion of conversion with its subsequent application to mission was not the operative issue in this change. After all, proselytizing had been practiced by Jews and Christians for centuries. Rather, the main motivator for the policy of forced imposition of the religion of the "chosen" seems simply to have been the acquisition of power.

When monotheism became the religion of empire through the Christianization of Rome, it naturally took on an imperialist worldview. This is ironic, considering that Christianity originated as a persecuted religious minority that struggled to survive in the face of the overwhelming power of a violently unsympathetic empire. On the other hand, it is not illogical, and Christian thinkers of the time wrote that history had proven the divinely chosen status of Christianity and the Church.[29] God's preference for the truth of Christianity was established as a divine sign in history through the Christianization of the most powerful empire on earth. After having gained the reigns of imperial power, then, Christianity became an imperialist religion itself. The imperial codes of the Christian Roman emperors, from Theodosius and Justinian onward, applied the power of the state to enforce religious ideology throughout the empire from the earliest period of Christian control.

We can observe a similar phenomenon occurring when Islam became an imperial religion. Like all new religious movements, Islam emerged as a minority faction and was opposed by the establishments that found it threatening. It managed to prevail, however, and eventually became the established religion of a Muslim empire, the caliphate. As in the case of Christianity, the elitist ideology of monotheism, combined with the power of the state and its state apparatuses, created an imperial religion that imposed its religious ideology by the power of the state. In the case of Christianity, the mechanism was the imperial codes mentioned above and reflective of the organization of the early Church. In the case of Islam, it was less centralized. Rather than caliphal decree, the political imposition of religious law and rule was authorized by the *shari'a*, the Arabic Islamic term for religious law, which developed only after Islam had become an imperial religion.[30] The very worldview articulated by *shari'a* with regard to non-Muslims is universal, triumphant, and reflective of a point of view shaped by the power of empire.[31]

There is a major difference, however, between the imperialism of Islam and that of Christianity, and that difference seems to be based on the particular historical contexts of transition from opposition (or persecuted) religion to religion of state. As Christianity emerged into history, it found itself in intense competition with one established religious community (Rabbinic Judaism) that claimed that only it represented the true will of the universal God. As Islam emerged into history, there were at least two and probably more established expressions of monotheism, each claiming a unique status as being the chosen of God.

We have noted previously how the elitism of chosenness may have been a common worldview of national religions in the ancient Near East. All religionists felt "chosen" by their particular God, and all observed that their neighbors had similar feelings of intimacy with their own deities. By the end of the Second Temple Period, however, the old national religions of the ancient world had died out or were absorbed by the dominance of Greco-Roman culture and religion. Only one of the ancient Near Eastern ethnicity-based religions survived, and that was the religion of Israel. Centuries earlier it had completed the transition from national polytheism to a vision of a single, monotheistic deity that ruled the universe, and it represented the only expression of monotheism when Christianity emerged as an independent religious movement. This Israelite monotheism included a variety of movements, each claiming to represent the true will of the one Great God, but all adherents of these movements called themselves Jews (or Judeans) and all retained the old feeling of a chosen relationship with their God – who was also the God of all creation.

This sense of chosenness was deeply entrenched in the Israelite monotheism of Judaism. It appears that all movements within Judaism retained that sense of chosenness. In fact, the ferocity of argument and polemic between the Pharisees, Saduccees and Essenes, for example, may be observed operating as such a high level precisely because each felt that it represented the one true expression of God's demands on the chosen people. Each was competing over who was the true chosen of God. Many factors certainly influenced the intense nature of the argument, including control of power and resources, status in the community, etc. It would be interesting to study internal religious arguments in monotheistic systems that identify themselves as chosen, and to compare them with religious systems such as the Hindu traditions that do not.[32] It seems clear from the scriptural sources cited above that chosenness became an identifying trait of monotheism in general, and also a trait utilized by polemical arguments between them.

As new forms of monotheism emerged in history, chosenness was one of the authoritative motifs that were understood to validate their truth claims. In the earliest period, when only one or two discreet expressions of monotheism existed, chosenness was a zero-sum equation. We have observed how this was the case with the emergence of Christianity. According to both Rabbinic Judaism and Christianity, only one of the two movements could be truly representative of the divine will. Only one was truly chosen. If one was chosen, the other was rejected.

The zero-sum equation was a natural conceptual paradigm for the particular historical context in which Christianity emerged as an independent religion. There were only two distinct expressions of monotheism, though each had within it some variations in theology and practice. Despite the different expressions or understandings within each system, however, it was the overall claims between the two that competed for the unique status of being divinely chosen. Only one could be true.

Islam, however, emerged centuries later and in a world in which there were a variety of competing expressions of monotheism. Not only were there "Judaism" and "Christianity," there were also well-developed and numerically significantly competing representations of each that had made their way into the Arabian Peninsula by the 7th century. Each one claimed to hold the proper understanding and response to the divine will. There is evidence of other expressions of monotheism at the time as well that were neither Jewish nor Christian, including indigenous Arabian monotheisms or proto-monotheisms.[33] To the early Muslims, therefore, it was not natural to conceive of chosenness as a zero-sum equation. The many expressions of monotheism contemporary to emerging Islam prevented an absolute zero-sum equation from obtaining among them.

The Qur'an represents the earliest layers of Islamic thought, and it mentions a number of times that any expression of monotheism merits the world to come (Q. 2:62, 5:69, 22:17). Not so early Christianity. The notion of salvation is repeatedly restricted in the New Testament to those who accepted belief in the saving power of Christ (John 3:36, 15:5–6, Acts 4:12). All others were excluded. Both the New Testament and the Qur'an were strongly influenced by the nature of the environments of their birth. The Qur'an is less exclusive than the New Testament because of the particular multi-monotheistic environment out of which it emerged.

To summarize our schema, therefore, we find the following.

- Long before the emergence of monotheism, all adherents of ethnically organized religion in the ancient Near East probably felt that they existed in a unique, "chosen" relationship with their primary national God.
- As monotheism emerged from this ancient Near Eastern world, it naturally retained the traditional notion of exclusive relationship inherent in national religion. The universalism of monotheism may have represented a challenge among some to the particularist notion of chosenness, but to others it may have even increased the sense of elitism because only Israelite monotheists understood the true universal nature of God.
- Before the notions of conversion, mission and reward and punishment in an afterlife, the notion of chosenness elitism had little impact on relations between religious communities.
- With the competing claims of different expressions of monotheism, chosenness became one of a core of items around which interreligious polemics were constructed. Chosenness thus became associated with monotheism in general and became a legitimizing trait of "true religion."
- Without control over political and military power, mission occurred on a largely even playing field. Jews and Christians each had an advantage over

the other at different periods during the first three centuries CE, depending on the political situation of each in relation to the Roman government.

- With the assumption of the tools of political power, it was natural for the sense of chosenness to be reflected in the policy of imperial law. Christianity, therefore, once it became the religion of empire, took on imperialist traits.
- Rabbinic Judaism, never the religion of empire, did not, although it is no less elitist and certainly would have if it could have.
- Because Christianity and Islam became the religions of great empires, they naturally engaged the powers of the state to increase their resources and numbers. Like Judaism, they developed expectations that they would become the universal religion of all humankind, but unlike Judaism, they were able to engage political and military power for the purpose of reaching this goal. Both thus became "imperialist" religions that developed justification for their use of power.
- Christianity, however, because of the particular historical environment in which it emerged, expressed the zero-sum equation in the nature of its imperialism. This resulted in an extreme form of imperialism – a kind of religious totalitarianism that stressed the requirement of membership in the Church for salvation. This development did not occur with Islam only because of the particular religious context in which it emerged and took on power.

All monotheisms feel a sense of chosenness. All are elitist. The three different historical modes of expressing that sense of election and elitism toward the Other vary in relation to history, namely, the histories of their emergence as religious systems and the histories of their ascension (or lack of ascension) to political and military power.

This exercise is an attempt at a historical deconstruction of theologies of chosenness and monotheistic elitism. It is presented here as a model for thinking about what seems to be the unending argument and competition between monotheistic religions and religious movements. It is my hope that it may stimulate more thinking and writing on the subject, and perhaps a re-evaluation of old theological assumptions.

Notes

1   "The Problem of Chosenness in Judaism, Christianity and Islam," The 2005 Sterling M. McMurrin Lecture on Religion and Culture, University of Utah (Salt Lake City: University of Utah, 2005). "Contextualizing Antisemitism in Islam: Chosenness, Choosing, and the Affects of the Birthing of New Religion," *International Journal of Applied Psychoanalytic Studies* 4:3 (2007) (www.interscience.wiley.com); "Chosenness and the Exclusivity of Truth," Institute for Advanced Catholic Studies (forthcoming). See also, Firestone, *Who is the real 'Chosen People'? The Meaning of Chosenness in Judaism, Christianity and Islam* (Woodstock, VT: Skylight Paths, 2008).

2 "Israel" is the designation for the Jewish people in traditional Jewish texts and general discourse. The actual name of the nation-state commonly known as Israel is "The State of Israel," meaning "the nation-state of the people called Israel."

3 Other forms of monotheism or proto-monotheism probably existed in the ancient world, though they could not be sustained (Donald Redford, "The Monotheism of Akhenaten," in Hershel Shanks and Jack Meinhardt, *Aspects of Monotheism* [Washington: Biblical Archaeology Society, 1996], pp. 11–26, Polymnia Athanassiadi and Michael Frede, *Pagan Monotheism in Late Antiquity* [Oxford: Oxford University Press, 1991].

4 The consonantal letters of the name are Y.H.W.H., which non-Jews have learned to pronounce as Jehovah or Yahweh. The actual name was probably used when the God was believed to be the particular national God of Israel. As Israel came to understand their deity as the God of the universe and all creation, the limitation associated with a proper name seems to have been problematic, with the likely result that articulation of the name ceased.

5 Nili Fox, "Concepts of God in Israel and the Question of Monotheism," in G. Beckman and T. Lewis (eds.), *Text, Artifact and Image: Revealing Ancient Israelite Religion* (Brown Judaic Studies, 2006), p. 342.

6 See also Romans 9:7–9.

7 It is not clear to me whether the use of a peoplehood or "race" reflects a lingering ethnic sentiment or use of a metaphor to provide meaning and relevance to the Hebrew Biblical notion in a cosmopolitan Greco-Roman world. I tend to think the latter, but more work needs to be done to parse out the meaning in the Greek and possible Hebrew/Aramaic subtexts.

8 It is tempting to rely on Cleary's translation here for *irtadaa*, " . . . which God has chosen for them" (Thomas Cleary, *The Qur'an: A New Translation* (n.p.: Starlatch Press, 2004), but although Cleary's translation is often quite insightful, the use of *irtadaa* here approaches but does not equal the meaning of chosenness.

9 For an analysis of the structural influence, see Martin Jaffee, "One God, One Revelation, One People: On the Symbolic Structure of Elective Monotheism" (*JAAR* 69:4 [2001], pp. 753–75). For an analysis of the historical influence, see Firestone (articles and monograph cited above).

10 Some scholars refer to the religion that is articulated in the Hebrew Bible as "Biblical Judaism." I prefer Biblical Religion in order to differentiate that from Judaism (or "Rabbinic Judaism").

11 "A Gentile once came to [Rabbi] Shamai and asked, "How many Torahs do you [Jews] have?" He answered, "Two. A Written Torah and an Oral Torah." (Babylonian Talmud, *Shabbat* 31a. See also *Yoma* 28b, *Kiddushin* 66a, *Exodus Rabbah* 47:3, etc.).

12 The literature treating the relationship between religionists and "the other" has grown significantly in the past few decades. See, for example, Laurence Silberstein and Robert Cohn (eds.), *The Other in Jewish Thought and History* (NY: NYU Press, 1994), Jacques Waardenburg, *Muslim Perceptions of Other Religions* (NY: Oxford, 1999).

13 Amos 9:7, Babylonian Talmud, Shabbat 88a, Acts 10:34; Q. 2:62, 5:69, 22:17.

14 The Hebrew word for "holy" is *q.d.sh*, and its base meaning is "separation" or "setting apart."

15 Or at least, that was the goal. Israel is criticized by the voice of the Hebrew Bible for *not* remaining completely loyal to their exclusive relationship with their God (Num. 25, 2 Kings 23, etc.).

16   A. D. Nock, *Conversion* (Oxford, 1933).

17   Matthew 28:18–20, Acts 10, 15; *Yebamot* 16a, 47a, *Kiddushin* 67a-b, 73a.

18   Cf. Jon Levenson, *Resurrection and the Restoration of Israel: The Ultimate Victory of the God of Life* (New Haven: Yale, 2008).

19   Fox, pp. 338–41.

20   David Biale, *Power and Powerlessness in Jewish History* (NY: Schocken, 1986), pp. 11–12.

21   H. H. Ben-Sasson (ed.), *A History of the Jewish People*, p. 219.

22   Lawrence Schiffman, *From Text to Tradition* (Ktav, 1991), p. 86.

23   See Salo Baron, "Population," *Encyclopedia Judaica* 13:870–72.

24   Although the New Testament cannot be considered an objective history, it is a historical document that chronicles Christian frustration and anger directed toward Jews who, in a natural response of establishment religion to the threatening claims of a new religious movement, were antagonistic toward it.

25   Ephraim Urbach, *The Sages* (Cambridge, MA: Harvard University Press, 1987), pp. 528–29.

26   Theodosius II (439 CE), Novella III: Concerning Jews, Samaritans, Heretics, and Pagans, cited in Jacob Rader Marcus, *The Jew in the Medieval World: A Sourcebook* (HUC Press, 1990), pp. 5–6.

27   The best known articulation of this is found in John Chrysostom (Robert Wilken, *John Chrysostom and the Jews* [Eugene, OR: Wipf and Stock, 2004], Paul Harkins, *St. John Chrysostom: Discourses against Judaizing Christians* [Washington, DC: Catholic University of America, 1979]).

28   "We desire that all the people under our clemency should live by that religion which divine Peter the apostle is said to have given the Romans. . . . We desire that heretics and schismatists be subjected to various fines. . . . We decree also that we shall cease making sacrifices to the gods. And if anyone has committed such a crime, let him be stricken with the avenging sword." (Cod. Theod. xvi, 1, 2; v, 1; x, 4)

29   See, for example, Eusebius, *Life of Constantine* 2:46: "But no, that liberty is restored, and that serpent driven from the administration of public affairs by the providence of the Supreme God, and our instrumentality, we trust that all can see the efficacy of the Divine power, and that they who through fear of persecution or through unbelief have fallen into any errors, will not acknowledge the true God, and adopt in future that course of life which is according to truth and rectitude." I am grateful to Prof. Joshua Holo for bringing this citation to my attention.

30   Joseph Schacht, *An Introduction to Islamic Law* (Oxford: Clarendon, 1964); N. J. Coulson, *A History of Islamic Law* (Edinburgh, University of Edinburgh, 1964).

31   See, for example, Abu 'Abadallah Muhammad b. Al-Hasan al-Shaybani, *Kitab al-siyar al-kabir* (Beirut: Dar al-Kutub al-'Ilmiyya, n.d., translated from the Arabic by Majid Khadduri as *The Islamic Law of Nations: Shaybani's Siyar* (Maryland: Johns Hopkins, 1966); Majid Khadduri, *War and Peace in the Law of Islam* (Maryland: Johns Hopkins, 1955), Rudolph Peters, *Jihad in Classical and Modern Islam* (Princeton: Markus Wiener, 1996).

32   See V. P. Varma, *The Political Philosophy of Sri Aurobindo* (Delhi: Motilal Banarsidass, 1998), pp. 58–60.

33   Uri Rubin, "*Hanifiyya* and Ka'ba: An Inquiry into the pre-Islamic Background of *din ibrahim*," in *Jerusalem Studies in Arabic and Islam* 13 (1990), pp. 85, 112;

Ella Landau-Tasseron, "Unearthing a Pre-Islamic Arabian Prophet," in *JSAI* 21 (1997), pp. 42–61, and G. R. Hawting, *The Idea of Idolatry and the Emergence of Islam: From Polemic to History* (Cambridge: Cambridge University Press, 1999).

CHAPTER

2

Interdependence of Scripture

BENJAMIN BRAUDE

The Bible, as conventionally imagined today, was invented by Luther, Gutenberg, and Gideon, with considerable help from the Prophet Muhammad. Most of us know Luther and Gutenberg and can imagine how each contributed to the invention of the current Bible. Luther was the first to showcase it as the fount of all Christian truth, *sola scriptura*. Gutenberg was the first to set it to the printer's font, fostering its ultimate emergence as the cheap, compact, convenient, medium that Gideon has placed in hotel rooms throughout the country. You remember Gideon. He was the one who left his Bible to help with Rocky Racoon's revival, according to the gospel of Paul . . . McCartney. However Islam's invention of the Christian Bible is not commonly taught in Sunday School. Yet Muhammad and his successors, including Luther's contemporaries, the mighty Sultans of the Ottoman Empire, have all played a role in creating a book whose existence is today taken for granted as a distinctly Judeo-Christian icon.

Conventional assumptions about Abrahamic scriptures typically treat them as three different developments of greater or lesser independence. The Jews had their Bible which they had gathered over the centuries. Around the 2nd century after the birth of Jesus Christ, the Christians added an appendix to the book the Jews had written, tagging their distinct addition the New Covenant or Testament, and the prior work the Old. In the 7th century Muslims developed a scripture of their own that came to be called the Qur'an, that is, the Recitation. This simpleminded history has provided one justification for contemporary political nostrums that contrast the so-called Judeo-Christian tradition with Islam, or the West with the East. Since Jews and Christians share, to a degree, a Bible and since Muslims do not, there seems to be a foundational difference between the first two religions and the last. However the conventional history is not merely simpleminded, it is wrong.[1]

The scriptural reality is far more complicated. Jews and Christians do not truly share the Old Testament, let alone the Bible as a whole. Quite apart from the elementary details of name, language, text, and, most important of all, hermeneutic, the actual books of the Christian Old Testament differ from what Jews put in their Scripture. It is a cardinal belief of the Christian biblical hermeneutic that the first part of their Bible is what was given to the Jews, but historically Jews have rejected that notion. Even among Christians there is no agreement as to what constitutes the Bible, for Catholics, Orthodox, and Protestants also differ with each other on its contents. To be sure *grosso modo*, Jews and Christians do share many of, but not all, the books of the Bible, a sharing in which Muslims do not participate. On the other hand, the Qur'an does include many of the stories of Torah and Gospel, including the latter's core. Jesus and Mary, important characters in the Qur'an, are absent from Hebrew Holy Writ. Thus in that crucial respect the Qur'an is closer to the New Testament than anything within the Jewish tradition. By contrast the role of scripture in Islam is far closer to its role in Judaism than in Christianity. Both Jews and Muslims believe that the most important gift God has given humanity is the Holy Word of Revelation. For Christians alone, Jesus Christ trumps Scripture. In sum the scriptural traditions of Judaism, Christianity, and Islam represent a complex changing nexus of divergence and convergence. Depending on the criterion, anyone's scripturality may or may not be more or less different from any other's.

None of this should be surprising once we recognize that, despite the current convention, the Good Book is not one book, but many. The history of the word reveals the history of its complexity. Hebrew has no true equivalent for Bible. Today the term most commonly employed for the Jewish scripture is not a word, but rather the initial letters of the Jewish holy writ's traditional three cores, *TaNaKh* – the acronym of *Torah* ("Teaching"), *Nevi'im* ("Prophets"), and *Ketuvim* ("Writings"). Translated into English the word would be TPW, hardly a term to inspire thoughts of divine revelation since it sounds like a manufacturer of automotive parts. The origins of the term *TaNaKh* are obscure, but seem to date no earlier than the sixth or seventh centuries, perhaps later.[2] "Bible" is not a Hebrew word nor is it, as conventionally understood, a Jewish concept. That word is derived from Greek. It was probably first employed by the Greek-speaking Jews of Alexandria in Hellenistic Egypt beginning in the 3rd century before the current era. They translated Hebrew holy writings into Greek, a text later known as the Septuagint, so called because by legend seventy or so scholars produced it. The words – note the "s" – they employed to describe this collective effort were *Ta Biblia*, literally "The Scrolls", a plural expression, reflecting many multiplicities, of the translators, of their sources, and of their products, as well as the medium through which this work circulated. What Greek-speaking Jewry regarded as holy writ, what they included among *Ta Biblia*, was not exactly what later Jews and many Christians have called the Bible. Although most of it would be familiar to today's believers much of it would not, since it included books which later came to be excluded from one canon or another. *Ta Biblia* illustrate an element of indeterminacy characteristic of the development of holy writ in general. It requires a very long process for the holiness of its component parts to be finally determined. And even believers who claim to subscribe to the same beliefs do not necessarily agree about the holiness of the same texts. So what emerges is a changing corpus of texts that we may call a loose canon, with all the flexibility, ambiguity, and potential divisiveness that such a term implies.

As *Ta Biblia*, suggest, one simple reason for the difficulty of defining the contents of scripture thousands of years ago was that, unlike today, they could not easily exist as a single physical unit. The physical medium through which Holy Writ is expressed is often ignored by believers and scholars alike. In fact the varied forms scriptures have taken offer one key to understanding the similarities and differences between Torah, Gospel, and Qur'an. Consider the written media available in the ancient world. Characteristic of Mesopotamia were clay tablets and cylinders, but such documents were too heavy to be long. About two thousand years ago, at the beginning of the current era, the clay tablet finally disappeared in the Mediterranean basin, though it survived further east. Within the Hellenistic world Nile papyrus beat Mesopotamian clay. The writing material which in turn supplanted papyrus, universally available and more resilient, was leather and, its later evolution, parchment. It was more durable than papyrus and certainly more widely available in and suited for different climates, but it was more expensive. It was tough enough for lengthy scrolls. It may be no accident that the earliest antecedent for Bible, *Ta Biblia*, dates from the century that, at least according to tradition, witnessed the popularization of parchment. However exactly when and where parchment became well-established is unknown and papyrus continued to be used, most notably in Egypt.[3]

The *sine qua non* of the modern Bible was the codex, a breakthrough that was to shape scripture in Christianity and Islam. The codex consisted of bound parchment or papyrus, later paper, on which a scribe transcribed text. Like the modern book its folios were composed of many large sheets carefully folded within each other and sewn together at one edge to create a tightly connected unit, usually put between two covers and bound. In many respects its invention was even more revolutionary than Gutenberg's moveable type. In no way is that to diminish the awesome consequences of the Gutenberg revolution, rather it is to underscore how significant the codex was. Gutenberg took this existing medium and mechanized the way it was written – moveable type replaced the scribal hand. The result of that mechanization created something that proved to be a huge source of cultural change through the diffusion of hundreds and later thousands of copies of the same text. However physically, the printed book did not look much different, at least initially, from the manuscript book.

The codex as opposed to the scroll, on the other hand, felt different, and was handled differently. With its own bound cover, the codex no longer needed pottery or pigeonholes to store and protect it. It was significantly more compact and much more easily transported in bulk, particularly for long texts, since unlike scrolls both sides of the page could be used. Most significantly of all, the angular codex imposed upon text the abstract Aristotelian notions of beginning, middle, and end in a way that the infinite curvature of a scroll could not. The scroll was an open expandable tube that curved in on itself. The codex was a closable box. Sew or paste another parchment or papyrus onto the scroll and it could keep expanding. The consequent bulk would set limits, but a bit here and there would not matter. Scrolls conveyed a marvelous sense of textual fluidity. While there were limits to what a single scroll could practically contain, scrolls could temporarily envelop scrolls, metaphorically signaling that while each component retained its own identity it still was part of a larger changing whole. Codices cannot contain each other. Rearrange, add, or subtract scrolls of *Ta Biblia* in their honeycombed shelving and the biblical order and canon was changed. If *Ta Biblia* are contained within a bound book, order and canon are bound as well.

Codex and Christianity

It has long been accepted by historians of the book that the triumph of the codex was somehow linked to the rise of Christianity.[4] The adoption of the codex despite its disadvantages of time and cost over the scroll – calculating the number of pages and sewing the sheets together in advance of the actual writing was a painstaking process – enabled Christianity to distinguish itself from Judaism not only in terms of belief and ritual but also in terms of the physical manifestation of its distinctiveness. One element which separated Christianity from Judaism was its conception and dating of a critical rupture in the history of divine revelation, a distinction between what it came to call the Old and the New Testaments. A version of this distinction appeared first in Paul's Second Letter to the Corinthians (3:6 and 14). It was elaborated by the founding Church Father of Christian exegesis, Irenaeus, in the 2nd century. The codex, as a closed book, metaphorically represented this distinctive rupture far more effectively than did the scroll. Putting the Jewish *Ta Biblia* into codices neatly conveyed two significant messages simultaneously. By using a new form Christianity was signaling its own novel departure from the old covenant. By putting its version of that old sacred text into a format whose beginning and end were immediately and clearly apparent, Christianity signaled that the book could now be closed on the old dispensation. Once Christianity adapted the codex for the original revelation to the Children of Israel, force of habit and established practice continued it for its own message.

Thus a basic difference between the Jewish and Christian understandings of *Ta Biblia* lay in the very forms in which each presented sacred text. But the degree of this difference in form should be qualified. True, Judaism was a scroll religion. Its continued insistence upon the scroll in its liturgical use of scripture – a single large scroll for the Pentateuch and scrolls of varying length for the other sections – can be understood as conservative resistance to Christianity's adoption of the new form. Christianity was a codex religion, but it first developed in a scroll religious context. Although Judaism liturgically revered Torah as a scroll, it apparently did adopt the codex, albeit in the study house not the house of prayer.[5] In the 4th century after Emperor Constantine accepted Christianity as a state religion, he ordered that dozens of elaborate parchment codices be prepared for the churches of his new capital, Constantinople. Thereby he proclaimed not only imperial support for this religion, but it also its distinctive textual medium.[6] Still the Eastern Churches did retain the scroll for its liturgy. Thus while recognizing the textual preferences within each religion it would be a mistake to insist upon a consistent categorical distinction.

One indication of the continuing plurality of media that was so characteristic of transitional scroll–codex culture was Jerome's late 4th century term for Bible, *Bibliotheca*, the sacred library, which he used in preference to *Ta Biblia*.[7] Since Jerome had translated its entirety from Hebrew and Greek, his judgment deserves respect. Had the only Bible Jerome known been the magnificent single volume codices of Constantine's donation, such a term would have been as strange to him as it might seem to us, 1600 years later. By adopting *Bibliotheca* Jerome acknowledged *Ta Biblia*, its many books, a library of sacred writ in Hebrew, Aramaic, Greek, and Latin, in scroll and codex, in parchment and papyrus, and his term captured the diversity of this literature. Jerome's *Bibliotheca* was retained into the Middle Ages, persisting in both Latin and Old English. In fact it seems to have been the original term used in both languages for what is now called the Bible. As to the content of this library, there are significant variations and conflicts. According to the usage of some early Christians, retained into the 16th century and persisting even today among a few dialects of modern English, the sacred library consisted of the Bible (i.e. the Old Testament) and the Testament (i.e. New Testament).[8]

Incremental Reluctant Canonization

The rise of Christianity helped force the canonization of *Ta Biblia*.[9] Its adoption and dissemination of the codex created a textual medium naturally more inclined to binding order and organization than the scroll. Its desire to categorize the historic *Ta Biblia* as the Old Testament, advanced the impulse towards the scriptural rigidity of a canon. The loose canon was starting to lose its looseness. To be sure within Judaism there had already been a tendency towards incremental canonization. Within centuries of their original composition and subsequent redaction the contents and order of different books became generally accepted as normative, ideally no longer subject to alteration or addition. While the first and second parts, the Torah had been set by roughly the 5th (if not earlier) century BCE, and the Prophets, a bit later, the third part, the Writings, were still a open grab-bag in the age of Jesus. In order to define a specific form of Judaism against rivals, notably other religions that have not survived and the one which proclaimed itself the continuation of the old, it was necessary metaphorically to close the book against what was perceived as an increasingly alien penetration, even though this was contrary to the psychology of scroll culture. Not only were Christian writings excluded, but also other religious texts of Jewish, Jewish–Christian, Jewish sectarian, or uncertain origin which for a variety of reasons were not considered appropriate by the rabbinical canonizers, though they had been part of the part of the community's holy legacy. Among these were the so-called Apocryphal or Deuterocanonical books, late writings of a scriptural character which are today accepted as Biblical and canonized into the Old Testament by the Roman Catholic Church and, to a degree, the Eastern Orthodox, but rejected by Protestants. These include the Books of Tobias, Judith, Ecclesiasticus (as opposed to Ecclesiastes), and Maccabees. Further differences arose within the Old Testament text itself. Christianity rejected the tripartite division of Jewish scripture. While Christianity proclaimed itself the fulfillment of *Ta Biblia* and accepted a version of this scripture as its own, there are some passages in works such as Jeremiah, Esther, and Daniel which appear in most Christian, but not the Jewish versions. Thus the differences between the Jewish and various Christian canons involved the organization and order of the books of the Bible, the presence or absence of specific books, and the actual contents of others. Judaism survived with a loose canon for a century or so after the birth of Jesus. With the rise of Christianity and a host of other increasingly vociferous cults within Judaism, the risks of a loose cannon became increasingly apparent.

The End of a Roll

Christianity and the codex were but two of the reasons for the decline of scroll culture. More important than either and in fact the cause of the first were the radical political challenges of the first and second centuries caused by Roman imperial expansion. The destruction of the Temple and the Judean kingdom in the year 70, the Roman suppression of repeated Jewish uprisings through the early centuries of the current era, coupled with the rise of the Jesus movement created an existential crisis of survival. The community of Israel had three pillars: the Judean commonwealth, the Temple in Jerusalem, and the Torah. The Roman conquest of 70 left only one standing. With the other major institutions of identity removed, a core scripture was forced to the sole foundation of the community together.

Nearly two millennia later after World War I the community of Islam faced a similar crisis following the collapse of the Caliphate. Like the Ottoman Caliphate, the Herodian monarchy in Palestine deviated from the pious traditions of their respective religions and provoked much internal opposition, but each acted as a recognized symbol of unity and identity for its community. The disappearance of the caliphate and the Ottoman Empire, for centuries bulwarks of Islamic power and self-confidence, compelled a greater reliance on the other elements of Islamic society, notably a reinforcement of its textual foundation, the Qur'an, and its normative elaboration, the Shari'a. The consequences of this unsettling shift are still unfolding. If the Jewish precedent is any indication, they will be far-reaching.

Within the Jewish tradition these challenges effected a radical change in the nature and interpretation of scripture. Otherwise, the grab-bag third part of *Ta Biblia*, *Writings*, might have continued to expand to include the Apocrypha, as it then existed, and also the later rabbinic writings which eventually took different formats, created different genres, and came to be called Mishnah, Talmud, and Midrash and so on endlessly. Physically, all such incorporation required was more space on the shelves for additional scrolls. Preventing this was an opposing preservative instinct which came to dominate in the midst of the crisis. The emerging rabbinic leadership could not tolerate the risk that Jewish holy writ would be undermined by the integration of doctrine which they dismissed as spurious and alien. Yet the older instincts of permanent scriptural expansion and inclusion could not be completely abandoned. Here there was an inherent conflict. A fluid notion of scripture had allowed those who called themselves successively and variously Hebrews, Israelites, Judeans and later Jews, to move from polytheist nature worship, to YAHWEH-focused sacrificial cult, to state-centralized Jerusalem Temple-based monotheist supremacy, and to the beginnings of deterritorialized text-based monotheism. But could this protean procession continue without end? If it did, would it not run the risk of transforming itself out of existence, particularly during the confrontation with the various millenarian movements that flourished after 70, Christianity included? The solution as it evolved in the second and third centuries was a classic example of attempting to eat one's cake while keeping it afterward. Part of the corpus would be declared inviolate and untouchable, still the scroll psychology of textual agglutination would continue. Teaching, Prophets, and Writings were not to be the alpha and omega of divine revelation according to Judaism. They were to be framed by the Oral Tradition, an umbrella category for the new rabbinic writings including the Talmud and Midrash, the former the legal-normative exploration of Scripture, the latter its homiletic-legendary exposition. The Oral Tradition occupied a position of authority different from that of the Written Tradition, as scripture (particularly the Pentateuch) was called. The Oral Tradition was an essential tool for collective survival. Two traditional pillars of communal existence had been destroyed and it was necessary to invent new institutions and practices to replace them. Still the principle of tradition had to be upheld even as its content of kingdom and sacrificial cult had been destroyed. Otherwise the surviving heirs might very well be destroyed as well, or at the very least disappear. Few moments in history are as fraught as the destruction that the community confronted. Torah and learning had to replace Temple and sacrifice. Torah had to be maintained as a firm pillar even as it assumed this new role as a flexible bridge to new forms of communal existence and religious ritual.

Unfortunately, the customary English terms, Written and Oral Traditions, misrepresent the original. The Hebrew for Tradition in each case is in fact Torah, the Memorized Torah and the Written Torah respectively – literally "the Torah on the Mouth" and "the Torah in Writing". The modern periphrastic preference for the word "Tradition" reflected the desire on the part of modern scholars to avoid any confusion between Torah and Torah. That misses the point. It is precisely the lack of boundary between these two which is at the heart of the Jewish concept of sacred textual space. The omnipresence and flexibility of Torah allowed for the expansion of the canon. Control of this loose canon had to be in the hands of those who devoted their lives to its mastery and study. Otherwise it could be dangerous. Reflecting the trauma caused by the secession of the followers of Jesus and other ancient dissidents, for many centuries the rabbis, invoking an oft-repeated story, refused to permit the writing down of the Memorized Torah lest it, like *Ta Biblia*, also fall into hostile hands.[10] And so the rabbinical tradition claimed that this Torah literally came to be committed to memory. Scholars and later scribes who preserved and propounded it gradually took over from prophets and priests who had first composed it.[11] Although the possibility of false messengers, fraudulent messiahs, and their followers was not eliminated, the arduous process of education and socialization necessary to achieve authority in this community of learning made interloping difficult.

Torah, thus understood, came to encompass the entire enterprise of Jewish learning, creating to a degree, an almost seamless web of intellectual devotion to text. It is this quality of Torah inextricably and almost indistinguishably enveloped within the warp and woof of an ongoing and evolving creative enterprise that makes the modern concept of Bible as a separate and distinct book apart, so alien to the Jewish tradition of open-ended scroll culture. That is one more reason to dismiss the Judeo-Christian tradition as a misnomer.

The Expansion of the Christian Great Bible

As we have already learned, Christians have read *Ta Biblia* differently from Jews. These differences were expressed not only through different languages, different canons, and in some instances, different contents, but also through a different set of exegetical principles and questions, an overarching hermeneutic. Christianity rejected, in principle, the Memorized Torah. However in practice the relationship between Christian and rabbinic interpretation was much more complex and interconnected. Since the 19th century a considerable amount of scholarly energy has been expended to ferret out the parallels between rabbinic and patristic explication of scripture, but similarity is by itself no proof of interaction and influence. In many instances these parallels may simply have reflected an earlier Israelite source common to both. Yet among such central figures in the history of the Church as Origen (185?–254?) and Jerome (340?–420) at least some rabbinic influence has been demonstrated.[12]

Despite such interaction there was an all-powerful difference between the two. For Christians, *Ta Biblia* were secondary to Jesus Christ. Revelation was overwhelmed by Incarnation. The Old Testament was problematic for early Christianity. It evoked two contradictory impulses. Some wished to abandon it completely in order to proclaim Christianity's total break with its Jewish past. But others, while accepting Jesus as the Christ, wished to hold on to the Israelite *Ta Biblia*. The compromise which eventually triumphed accepted *Ta Biblia*, but with the insistence that it be read to prove that Jesus was indeed the Messiah promised by Israelite prophecy. This hermeneutic began in the New Testament and was continued by the Church Fathers. The effect was structurally similar to the Memorized Torah in Rabbinic Judaism. While the Fathers rejected its claims, they accepted the underlying principle behind it, namely that there must be a tradition of interpretation, in this case, the Magisterial Teaching of the Church, that offered the only correct way to understand sacred writ. The Church Fathers accepted this notion of an expanded bible, but to a more limited and precise degree than did the Rabbis. The Christian hermeneutic had to adhere to a rigid discipline of purposeful and consistent interpretation to ensure that its Old Testament not be allowed to deviate from the correct theological line. Those parts of the text which did not lend themselves to such interpretation were neglected. The mental discipline required to navigate the extremely narrow passage between rejection and acceptance of the Israelite *Biblia* was extremely demanding.

By the dawn of the 7th century, before the age of Muhammad, both Judaism and Christianity had developed similar bibles. Each took as their foundation ancient Near Eastern Hebrew and Aramaic texts preserved by the Israelites and the Judeans. Their selection of texts from this corpus overlapped, but was not the same. Each employed a tendentious hermeneutic lens to understand these texts, thereby shaping and expanding the content and meaning of the original stories, in order to create their respective Great Bibles. The rabbinic lens was intended to facilitate the transition from a temple-centered polity to a state-free text-based community. The patristic lens was intended to facilitate the transition of those texts from their roots in that prior polity and community to the savior-based faithful. Together Judaism and Christianity had established and diffused a dominant narrative discourse that drew upon and expanded a corpus of stories now universalized beyond their distinctive origins to become a kind of religious lingua franca. That expanded narrative created a sacred textual space in which both participated, whether in concord or discord. Soon a third joined that community of discourse.

The Development and Influence of the Muslim Bible

Islam succeeded in the 7th century because Christianity destroyed itself. Islam can be understood as the resolution of two nearly fatal original problems in Christianity – Christology and *Ta Biblia*. The nature of Jesus Christ – divine, human, or some mysterious position in between or combining both – was the central question fissuring Christianity in the centuries before the rise of Islam. It had led to civil wars, exacerbated by the Roman imperialization of Christianity under Constantine. Only after Islam conquered the Byzantine territory dominated by one disaffected faction – the so-called Monophysite position – and effectively took them out of combat, did this war end. Ultimately the civil wars and the rise of Islam effectively ended Christian control of its heartland. The Muslim conquests of the 7th century completely disrupted the balance of ecclesiastical power, transforming the church forever. Undermining the historic centers, Alexandria, Antioch, and Jerusalem, Islam made Rome stronger than it had ever been. The other hierarchical imperial late-comer, Constantinople, though weakened did survive. Eight centuries later the Ottoman conquest of Constantinople undermined Rome's only surviving rival and gave the Bishop of Rome more power than he had ever known. Muhammad and his followers have proved to be allies of the papacy, perhaps the greatest.

In reaction to the mystery of incarnation and all the theological gymnastics and civil wars that followed, Islam reasserted absolute monotheism. Islam's creedal statements can be read as a direct polemic against the Trinity – "There is no God, but God" and "He begetteth not, nor is He begotten". The second problem, *Ta Biblia*, has received less attention, but was also addressed by Islam. Islam resolved to avoid the textual bigamy which Christianity imposed on what it called the Old Testament. Instead of trying to claim for itself that same coveted text through editorial and exegetical sleight of hand, Islam offered its own, a kind of *Reader's Digest* revised version of the existing Great Bible. Its stories are to be found in the Qur'an, but now conform to the new dispensation. The Jewish Great Bible is denuded of family history and genealogies. The Christian Great Bible is stripped of any hints at the divinity of Jesus. There are few names and places in the Qur'an – to the point that not even Mecca or Jerusalem, as such, merit a mention. Much that appears in the biblical accounts is absent from the Qur'an, while other stories and episodes, though presented with the same authority as those to be found in the Torah (narrowly defined) or the Gospels, in fact do not originate there. Where did they come from? While absent from *Ta Biblia* these stories do reflect the contents of the Great Bibles, the shared sacred scriptural space that was pervasive in the orally-attuned ancient world of late scroll culture, preserved and promulgated in the expanded genres of Jewish and Christian exegesis.

Dominating the Qur'anic narrative are two themes, the transcendence of the One God, and the history of His revelation, conveyed through a succession of prophets, culminating in the seal of the prophets, Muhammad. Islam's understanding of prophethood differed, although most of the Qur'an's cast of prophetic characters did appear in the Jewish or Christian Great Bibles. The most important of the Prophets were transmitters of a revelation from God, and as such, though never divine, the closest on earth to God. Muhammad, as the last best hope of humanity, was the closest to God that has ever been or will be.

The importance of scripture to Islam cannot be overestimated. The Qur'an is to Islam what Christ is to Christianity. Islam reversed a relationship established when Christ's incarnation overwhelmed Israel's revelation. Now text trumped all. Although Christianity has been linked to the codex, it began in a scroll culture. Islam was the first codex religion. It arose in the 7th century, long after this form had been well-established. The implications of this fact are significant. While the scroll-culture Torah became a term infinitely expanding to encompass ever more Jewish learning, the Qur'an never designated anything but itself. And while Islam developed an interpretive tradition for the Qur'an, the distinction between this tradition and the Qur'an itself was scrupulously maintained. For instance the gloss-enveloped or bordered *Ta Biblia* such as the medieval *Biblia Latina cum Glossa Ordinaria*, the Reformation *Geneva Bible* or the Hebrew *Mikraot Gdolot* has no equivalent in Islam. When gloss or commentary accompanied the text of the Qur'an such a volume could never be called a Qur'an in traditional usage, but rather was named after its commentator alone. Nonetheless the Qur'an did not emerge as a neatly-bound self-contained volume out of the head of Zeus, or, in this case, the angel Gabriel, but instead rapidly experienced all of the historic stages involved in the preservation of divine revelation. The Qur'an literally means "Recitation." Its verses were first preserved through memory, palm-branches, tablets, flat stones, and whatever else was handy. According to later traditions, as pious Qur'an memorizers started to be lost in the early battles of Islam, steps were taken within a decade of the death of the prophet Muhammad to compile their verses into a book. Its scattered origins as well as its *Ta Biblia* antecedents are reflected in its synonym, the collective *al-Mushaf*, i.e. *The Collection of Pages* or *The Texts*, the name given by the companion of the prophet, Salim, who was one of the early collectors of Qur'anic texts. Significantly that *Collection* Salim had first heard in Christian Ethiopia, whose Eastern Christianity preserved a scroll culture distant from Constantine's codex donations. The operative process is revealingly described as "to collect the Quran between two covers," a physical conception of sacred text not employed at so early a stage by Islam's predecessors.[13] The process of creating a canon that took at least six centuries in Judaism and about three in Christianity, in Islam took a matter of decades. With the rise of Islam, codex culture had fully triumphed.

In Islam The Book became literally a matter of life or death. Islam divided non-Muslims into two categories, those who had a Book and those who did not. Life, with certain restrictions, was allowed the first. Death or conversion to Islam was theoretically the fate of the second. As presented in the Qur'an, the first category covered Jews and Christians who were clearly heirs to the Great Biblical prophetic tradition, as well as the obscure Sabians. The Qur'an called them *ahl al-kitab*, literally People of the Book. The second group was more difficult to define. It included those outside this tradition, primarily the idol-worshipping polytheist pagans who had been Muhammad's first adversaries in Mecca, and others who could be described as beyond the pale of properly organized religion. As Islam came into contact with Zoroastrians and Hindus, problems arose. The second category seemed to apply to both groups, but the practical difficulties of mass forced conversion or mass murder prevented the consistent application of either policy. One solution was the quickie book. Muslim jurists started to recognize as a Book the fluid sacred textual traditions in each of these religions, which could be linked to the Sabians. While Judaism and Christianity were not under such pressure, the Islamic life or death insistence on having a book – some academics might claim it reminiscent of the tenure process – gave impetus to focus on their respective *Biblia*.

In Judaism this was reflected in even greater attention to the work of the Masoretes, the scribes and scholars who preserved the text of Hebrew scripture. Around the time of the rise of Islam, the culmination of their work was achieved, the vocalization – that is the addition of vowel marks – of the text, which, remember, had survived in the consonant-only vowel-free alphabet characteristic of Semitic languages. Out of this enterprise the acronym *TaNaKh*, the closest Hebrew equivalent to the term Bible developed, as we have already learned. But since these events cannot be dated precisely, the causal relationship remains uncertain. It is worth noting that vocalizing the *TaNaKh* produced a text that in that respect closely resembled the Qur'an which had been painstakingly vocalized by Arab grammarians. Suffice it to say that both the collection and preservation of the Qur'an and the work of the Masoretes were closely parallel activities. The connection is much more compelling in another development which clearly did emerge after the message spread by Muhammad. The Karaite challenge to Rabbinite Judaism arose in the 9th century within the lands of Islam. It insisted on the primacy of the entire Written Torah, Prophets, and Writings and rejected the Memorized Torah. In practice the Karaites adopted their own interpretive devices which bore similarities even to their Rabbinite opponents.[14] Karaism's claim to get back to the text echoed Islam's own text-based identity and anticipated by seven centuries a similar effort by Luther and the Reformation. Both its name, Karaite (or Qaraite) – etymologically related to Qur'an – and its focus clearly reflected its interaction with Islam. Although Karaism never displaced Rabbinite dominance, it did force Judaism to give greater attention to its scriptural heritage.

Since the extra-biblical genres in Christianity never assumed the bulk and importance that rabbinic literature did in Judaism, it did not respond to

Islam's challenge with the same convulsions as the earlier religion. However in the aftermath of the rise of Islam an almost imperceptibly subtle change did take place in the Christian attitude toward its scripture. The Greek neuter plural, *Ta Biblia*, "The Scrolls," had smoothly been accepted in Latin as the same gender and number, *Biblia*. But at some point in the middle ages – it is attested by at least the 11th century – *Biblia* started to become a Latin feminine singular.[15] Conceptually a single unit, a book, began to replace a collection of scrolls, only three-quarters of a millennium or so after the invention of the codex. The Christians now at last had a *Kitab*.

The Qur'an is an admirably austere and seemingly universalist book with few betrayals of its origin. The transcendence of its God, the virtue of His messengers, the over-riding purity of its ethics are messages repeated again and again, with remarkably few details of time, place, and person. The contrast to the gossipy, anecdotal, exuberant digressiveness of biblical tales is striking. How could the Qur'an maintain such laconic consistency? Islam itself has claimed that the Qur'an was the original essence of the message given all God's messengers from Adam on and that the superfluities of the Jewish and Christian writs represented the accretions and distortions caused by a centuries-old game of broken telephone and worse. As dismissive as Islam was of all that accumulation of misinformed gossip, Muslims not only heard it and knew it very well, but also, to a large measure, came to accept it and understand the Qur'an through it. The possessors of the Qur'an exploited what economists call the free-rider principle. That is the ability to take advantage of generally available benefits without having to pay for them. Muslims could maintain a comparatively pristine and consistent text bearing a clear ethical message, without having to be distracted by the messy narrative contradictions and complexities of time, place, and personality, because all those missing details were already supplied and paid for by the well-known accounts of the Jewish and Christian Great Bibles. Whatever problems arose out of those details were not the concern of Islam, but rather reflected the misunderstandings piled on the true original text – as preserved in the Qur'an – by those less reliable Jews and Christians.[16]

Despite professed disdain, elements of their Great Bibles rapidly came to be assimilated into the accepted interpretation of the Qur'an. Like the Memorized Torah for the Jews, and the New Testament and Magisterial Teaching of the Church for Christians, Muslims too acquired a tradition of interpretation by which their scripture could reliably be understood. This was called the *Sunna*. Like the Memorized Torah, the *Sunna* was not a specific text, but rather originally an oral tradition. At its core were the events or sayings attributed to the Prophet Muhammad or his close companions by a meticulously studied chain of tradition, known as *hadith* ("deed" or "utterance") literature. This literature was immense and offered a diverse abundance of grist for the interpretive mill. The earliest efforts at understanding the Qur'an were expressed through the careful collection of such stories and the systematic verification of the reliability and existence at the time and place in question of each individual who, purportedly, witnessed or transmitted the saying or event. Of prime importance were the Sayings of the Prophet about the meaning of the Qur'an. But what his followers had to say – though clearly of lesser authority – was not ignored. Those known to be learned in the Jewish and Christian Great Bibles were an important direct source for Muslim interpretation. Revealingly, attitudes toward the value of their accounts in explicating the Qur'an have varied over the centuries of Islam. Initially they tended to command respect, but subsequently they came to be dismissed.

In the late 9th-early 10th century Qur'anic studies matured beyond the collection and verification of the *hadith* to its next stage, *tafsir*, that is the explication of the meaning of the text on the basis of the Sayings of the Prophet and his companions. The earliest major work in this genre was by Abu Jafar Muhammad ibn Jarir al-Tabari (839–923), a Persian who wrote in Arabic and was one of the most accomplished and prolific scholars in the history of culture. His wide-ranging erudition, literary style, and critical judgment were astounding. He carefully assessed the corpus of Muslim traditions and proposed his own interpretations to resolve their contradictions and disagreements, an effort which fully justified the title he gave it, *The Complete Clarification of the Interpretation of the Verses of the Quran. The Complete Clarification*, usually called *The Tafsir*, was completed sometime between 896 and 903 and fills some sixteen volumes in modern printings.[17] What he had learned and could not incorporate into his commentary he assembled for his next mammoth project, a history of the world, based upon his own Muslim Persian perspective, from creation until 915, *The History of Prophets and Kings*. Its English translation consumes forty volumes.[18] As the title suggests, Tabari's interests were not limited to royalty but encompassed as well the very same prophets whose divine messages formed the Qur'an.

Tabari was highly influential. He was not only prolific, but popular. Copies of his works – in the original and, for the *History*, in abridgement and translations as well – spread throughout the Muslim world. One reason for such widespread diffusion was the last major innovation in the technology of the book, before printing itself, the invention and adoption of paper. The Chinese invented paper probably about two millennia ago, but Muslims started to use and manufacture it many centuries before Europeans. It was already well-established in Baghdad when Tabari embarked upon his voluminous production. Paper was far cheaper, lighter, and more manageable than parchment. It was also more widely available and flexible than papyrus, whose continued use by this period was largely confined to Egypt. Paper made books far cheaper and more easily available, but paper did not immediately effect production of the Qur'an. Just as a conservative impulse maintained the scroll for Torah in Judaism so parchment survived for the Qur'an in Islam, but Muslim conservatism was weaker than Jewish and by the 10th century paper Qur'ans started to appear.

Paper took longer to reach Europe. It did not make its way directly from

China, but rather through the Islamic world. The first areas to use it were the closest to Islam: Italy, starting in the late 11th century, and Spain. By the 13th century the material had become so common that Europeans started to manufacture it themselves widely. Taking advantage of widespread water-power to run the mills, their paper was cheaper and soon it flooded the entire Mediterranean market, Muslim as well as Christian. Paper was the essential raw material for that next innovation, the printing press. Just as Islam had been the first of the three Abrahamic religions to insist that divine revelation be a book, so it was the first to adopt and spread the technology, paper, that ultimately made that medium an affordable commonplace.[19]

The Development of the Christian Great Bible

Compared to the abundant attention to scripture displayed by Jews and Muslims, and despite their early efforts Christians still lagged behind. Its major breakthrough did not occur until quite late, the 12th century, after scripture started to become a feminine singular. Not coincidentally this was during the very period which saw Peter the Venerable organize in Cluny, almost four hundred kilometers from Paris, a team of scholars to translate the Qur'an and other Muslim texts into Latin. Around the mid-12th century in Laon, much closer to the metropolis, another school of scholars completed the *Glossa ordinaria*, extracts mainly from early Church Fathers, organized as a running commentary on the whole Bible. At the beginning of that same century the Abbey of St. Victor in Paris was founded. It transformed biblical study in Christendom, producing a series of works, in the Great Biblical tradition, which defined the subject for the rest of the Middle Ages. The most important of these was the *Historia Scholastica* of Peter Comestor, who was to become the chancellor of the cathedral school of Paris.

Peter the Eater, to give his name its literal translation, like the great medieval Jewish commentator Rashi (Rabbi Solomon bar Isaac), came from Troyes, about one hundred miles east of Paris. He was born around 1100 just five years before that rabbi's death. Whether or not the work of Rashi and his colleagues and successors were directly known to Comestor remains a matter of scholarly debate, though the coincidence of their near contemporaneity, shared origin, and common enterprise has made the assumption of a connection tempting. Whatever the sources and influences, Peter's book represented the most successful revolution in the history of Christian biblical exegesis from its origins until the era of the Renaissance, printing, and the Reformation. It rescued *Ta Biblia* from the strait-jacket of theology in which Irenaeus had protectively placed it in the 2nd century. In terms of the history of the Great Bibles, Peter finally introduced into Christianity literary forms and approaches which had existed in Judaism and Islam for centuries, the rewritten Bible, e.g. Jubilees (a work preserved largely in a 6th-century Ethiopic translation, but believed to have originated in Palestine, around two centuries before Jesus), the Dead Sea Scroll text known as *The Genesis Apocryphon*, and Tabari's *History*. It is not that Christianity had neglected *Ta Biblia*. Christians had given much devotion to their study, but they pursued narrow well-trodden paths, directed primarily to the New Testament. And their approach to the Old Testament reaffirmed the typological approach that made every Old character anticipate the New. While Comestor in no way whatsoever departed from those principles, his method created tensions that opened *Ta Biblia* to other perspectives and interpretations. Some of his contemporaries warned that Comestor's presentation of the literal narrative undermined the far more important attention to allegory, which was the highest level of interpretation.[20] The title and continuous structure of the book created a linear logic of its own. It had to present the subject and its stories on their own biblical terms. Nearly three-quarters of *Historia Scholastica* dealt with Old Testament subjects. As a *Historia*, it was concerned with the literal reality of the characters in *Ta Biblia*. In popular terms, the *Historia Scholastica* became the bible of Latin Christendom for some five centuries, from its completion around 1173 until finally it started to be displaced by Luther and his contemporaries in the 16th century. The work was an immediate success by almost every conceivable indicator. It represents a close parallel to Tabari's own work of history. And similarly it too benefited from the spread of paper that allowed it to be cheaply reproduced all over Europe.

In many respects the *Historia Scholastica* helped prepare the way for what Jaroslav Pelikan has called the reformation of the Bible and the Bible of the Reformation.[21] There was still a considerable distance in time and understanding between that Reformation achievement and the Great Christian Bibles of the late middle ages. The basic difference is that while Comestor's work stirred interest in *Ta Biblia* for their own sakes, it was not itself the Bible.

The more proximate causes for the invention of the Bible as we now know it were the three closely related developments of the fifteenth and sixteenth centuries: the Renaissance, printing and the Reformation. On its face the Renaissance seems unlikely since conventionally it is supposed to have focused on the Greek and Latin heritage of Europe. However by paying attention to the authentic remains of one part of the ancient world, the Renaissance willy-nilly raised questions about the others. The philological skills first applied to the classics of pagan culture soon were transferred to patristic writings. Refined mastery of Greek fostered reexamination of the Septuagint. Hebrew naturally followed, leading to direct study of what Jerome had a millennium earlier called, the Hebrew Truth. Instigating the attention to Greek culture had been the migration of Byzantine scholars and manuscripts from the Eastern Mediterranean to Italy which increased after the fall of Constantinople to the Ottoman Turks in 1453. Over the same century a similar process of migration occurred from the Western Mediterranean to Italy. In this instance the scholars were Jews and the manuscripts largely in Hebrew. The impetus was the more than century-long Iberian Christian campaign against Jews (and Muslims) that culminated in the Expulsion of 1492. Without benefit of new human resources a third element of the ancient world reemerged, though this recovery was more tenuous than the others. Ancient Egypt assumed an important role in the European cultural imagination.[22] The Renaissance was animated by the belief that it could leap over the centuries to recover ancient truths obscured by the neglect, ignorance, and corruption of the centuries. At the heart of the Reformation was the very same claim.

If the Renaissance fostered the culture of textual authenticity, the print revolution fostered the culture of textual availability. Taken together these two elements distinguished the success of the Reformation in Christianity from the failure of Karaism in Judaism centuries earlier. Karaism could not build upon the kind of general transformation in hermeneutic consciousness wrought by the Renaissance. Nor could it diffuse its message through the technological breakthrough wrought by movable type. The effect this had on *Ta Biblia* was revolutionary. In the Christian Middle Ages a complete manuscript of scripture was a rare commodity. People did not know scripture directly, but through a variety of other media – liturgy, sermons, public art, and elaborated popular tales for the common folk, works of theology for the educated, and the *Historia Scholastica* for both. The diversity of forms that *Ta Biblia* took created a diversity of meaning for its contents. As long as *Ta Biblia* themselves were a rarely accessible icon, any number of theologically irrelevant claims could be made in its name with little fear of contradiction. But as the Bible came to be more widely available, it also grew smaller in size. Printing invented the Little Bible, replacing the Great Bibles which had evolved over the centuries. Luther built upon this foundation, making the Bible his pillar to replace the papal hierarchy similar to the way in which the Rabbis used a version of it to replace the fallen Temple and Judean commonwealth.

These were the proximate causes, but there was another. Underlying this movement, purportedly back to the book was something else, the impetus for putting revelation between two covers, the impulse that had led to the creation of the first Abrahamic comprehensive book of Holy Writ, the Qur'an. Islam's codex-*kitab* culture set forth a model for religious text that repeatedly intrigued its co-Abrahamites. It would be contrary to the conventions of religious belief to acknowledge explicitly that any other religious belief was influencing its own. However such interaction is the very essence of religious existence for no one could survive without the other. The Jews would long since have disappeared if Christians and Muslims had not also believed and propagated the stories they first told in their own scripture. Without a foundation drawing upon the Israelite textual tradition, Christianity would have gone the way of Gnosticism, the mystery religions, and the other spiritual curiosities of the Hellenistic world. Without the other two Abrahamic religions, the Qur'an would have made little sense in a world filled with the sacred textual space created by its established precursors. The Abrahamic religions are a three-legged stool. No one leg can stand on its own.

Faith follows power, although pious protests might deny that fact. Without the conquests of the 7th century Islam would have long since disappeared into the Ka'aba. The Renaissance and Reformation witnessed the most dramatic intrusion of Islam into Christendom since that first triumph. Constantinople fell in 1453, and Rome and Vienna quickly became the next Ottoman targets. One Pope was reported to have offered Rome to the Sultan for a mass, but Mehmed could not be bought as easily as Henri IV and Rome is not Paris. Astute political observers such as Machiavelli and Ogier de Busbecq, a high-ranking Habsburg diplomat, sought to learn the lessons of Ottoman success. Religious observers could not cite such lessons as openly, but given the scriptural interaction that had constantly characterized the history of these three religions, it makes sense that the primacy of the Qur'an in an Islam that was ever more successfully penetrating Europe, would have prompted Christians – perhaps unconsciously – to hearken more fully to their own scripture. Luther was acutely aware of the Turkish threat. He repeatedly preached against it as it moved ever closer to the German lands. It was certainly one of the many reasons that moved him to make the Bible the centerpiece of his own theology. Whether Luther knew it or not, his emphasis on what had now become a book drew upon a long and complicated history in which Islam played a crucial part.

By Way of Conclusion

A comparison among any of the three Abrahamic religions, as opposed, perhaps, to an exercise of comparing any one of them to a more distant system of belief and practice, such as North American animism or Japanese Buddhism – somewhere in the middle are the relations between Islam and Hinduism – runs afoul of the lack of an uncontaminated sample. Each self-consciously recognizes and, to a degree, perhaps unconscious, reflects the other. What the Abrahamic religions create is a complex commingling of identities. Is it possible to distinguish between truly Islamic as opposed to Jewish as opposed to Christian? Of course, one may identify distinguishing characteristics for each and there are differences, but there is also such a range of commonalities that in some areas the distinctions are very hard to draw. Furthermore this range of commonalities is so strong that it is very easy for any one of the three either to appropriate something from the other and claim it as its own or attribute something to the other that is in fact its own invention or to indulge a complex mixture of the two. It is also possible for each to work together interactively all the while denying or pretending to deny that very fact.

The commonalities and divergences are particularly noteworthy with regard to Scripture. Christians, Jews, and Muslims do and do not "read" the same sacred text. I put "read" in quotation marks since historically most Muslims, Christians, and many Jews heard rather than read sacred text. Two share more scripture with each other than they do with the third, but the sacred words of Jews are not exactly the same as the sacred words of Christians. The Qur'an of Islam represents not only a triumph of Arabic letters, but also a deracinated distillation of both Jewish and Christian Scriptures. Read on its own, the Qur'an can seem like the sound of one hand clapping. Through ancillary quranic genres that incorporate both Muslim insight and abundant Jewish and Christian biblical traditions, the second hand appeared. In this regard, Islam was by no means exceptional. Each sectarian tradition must be understood as part of a hermeneutic enterprise that is greater than any one text alone. The interconnectedness of the three demonstrates that despite these many differences, Judaism, Christianity, and Islam share the same sacred textual space. In that sense the three do read the same sacred text.

At the outset I dismissed the Judeo-Christian tradition. In the course of this essay in what might seem to be a contradictory mode I have also argued for Abrahamic commonalities. In fact my objection to the Judeo-Christian tradition is not so much that it is wrong, but rather that it is incomplete. All three religions together form a triune community. The correct term should be the Judeo-Christian–Muslim tradition.

Notes

1 For a general introduction to this topic see Frances E. Peters, *The Voice, The Words, The Books, The Sacred Scripture of the Jews, Christians, and Muslims* (Princeton, 2007). I thank Mark Cohen for calling this recently published work to my attention.

2 Marc Brettler has called my attention to Israel Yeivin, *Introduction to the Tiberian Masorah* (Missoula, Montana, 1980), which addresses this issue.

3 David Diringer, *The Hand-Produced Book* (London, 1953), p. 93, and more generally, Alberto Manguel, *A History of Reading* (London and New York, 1996).

4 Colin H. Roberts and T. C. Skeat, *The Birth of the Codex* (London, 1983).

5 Saul Lieberman, *Hellenism in Jewish Palestine, Studies in the Literary Transmission, Beliefs, and Manners of Palestine in the I century* B.C.E.–*IV Century* C.E. (NY, 1950), p. 205 provides rabbinic references. However the rabbinic term which most closely approximates codex, *pinkas*, may also mean wax tablet or more generally written records. The Latin word codex itself can also mean tablet. It should be no surprise that in a largely oral culture the terminology for written media was not precise and consistent.

6 T. C. Skeat, "Early Christian Book-Production: Papyri and Manuscripts", in G. W. H. Lampe (ed.), *The Cambridge History of the Bible*, volume 2, *The West from the Fathers to the Reformation* (Cambridge, 1969), p. 75.

7 *Oxford English Dictionary*, on-line, q.v., Bibliotheca.

8 *Oxford English Dictionary*, on-line, q.v., Bible

9 Moshe Halbertal, *People of the Book* (Cambridge, MA., 1997), argues for an earlier date, but acknowledges the varied opinions. The disagreements reflect to a degree varying definitions of canonization. Is it merely the ideal that there should be a group of writings which are divinely inspired and apart from all others? Accordingly an early date makes sense. Or is it a precise and universal agreement on what those writings are, coupled with the thought that any further additions

are inconceivable? I favor this far more restrictive definition and accordingly prefer the later date.

10 Lieberman cited n. 5, pp. 206–7 provides abundant rabbinic references.

11 Anthony J. Saldarini, "'Is Saul Also Among the Scribes?' Scribes and prophets in Targum Jonathan" in *"Open Thou Mine Eyes . . . " Essays on Aggadah and Judaica, Presented to Rabbi William G. Braude on His Eightieth Birthday and Dedicated to His Memory* (Hoboken, N.J., 1992), pp. 239–53.

12 Nicholas de Lange, *Origen and the Jews: Studies in Jewish–Christian Relations in Third-Century Palestine* (Cambridge, 1976); David Paul McCarthy, "Saint Jerome's Translation of the Psalms: The Question of Rabbinic Tradition", in Blumberg and Braude, pp. 155–91.

13 John Burton, *The Collection of the Quran* (Cambridge, 1977), p. 122, quoting Abu Bakr Abdullah ibn abi Daud, Kitab al Masahif, ed. A. Jeffery (Cairo, 1936/1355), pp. 5, 6, 10; Abu Bakr awwal man jama'a al-Qur'an baina lawhain.

14 On this latter point see Philip E. Miller, "Was There Karaite Aggadah?" in Blumberg and Braude cited n. 11, pp. 209–18.

15 *Oxford English Dictionary*, on-line, q.v. Biblia.

16 Hava Lazarus-Yafeh, *Intertwined Worlds: Medieval Islam and Bible Criticism* (Princeton, 1992).

17 *Tafsir al-Tabari: Jāmi al bayān an tuwil ul-Quran*, ed. Muhammad Shakir and Ahmad Shakir (Cairo, 1954).

18 Ehsan Yar-Shater (ed.), *Tarikh al-rusul wal-muluk, The history of al-Tabari* (Albany, 1985–2007).

19 Jonathan Bloom, *Paper before Print: the History and Impact of Paper in the Islamic world* (New Haven, 2001).

20 Beryl Smalley, *The Study of the Bible in the Middle Ages*, second edition (Oxford, 1952).

21 Jaroslav Pelikan, with Valerie R. Hotchkiss and David Price, *The Reformation of the Bible, The Bible of the Reformation, Catalogue of the Exhibition* (New Haven, 1996).

22 Brian Curran, *The Egyptian Renaissance, the Afterlife of Ancient Egypt in Early Modern Italy* (Chicago, 2007).

CHAPTER

3

The "Convivencia" of Jews and Muslims in the High Middle Ages

MARK R. COHEN

The notion of "convivencia" was invented by Spanish historians to describe Christians, Jews, and Muslims living together more or less peacefully in medieval Christian Spain.[1] But the concept, if not the word itself, can equally be applied to Jewish–Muslim co-existence in the medieval Arabic-speaking Islamic world. Also commonly known as the "Golden Age" of Jewish–Muslim harmony, the idea especially pertains to Islamic Spain, from the mid-10th to mid-12th centuries, but it extends to the Judaeo-Arabic symbiosis in the entire Islamic world. The convivencia of the Islamic world and Reconquista Spain, taken together, is traditionally contrasted with the far less harmonious and culturally less integrated era of Jewish–Christian relations in the Ashkenazic lands of northern Europe.[2]

To be sure, many Spanish historians today would distance themselves from the rosy picture of convivencia in Catholic Iberia, just as many Jewish writers have done for the Islamic–Jewish experience. A recent statement in this mood comes from a Spanish literary scholar, Darío Fernández-Morera, writing about "The Myth of the Andalusian Paradise" (2006).[3] The opposite pole has been reiterated in recent years in the encomium for the Spanish convivencia by Maria Rosa Menocal in her book *Ornament of the World: How Muslims, Jews, and Christians Created a Culture of Tolerance in Medieval Spain* (2002).[4]

The debate about the convivencia of Jews and Muslims in Muslim Spain and elsewhere in the medieval Islamic world stems from opposing political motives. One side, which we may label the Muslim side, portrays Islamic–Jewish relations in terms of tolerance (*samaha* in Arabic) and harmony. This viewpoint originated among 19th century central European Jewish historians, who had their own political axe to grind. Living as they did with the unfulfilled promise of emancipation they yearned, nostalgically, for the "freedom" and "tolerance" – a veritable "interfaith utopia" – they thought they found in Spanish Islam. As taken up by Arabs and pro-Arab western writers, this theory blames Zionism for undermining the harmony of the past. The opposing side is represented by Jewish and Zionist writers who portray Jewish life under Islam in the Middle Ages as an unmitigated disaster and assert that Arab anti-Semitism of the 20th century is firmly rooted in a congenital, endemic Muslim/Arab Jew-hatred. Both claims, however, are based on historical myths.

The truth, as always, lies somewhere in between. The convivencia of Jews and Muslims in Muslim Spain and elsewhere in the medieval Islamic world was real, but its harmony had limits. It was marked by a legally-prescribed regime of discrimination and even witnessed periodic outbursts of violence. Nonetheless, the cultural achievement of Arabic-speaking Jewry; the political influence that some Jews attained in Muslim courts and in Muslim intellectual circles; and the substantial security Jews experienced living among Muslims cannot be denied. Moreover, notwithstanding attempts in recent years to prove the contrary, anti-Semitism, properly understood as the irrational belief that Jews, allied with Satan, control the wheels of government and commerce and wantonly kidnap and kill helpless gentile children, simply did not exist in the Islam of the Middle Ages.

How shall we explain the wholesale Jewish adoption of Greco-Arabic science, as well as philosophy and medicine, culminating in the works of Maimonides, the intellectual acme of the Jewish–Arab cultural convivencia in the 12th century? How shall we account for the new Jewish enthusiasm for Hebrew grammar, or the remarkable innovations in Hebrew poetry? How, too, shall we account for the unprecedented role played by some Jews in the corridors of Islamic power? And we need also to understand why the Jews of Islam, in stark contrast with their brethren in Christian lands, who constructed their history as a long chain of suffering, preserved very little collective memory of Muslim acts of violence, or of being victims of anti-Semitism.

The answer to these questions does not lie in a simple contrast between tolerance (Islamic) and intolerance (Christian). It entails fundamental religious, political, economic, and social realities of the Islamic world – realities that contrast with those of northern Europe and, by comparison, explain more completely the symbiosis of Judaeo-Arabic civilization. And it is predicated on the reasonable assumption that a people, particularly a minority considered inferior by the majority ruling population, does not accept or adapt the culture of its surroundings so heartedly unless it feels relatively secure living in its midst.

Jewish receptivity to Arabic and Islamic cultural modes was, at a very basic level, reinforced by the fact that Islam and Judaism share much in common. This was the product of a symbiotic relationship of mutual dependency, in which influence moved in both directions, from Judaism into Islam in the early centuries and from developed Islam into Judaism later on.

The result was an Islam that was easily recognizable by Jews, with similar religious ideas and practices, a similar structure of law, and similar exegetical strategies.

This interplay of Islam and Judaism fostered Jewish comfort in the Islamic milieu. Judaism's unequivocal monotheism made Islam more tolerant of Jews than of Christians, whose Trinity smacked of polytheism (*shirk* in Arabic, the cardinal sin in Islam), and for similar reasons, Islam's monotheism made it more tolerable in Jewish eyes than the Christian faith. Bernard Lewis' term "Judaeo-Islamic tradition" aptly describes this culture of living together.[5]

My own approach to this question, going beyond that of Lewis – an approach developed in great detail in my book, *Under Crescent and Cross: The Jews of the Middle Ages* (Princeton University Press, 1994) and in a sequel article[6] – is comparative. In order to appreciate more fully the co-existence of Muslims and Jews in the Middle Ages I compare the situation of the Jews in the Islamic world with that of their brethren in Ashkenazic northern Europe. It has seemed to me that the most fruitful way to illuminate differences in a comparative study is to take cases that are palpably different. To be sure, recent scholarship has argued that the Jews of Ashkenaz suffered rather less than traditional historiography has presumed and that they were much more aware of Catholic culture than previously recognized, and interacted in a much more relaxed manner with Christians. It has been argued that they even absorbed Christian ideas into Judaism, if only for polemical reasons – what Ivan Marcus has felicitously called "inward acculturation."[7] This revisionism has been extended to Christian Spain. At least one scholar has argued that the interfaith convivencia there reasserted itself during the darkest period of Jewish–Christian relations in the Catholic sector in the 15th century.[8]

The acculturation of the Jews in Islamic lands was more far-reaching, both inward *and* outward, than in Ashkenazic lands, a symptom of the greater comfort level experienced by Jews in the Arabic-speaking world. The comparative method offers a paradigm that explains not only why the Islamic high Middle Ages (the period between the rise of Islam and the Mamluk period, beginning in 1250) were far more peaceful and secure for Jews than life in northern Christian Europe, but also reciprocally, and from a new perspective, why Jewish–Christian relations deteriorated so drastically during the central European Middle Ages. The paradigm also helps explain why Jews lived more securely in "other Christendoms" in the Middle Ages, and why, despite the general decline in the Muslim world in the later Middle Ages, things never reached the low-point they did in northern Christendom or in Christian Iberia, where massacres, forced conversions, economic oppression, and ultimately expulsion – all of this accompanied and fed by irrational anti-Semitism – largely emptied western Europe of its Jewish population by the end of the Middle Ages.

In what follows I summarize the interrelating factors that made the Islamic/Arabic environment relatively more comfortable than life was for their brethren living in northern Christendom and in late medieval Spain, and which, in turn, fostered the cultural developments to which the literary sources so abundantly attest.

Explaining Jewish–Muslim Relations: The Comparative Perspective

Using historical data and some social-anthropological concepts, I construct the paradigm that I mentioned above to understand Jewish–gentile relations in general in the Middle Ages, and to attempt to explain what in the medieval Middle East appears to be a "tolerant" relationship between Muslims and non-Muslims, though, of course, I do not mean "tolerant" in our modern, liberal sense of full equality (this kind of tolerance as we know it in modern times was not celebrated as a virtue by monotheistic religions in the Middle Ages). The paradigm claims that anti-Jewish violence is related, in the first instance, to the primacy of religious exclusivity. Historically, religious exclusivity characterized both Islam and Christianity. But anti-Jewish violence was more pronounced in Christendom because innate religious antagonism, there from the time of Jesus himself, was combined with other erosive forces. The first was legal status, namely, the evolution of a special law for the Jews and a system of baronial or monarchical possessory rights – though varied in character and uneven in its application in different times and places[9] – that could be manipulated in an arbitrary manner. The second lay in the economic circumstances that excluded the Jews from the most respected walks of life. Religious exclusivity, a special, arbitrary legal status, and economic marginalization combined with another adverse factor, social exclusion, to rob the Jews of their rank in the hierarchical social order. The gradual replacement of the ethnic pluralism of Germanic society of the early Middle Ages by a medieval type of "nationalism," paralleling the spread of Catholic religious exclusivity to the masses and the rise of the crusading spirit in the 11th century, also contributed to the enhancement of the Jew's "otherness" and to his eventual exclusion from most of western Christendom.

In the Islamic world, these erosive factors were muted. Religious exclusivity was modulated by the continued, tolerated presence of non-Muslim religions: Jews, Christians, Zoroastrians, and, in India, Hindus. The Qur'an, for all its harsh language referring to Christians and Jews, contains the nucleus of a kind of religious pluralism. Non-Muslims are not to be forcibly converted. Jews and Christians, "people of the book," were allowed to live securely in their autonomous communities and to develop.

Legally speaking, Jews shared with other non-Muslims the status of *dhimmis*, or "protected people." They enjoyed security in return for the payment of an annual poll tax and adherence to other discriminatory regulations, and so long as they acknowledged the superiority of Islam. Outbursts of anti-Jewish, or usually it was anti-*dhimmi*, violence typically occurred when non-Muslims were perceived to be ignoring the laws of the *dhimma,* for instance, by lording it over Muslims in public office. Or it transpired when Islam itself felt under attack from outside forces, like the Crusaders or the Mongols. It should be added that most of the time when Jews and Christians failed to abide by the restrictions of the *dhimma* system, they did so with the tacit approval of the ruling authorities, even as Muslim clerics, the *'ulama,* periodically objected to this latitudinarianism.

Economically, the Jews of medieval Islam were not limited to a small range of pursuits, isolated from the rest of the population in deplored professions, like moneylending, as in Europe by the high Middle Ages. The Islamic market-place, in fact, was marked by a substantial degree of inter-denominational cooperation. Jews mixed freely with their Muslim counterparts, even forming business partnerships, with a minimum of friction. When, after about the 12th century, Jewish economic circumstances declined, this was not a confessional phenomenon alone, but one which Jews shared with others, including the Muslim majority.

In social-anthropological terms, Jews held a permanent niche within the normal hierarchical social order of Islam, and while they were marginalized, they were not ostracized or expelled. They continued to hold their place, with a recognized rank in society. The original and long-lasting ethnic pluralism of Islam and the diffusion of triumphalist superiority over non-Muslim "disbe-lievers" among two and in many places three religions, also helped secure their position, mitigating their "otherness" and preventing the emergence of the irrational hatred we call anti-Semitism. It also meant that Jews – in general, and not just the philosophers and the physicians – fraternized with Muslims on a regular basis, with a minimum of hostility. This sociability constituted an essential ingredient in the cultural interchange between Jews and Arabs of the high Middle Ages.

For all these reasons, the Jews of Islam had substantial confidence in the *dhimma* system. If they kept a low profile and paid their annual poll tax, they could expect to be protected and to be free from economic discrimination – not to be forcefully converted to Islam, not to be massacred, and not to be expelled. To be sure, the system occasionally broke down, as it did most excep-tionally during the mid-12th century, when the fanatical Muslim Berber Almohads, the Islamists of their time, destroyed entire Jewish communities in North Africa and Spain and forced thousands of Jews and Christians to accept Islam, even as they imposed their own stringent Islam upon those considered impious Muslims. Also notorious, because of the unique preservation of detailed Islamic sources, was the destruction of houses of worship and forced conversions ordered by Caliph al-Hākim in Egypt and Palestine at the begin-ning of the 11th century, and the the assassination in 1066 of the "haughty" head of the Jewish community of the Muslim principality of Granada, Spain (the adjective "haughty," was applied to him by a Jewish writer a century later), which was followed by a mini "pogrom" when a mob attacked the Jewish quarter of the city, with great loss of life. During these rare episodes,

Jews felt the impact of violence no less than the Ashkenazic Jews of Europe, but they did not preserve them as part of a collective memory of suffering the way their Ashkenazic brethren did. They recognized these as temporary lapses of the *dhimma* arrangement and trusted that forced conversions, a violation of Qur'anic law, would be reversed after the initial zealotry faded. Doubtless this is one factor among others that explains why Jews in Islamic lands under threat favored superficial conversion (like the Islamic *taqiyya* recommended for Muslims faced with persecution) over martyrdom, unlike their self-immolating Ashkenazic brethren, who had little hope of being officially allowed to return to Judaism after their baptism (though on occasion a secular ruler, for political reasons, might permit this). In this respect the Jews of Islamic Spain and other places in the medieval Islamic world where temporary acts of intolerance threatened Jewish life, anticipated the response of Jews in Christian Spain – the so-called Marranos – who converted to Catholicism rather than accept a martyr's death during and after the pogroms of 1391.

Judaeo-Arabic Culture

The paradigm developed in *Under Crescent and Cross* and summarized briefly in this essay helps explain, not only Muslim–Jewish co-existence, but also why Jews were so ready to adopt Arab-Islamic culture. It was not my intention in the book to retell this remarkable saga, which has been so well treated by others. Let me, however, make a few comments here in order to fill in this gap and explain what the convivencia consisted in as a cultural phenomenon.[10]

Here, again, the comparative perspective informs our understanding. When Jews, predominantly from the Middle East, settled in Europe, they did what Jews did everywhere – they gave up their "Jewish" language for the local spoken tongue. The Jewish language they abandoned was Aramaic, which had replaced Hebrew in late Antiquity as the medium of communication, verbal and to a certain extent also written (for instance, in the Talmuds). In place of Aramaic they adopted Old French in the Frankish realm (and in England, when they migrated there with Christians following the Norman Conquest in 1066), Italian in Italy, Anglo-Saxon in the German domains, and romance dialects that crystallized into Spanish in the Catholic parts of the Iberian Peninsula. Like most of the masses, Jews did not know Latin, the language of high culture. Since, moreover, Latin was the language of the hostile Church, there was an additional barrier to its reception into Jewish life. However, this did not constitute a great loss for Jews, who were by and large content with their traditional, textually-based religious civilization, which continued to develop in new and creative ways. Some of this bore the imprint of Christian influence, to be sure, though more often in defense of Judaism rather than branching off into new forms of cultural expression. The rational mode to which some Jews in Hellenistic antiquity in places like Egypt had been attracted (Philo of Alexandria in the 1st century is the most famous example), did not itself emerge in Latin Europe until the 12th century, and when it did, it held little attraction for Ashkenazic Jewry. Jews there did not have direct access to the religious philosophy of such scholars as Thomas Aquinas written in Latin, and little of the Judaeo-Arabic philosophical oeuvre of Jews from Islamic lands, as translated into Hebrew in the 12th century in southern France, made its way north.

Things were different in the Middle East after the Islamic conquests. There, too, Jews abandoned Aramaic for the new language, but Arabic functioned both as the language of high culture *and* the common tongue of Jews and Arabs in everyday exchange. It was at the same time linguistically akin to Aramaic and Hebrew, with morphological forms and cognates that facilitated transcribing Arabic into Hebrew letters and reading it – the form of Arabic we call Judaeo-Arabic. Thus, assimilating Arabic was even less of a "leap" for the indigenous Aramaic-speaking (and sometimes Hebrew reading) Jews of the Middle East than it was for Jewish immigrants in Europe transitioning from Aramaic to European vernaculars. Furthermore, while Arabic was, like Latin, the language of the dominant religion, as we have seen the Islamic "church," so-to-speak, was far less hostile to Judaism than the Latin clergy. By the 10th century, some two and a half centuries after the rise of Islam, Jews had made a total and largely effortless transition from Aramaic to Arabic and now used Arabic, not only in daily speech, but for nearly everything they composed. This prepared them to share lock, stock, and barrel in the high culture of Islamic society.

Islam came into contact with the science, medicine, and philosophy of the Greco-Roman world centuries earlier than European Christendom. Translated early on into Arabic, these works gave rise to what a German scholar, Adam Mez, called, not without good reason, "Die Renaissance des Islams" of the 10th century.[11] Jews of the Fertile Crescent, the heartland of the Islamic Empire and the first center of the new Arabic science, medicine, and philosophy, had both access to and interest in the translated texts read by Muslim intellectuals. This facilitated the cultural convivencia of the Judaeo-Arabic world, which began in the eastern Islamic domains and spread to the Muslim West. It led to Jewish assimilation of philosophy, science and medicine – philosophy serving as handmaiden of religious truths, as it did for Islamic religious leaders themselves.

The Arabic and Islamic "renaissance" laid the groundwork for other Jewish cultural developments. The Bible was translated into Arabic. Hebrew as a language began to be studied "scientifically," so-to-speak, using linguistic measuring rods in vogue among Arab grammarians. But nearly everything Jews wrote they wrote in Arabic, and this was not limited to philosophy, for which Hebrew entirely lacked a vocabulary. Poetry, the major exception, was composed in Hebrew. But this too imitated its Arabic model. Jewish poetry before the Arab conquests – the *piyyut* – was liturgical, composed for recitation in the synagogue and sung by cantors as part of the worship service. It differed from Biblical poetry (as in the Song of Songs) by replacing the parallelism of words with the repetition of rhyme syllables. The language, post-Biblical Hebrew, was often obscure, difficult to understand for modern Hebrew speakers and probably for the average contemporaneous Jew himself. The popularity of the genre may have stemmed from the poetry's numinous quality and from the cantillation itself.

The Hebrew poetry of the Islamic period displayed several innovations. It introduced metrics based on the quantitative patterning of syllables, mimicking the metrics of Arabic poetry. Arabic rhyming schemes were also adopted. The themes, too, were new – secular themes like nature, love, wine, panegyric, the beauty of women and young boys, even in the case of one poet, war – all borrowed from the Arabic poetic arsenal. Even the choice of Hebrew was imitative. Arabic poets prided themselves in writing in the language of holy scripture, the Qur'an, believing Arabic to be the most beautiful of all languages. Jews followed suit with their Biblical Hebrew poetry, asserting the wonderment and uniqueness of the language of their own scripture. The social setting for this new poetry also followed the Arabic model. The poems were recited and sung in gardens, like the gardens of the caliph's palace or of private homes, which formed the physical setting for Arabic poetry. Jews continued to write religious poetry, but it too employed Biblical Hebrew and Arabic meter and borrowed themes from Islamic pietistic thought.[12]

One of the greatest rabbis of the Middle Ages, Saadya Gaon (d. 942), in many ways the "father" of Judaeo-Arabic culture, wrote poetry. He served as head of the great yeshiva located in Baghdad, one of two that became the religious centers for Jews throughout the Islamic domains. He composed the first comprehensive Jewish prayer book, writing the directions for the worshiper in Arabic (the prayers, of course, remained in their original Hebrew) and including poems of his own. Saadya also compiled books of Jewish law in Arabic, as did other Geonim, or heads of the yeshiva. Thus, even the supposedly sacrosanct realm of Jewish law was not immune to Islamic influence. In fact, the entire structure of Jewish legal discourse was altered in accordance with Islamic categories, while some of the content of Islamic law influenced Jewish legal thought as well.[13]

Other religious developments within Judaism also drew inspiration from Islam. The Karaite movement – the first oppositional movement in Judaism since the ascendancy of the Talmudic rabbinic scholars in late Antiquity – arose in the eastern Islamic world at just about the same time and in the same place that Shi'ism began to flourish, in opposition to the dominant Sunni "orthodoxy." Later on, Sufi pietism exerted a powerful influence on Jewish religious thought and practice, as early as the 11th century in Spain and then, beginning in the early 13th century, in Egypt. Abraham the son of Moses Maimonides (d. 1237) was a "Jewish Sufi," as were his descendants, the leaders of the Jewish community in Egypt for several more generations.

The Arabic language gave Jews entrée to the corridors of Muslim power and made possible the remarkable careers of such luminaries as Samuel ha-Nagid ibn Nagrela in the 11th century, head of the Jewish community, poet,

Talmudist, and vizier of Granada (the father of the Jewish vizier assassinated in 1066), as well as scores of other Jewish denizens of Islamic courts, many of whom occupy pages in Islamic chronicles. Other dignitaries, as well as merchants, less well known because they did not leave books behind, are no less important as Jewish exemplars of the convivencia that reigned for several centuries during the Islamic high Middle Ages. For all the reasons given here, Muslim–Jewish co-existence was free from the kind of anti-Semitism that reared its ugly head in Christian Europe during the high Middle Ages.

Islamic Anti-Semitism Today

The book on which this essay is based was published in 1994, a year after the signing of the Oslo Accords and the famous handshake of Yitzhak Rabin and Yasir Arafat on the White House lawn. At the time of its publication, it was taken by some as being supportive of the new, emerging rapprochement between Israelis and Palestinians, even though the research for the book ante-dated Oslo by many years. Events occurring since 1994 – the attacks of 9/11/2001 and other terrorist plots in Europe; the wars in Afghanistan and in Iraq; the growing hostility especially in Europe between Europeans and Muslims; and the emergence of a new anti-Semitism propagated largely by Muslims – have, however, strengthened the historiographical polarization I came to correct. The mutual hostility between Israelis and Arabs, especially Palestinians, has raised anew the question whether this hostility might have its roots in the historical relationship between Jews and Muslims, bolstering one of the two myths that *Under Crescent and Cross* was meant to dispel.

The idea that modern Muslim anti-Semitism comes from a medieval, irrational hatred of the Jews, similar to the anti-Semitism of Christianity with its medieval origins, cannot be sustained. Understood as a religiously-based complex of irrational, mythical, and stereotypical beliefs about the diabolical, malevolent, and all-powerful Jew, infused in its modern, secular form with racism and the belief that there is a Jewish conspiracy against mankind – anti-Semitism is not an indigenous or inherent phenomenon in Islam.[14] As Bernard Lewis explains, it was first encountered by Muslims at the time of the Ottoman expansion into Europe, which resulted in the absorption of large numbers of Greek Orthodox Christians.[15] This Christian anti-Semitism became more firmly implanted in the Muslim Middle East in the 19th century, thanks mainly to European Christian missionaries, who played the major role in introducing western Jew-hatred into the Arab world. In the mid-20th century, this anti-Semitism was given a new boost thanks to Nazi propagandists currying favor with Arab leaders as part of their military strategy to rule the world and destroy the Jews,[16] and ultimately by Arab objections to the establishment of the State of Israel.

Christian-style anti-Semitism has since become absorbed into the fabric of Islam as if it were there from the start, when it was never there from the start

at all. Often cited as proof of the contrary are the widely read Arabic translations of the early 20th century Russian forgery, "The Protocols of the Elders
of Zion," which purports to tell the story of a Jewish and Masonic plot to
take over the world. The "Protocols" is not an Islamic text, though it seems
Islamic to many Muslims, because it echoes old themes in the Qur'an and elsewhere of Jewish treachery toward Muhammad and his biblical prophetic
predecessors. The "Protocols" seems all the more credible in the light of the
political, economic and military success of Israel.

Sadly, the pluralism and largely non-violent attitude towards the Jews that
existed in early and classical Islam seems to have lost its public face. Equally
sad, age-old Jewish empathy with Islamic society among Jews from Muslim
lands, and their memory of decent relations with Muslim neighbors in relatively recent times, have similarly receded. Comparative study of
Jewish–gentile relations in Christendom and in Islam may explain the difference between the two societies. But it does not make present-day Arab
anti-Semitism any less unfortunate than its Christian roots. Equally unfortunate is present-day anti-Muslim feeling in the Jewish (as in the non-Jewish)
world. One can only hope that a time will come when a just and peaceful solution to the Arab–Israeli conflict will allow a correct memory of the past to
play a role in attitudes of the present.

In closing, and in tribute to the concept animating this conference, I would
like to quote something very relevant. It comes from the pen of Naguib
Mahfouz, the Egyptian writer and winner of the Nobel Prize for literature. In
a letter to his friend, Professor Sasson Somekh, the noted Israeli scholar of
modern Arabic literature and himself a native-born Iraqi Jew, Mahfouz wrote:

> Our two peoples knew extraordinary partnership for many years – in
> ancient days, in the Middle Ages, and in the modern era, with time of
> quarrels and disputes few and far between. Unfortunately, we have docu-
> mented the disputes one hundred times more than the periods of
> friendship and cooperation. I dream of the day when, thanks to the coop-
> eration between us, this region will become a home overflowing with the
> light of science, blessed by the highest principles of heaven.

This letter is excerpted in Somekh's memoirs, *Baghdad Yesterday: The
Making of an Arab Jew*, recently published in English translation from the
Hebrew.[17] This memoir itself stands as testimony to the relatively harmonious
relationship between Jews and Arabs in Arab lands up through the first half
of the 20th century, as well as to the embeddedness of some Jews in high
Arabic culture right down into modern times.

Notes

This essay represents a longer version of the paper I delivered at the conference on
"Children of Abraham: A Trialogue of Civilizations," held at Harvard University's

Weatherhead Center, October 22–24, 2007. It is based on my book, *Under Crescent and Cross: The Jews in the Middle Ages* (Princeton, 1994; 2nd ed. forthcoming 2009); Turkish, *Hac ve Hilal Altindar: Ortacagda Yahudiler*, translated by Ahmet Fethi (Istanbul: Sarmal Yayinev, 1997); Hebrew, *Be-tzel ha-sahar veha-tzelav; He-yehudim bimei ha-beinayim*, translated by Michal Sela (Haifa University Press and Zmora/Bitan-Dvir Publishers, 2001); German, *Unter Kreuz und Halbmond: Die Juden im Mittelalter*, translated by Christian Wiese (Munich: C.H. Beck Verlag, 2005); Arabic, *Bayn al-hilal wa-l-salib: Al-yahūd fi'l-'usūr al-wustāa*, translated by Islam Dayeh and Moez Khalfoui (Cologne, Al-Kamel Verlag, 2007); French and Spanish translations to appear: Paris, Editions du Seuil; Valencia, Universidad de Valencia Press), and on a sequel article, "Anti-Jewish Violence and the Place of the Jews in Christendom and in Islam: A Paradigm," in *Religious Violence between Christians and Jews: Medieval Roots, Modern Perspectives*, ed. Anna Sapir Abulafia (Basingstoke, Hampshire: Palgrave, 2002), pp. 107–37, transl. into Romanian by Felicia Waldman in *Studia Hebraica* (Bucharest) 6 (2006). The argument of those publications is augmented here in the context of the Harvard conference.

1 See Thomas Glick's introductory essay to, and the other essays in, the Jewish Museum exhibition catalogue, *Convivencia: Jews, Muslims, and Christians in Medieval Spain* (New York, 1992).
2 See Chapter One in my *Under Crescent and Cross: The Jews in the Middle Ages.*
3 In *The Intercollegiate Review* 41 (Fall, 2006), pp. 23–31.
4 Boston: Little, Brown, 2002; also translated into French and Spanish.
5 See his *The Jews of Islam* (Princeton, 1984).
6 See above note 1. The present essay omits footnotes, preferring to let the interested reader follow the documentation by referring to the book and that article.
7 See especially his article "A Jewish–Christian Symbiosis: The Culture of Early Ashkenaz," in *Cultures of the Jews: A New History*, ed. David Biale (New York, 2002), pp. 449–516. Other representatives of this revisionist school – what I would call the "neo anti-lachrymose school" – include: Israel Jacob Yuval, *Two Nations in Your Womb: Perceptions of Jews and Christians in Late Antiquity and the Middle Ages*, trans. Barbara Harshav and Jonathan Chipman (Berkeley, Los Angeles, London, 2006) from the Hebrew original of 2000; Johannes Heil, "'Deep Enmity and/or Close Ties?' Jews and Christians before 1096: Sources, Hermeneutics, and Writing History in 1996," *Jewish Studies Quarterly* 9 (2002), pp. 259–306; Elisheva Baumgarten, *Mothers and Children: Jewish Family Life in Medieval Europe* (Princeton, 2004); and Jonathan Elukin, *Living Together, Living Apart: Rethinking* Jewish–Christian *Relations in the Middle Ages* (Princeton and Oxford, 2007).
8 Mark D. Meyerson, *A Jewish Renaissance in Fifteenth-century Spain* (Princeton, 2004), based on data from one Jewish community in the kingdom of Valencia.
9 A good statement of the variations in the status commonly called "Jewish serfdom" can be found in Simha Goldin, *Ha-yihud veha-Yahad* (Uniqueness and Togetherness: The Enigma of the Survival of the Jews in the Middle Ages) (Tel Aviv, 1997), pp. 14–30.
10 For an overview and for further reading see several chapters in the *Oxford Handbook of Jewish Studies*, ed. Martin Goodman, with Jeremy Cohen and David Sorkin (Oxford, 2002) and *The Literature of Al-Andalus*, ed. Maria Rosa

Menocal, Raymond P. Scheindlin, and Michael Sells (Cambridge, 2000), which integrates Jewish literature into the literature of the age generally.

11 The book was published in 1922 and has been translated into many languages, including English and Arabic.

12 This latter phenomenon is discussed thoroughly and authoritatively by Raymond P. Scheindlin in *The Song of the Distant Dove: Judah Halevi's Pilgrimage* (Oxford, 2008).

13 The influence of formal features of Islamic law on Judaism has been the subject of much scholarship, while the most important work on the influence of the *content* of Islamic law on the Jews has been dominated by the fruitful investigations of Gideon Libson.

14 This point has been made by Bernard Lewis and many other scholars. For a recent discussion of contemporary Islamic anti-Semitism in context, see the essays in the thematic issue on anti-Semitism in the Muslim world guest edited by Gudrun Kraemer, *Die Welt des Islams* 46 (2006), especially Kraemer's introductory essay, "Anti-Semitism in the Muslim World: A Critical Review," and Michael Kiefer's, "Islamischer, Islamistischer oder Islamisierter Antisemitismus."

15 Bernard Lewis, *Semites and Anti-Semites: An Inquiry into Conflict and Prejudice* (New York and London, 1986), 132.

16 This aspect has been thoroughly studied in a 2002 German book by Matthias Küntzel, now translated into English as *Jew-Hatred and Jihad: The Nazi Roots of the 9/11 Attack*, trans. by Colin Meade (Telos Press, 2007).

17 (Jerusalem, Ibis Editions, 2007).

CHAPTER

4

Muslim–Jewish Relations in Ayyubid Egypt, 1171–1250

MOHAMED HAWARY

Egypt had a very sizable Jewish population during the twelfth and thirteenth centuries. Over ninety cities, towns, villages, and hamlets with Jewish inhabitants are known. Fustat had a Rabbanite Jewish community numbering some 3,600 souls. In addition, there was the much smaller Karaite community and a small congregation in nearby Cairo, bringing the total Jewish population in the capital to well over 4,000. The history of the Jews in Egypt since the Arab conquest (AD 630–41) till Jawhar's entry into Fustat at the head of the Fatimid army (AD 969) is almost entirely shrouded in obscurity. The earliest reference to the Jews in Fustat, so far as is known, is a document from the year AD 750. But very little indeed do we know of the life of the important Egyptian Jewry during more than three centuries.

Many of the Jewish communal officials in Egypt were connected in some way or other with government. The Jews no doubt were treated in the same manner as the other non-Muslim inhabitants, the people of the tribute (*ahl al-dhimma*). The Fatimids and their successors, the Ayyubids (AD 1171–1250), employed *ahl al-dhimma* in their administrations far beyond their proportion in the general population. The Jews in Egypt used to be distinguished in this period by a different dress.

The Jewish community of Egypt in the High Middle Ages was affluent, influential, and on the whole stable and secure. The Jewish community of Egypt was well organized. In short, it was bourgeois but not particularly creative in the spiritual or intellectual spheres. The Jews of Egypt were pious and hardworking, and they took care of the less fortunate among them through admirable social services. They were generous in supporting Jewish institutions at home and in the spiritual centers of Palestine and Iraq. There were some men of learning among them, none truly outstanding, and even some of these had come from elsewhere.

This essay deals with the Egyptian Jews under the Ayyubid (AD 1171–1250) rule. There were three prominent Jewish sects in Egypt during that time: Rabbanites, Karaites, and Samaritans. The history of the Jews in Ayyubid Egypt occupies an important part in the general course of Egyptian history. The Jews, at that particular period, were not isolated from the whole community, either politically, economically, or socially. In general, they performed their role freely, like all other segments of society. During that time, the Jews constituted an inseparable part of the Egyptian society in its entirety.

The Protected People (*ahl al-dhimma*)

The Protected People (*ahl al-dhimma*), in Islamic countries, were the members of the revealed religions, namely the Jews, the Christians, and the Sabians, who had entered into covenant with the Muslims. As believers in the true God, they were tolerated by Prophet Muhammad [PBUH] but were disarmed and made to pay tribute for the protection afforded them.

Thus, the *dhimmi* is the Arabic term that refers to the non-Islamic-embracing population. In a similar manner to the Jewish reference to a non-Jew as being a *goy*, so too the term *dhimmi* refers to non-Muslims.[1] According to Islamic law, both Christians and Jews were merely promised protection in return for the payment of a tribute (Landshut 1976, 5).

Prophet Muhammad (PBUH) first codified the treatment of minority religions (*ahl al-Kitab* – the "People of the Book") in Islamic territories with the institution of special taxes on unbelievers. The relevant passage in the Qur'an (IX, 29) states: "Fight against those who do not believe in God or in the Last Day, who do not forbid what God and his Prophet have forbidden or practice the true religion, among those who have been given the Book, until they pay the *jizya* [poll tax] from their hand, they being humbled." This passage has traditionally been interpreted to indicate that the *jizya* was intended as a symbolic expression of humiliation and subordination of those who rejected Prophet Muhammad and Islam.[2]

The basis of the Islamic legal approach to *dhimmis* is to be found in the Qur'an and continued in the Pact of Umar, attributed to Umar Ibn al-Khattab (634–644), which is a form of agreement in which non-Muslims agree to a host of regulations – such as the payment of the *jizya* tax, the wearing of special clothes, and the exclusion from public office[3] – in return for protection. However, with the exception of the *jizya*, these were often honoured more in their breach than in their observance. Indeed the ubiquitous presence of *dhimmi*s in Arab ruling circles involved them in the business of state in ways unimaginable for Jews in Christian northern Europe (Cohen 1994, 65–66). Mark Cohen says that the Pact of Umar operated differently from the charters of privileges granted to the Jews in Europe, and it was more beneficial to the Jews than the European charters because it did not have to be renewed with each change of ruler, and thus offered a certain stability in the basic law regarding the legal status of Jews in the Muslim world which had no parallel in Christendom (Cohen 1994, 73).[4]

The need to maintain undisturbed relations with those on whom the existence of an economic structure depended gradually shaped the Muslim attitude towards the 'peoples of the Book' who refused to accept Islam. The attitude toward these non-Muslims in Islamic territories was shaped in principle in accordance with the concept of *dhimma*, meaning protection granted to them by agreement or treaty.

The major expressions of *dhimmi* status were the poll-tax or *jizya*, which all male non-believers above the age of fifteen had to pay, and the special land-tax, known as the *kharaj*. In return, their lives and property were protected and, in accordance with the general attitude of Islam to unbelievers, they were assured liberty of faith and worship. They were also permitted to organize themselves as they wished, and the Jews fully availed themselves of that permission. Naturally there were changes for better or for worse in various places and at various times; but the principles established in the early days of Islam continued to serve as the basis for the relations between Muslim and *dhimmi* throughout the ages.

Muslims and Jews in Ayyubid Egypt

By 1171, the Fatimids had lost power to an expanding group of Kurds from Syria, called the Ayyubids. When Saladin became the ruler of Egypt, he left a great impression on Cairo. He refused to live the grand life of the Fatimid caliphs, and he did not want to be seen as a religious ruler.

It has often been emphasized that the Fatimid period was the golden age of government officials coming from the minorities (Qasim 1979, 52). The same was true for the subsequent Ayyubid period. Both in number and power, the Christian government servants far outstripped the Jewish – a fact fully evidenced in the Geniza records. Still, Jews frequently attained positions of powerful influence, as illustrated in the following often quoted verses of an Egyptian poet:

> The Jews of our time have attained the goal of their aspirations:
> The honors are theirs and so are the riches.
> Counselors and kings are taken from their midst.
> Egyptians! I advise you, become Jews, for Heaven itself has turned Jewish.[5]

Christians, Muslims and Jews have always had a close relationship in Egypt. The Jews under Fatimid and Ayyubid rule were integrated into contemporary society, buying, selling and renting property from their neighbors and practicing the same trades. Many of the documents found were written in Judeo-Arabic, a form of medieval Arabic written with Hebrew letters, indicative of the Jewish integration within the greater Arabic-speaking community.

"During medieval times, the Jews were attacked in Europe. But life was easier in Middle Eastern countries then, so we see a huge migration from Europe and a corresponding proliferation of synagogues and Jewish scientists." This includes Maimonides, who settled in Egypt after he was forced out of Spain by a fanatic Muslim ruler, later becoming the personal physician of Saladin's vizier al Qadi al-Fadil (al-Qawsi 2001, 148–50). [6]

Jews did not serve in the army, but neither did the Muslims and Christians belonging to the sedentary local population. The Ayyubids, who were Kurds themselves, maintained a predominantly Kurdish and Turkoman officers corps with mercenaries drawn from many different ethnic groups. We find Jewish physicians attached to the Egyptian army and navy (Goitein 1967, 72–73).

At that time, Egyptian Jews possessed agricultural land and sometimes supervised in person the harvest and of course such operations as grape pressing and cheese making which involved religious taboos, but the soil was tilled by non-Jewish fellahin exclusively. Even orchards belonging to the Jewish community were leased to Muslims against a yearly payment. Jews had an important part in the processing of flax, the staple export of Egypt, but only after the peasants had cut, soaked, and dried it. The manual occupations of Jews were those of artisans and craftsmen (Goitein 1973, 175).

Tanning and dyeing are very conspicuous occupations, because the hides and textiles treated are spread out for drying in open spaces in or outside a city. Muslims normally did not pay much attention to Jews, but the Jewish tanners and dyers could not escape them because of the very conspicuousness of their trade. Thus Muslims were prone to assume that most Jews were engaged in these occupations (Goitein 1973, 176).

From Muslim descriptions of Old Cairo it was already evident that sugar production must have been one of the major, if not the greatest, industry in that town during the Fatimid and Ayyubid periods, and from the same sources it appears also that the share of the Jews in this field was very extensive (Goitein 1967, 125–26). In this respect it is necessary to dispel certain notions that appear again in some historical writings, namely that the Jews were concentrated mainly in occupations despised by Muslims (Goitein 1973, 175).

The Jewish and Christian populations were allowed to go on living under the same laws as had been enforced before their conquest, except that these laws were now administered by religious, instead of civil, authorities. The head of each community was thus able to perform a very useful function in that it was on him that rested the responsibility for the collection of taxes had been imposed by the Muslim conquerors (Landshut 1976, 7).

Saladin and the Egyptian Jews

The early period of Islamic rule had been one in which relations between Christians, Muslims, and Jews were generally fruitful. The Ayyubid government adopted a new attitude toward the non-Muslim communities. The ancient discriminatory laws were renewed or their renewal was attempted, while the Sultans and their entourage were still in close contact with people of other creeds, and amiable, and sometimes even cordial relations existed between both sides (Goitein 1967, 38).

The greatest figure of medieval Judaism, Maimonides, traveled east to Egypt where he thrived as a court physician to members of the Ayyubid dynasty and its most famous son, Saladin. Shortly after the abolition of the Fatimid caliphate, Maimonides was recognized by the new regime as the *reshut*, or official authority, and was even acclaimed as *ra'is al-yahud* (head of the Jews) (Kraemer 1991, 8; Ehrenkreutz 1991, 305).

Maimonides clearly found a freer environment in Cairo under the Ayyubids than in the Andalus from which he came. His *Guide of the Perplexed*, written in Arabic, was a philosophical interpretation of religion and other works in Arabic and Hebrew. His life of thought gives evidence of easy relations between Muslims and Jews of education and standing in Egypt of his time.

Maimonides was a protégé of Saladin's minister al-Qadi al-Fadil. In the last years of his life Maimonides treated the members of the royal house (Ashtor-Strauss 1956, 312). There were a number of Jewish physicians who attended Saladin personally. But, in addition, there were court-physicians who had the care of the king's wives, children and domestics. Naturally these physicians received monthly salaries, and their posts were eagerly coveted. One of them was Saladin's personal physician (Ibn Abi Usaibi'a 1965, 538). Jewish physicians had private patients who were Muslim, both dignitaries at court and ordinary people (Cohen 1994, 134). Other Jewish physicians were appointed to posts in the public hospitals which had been founded at that period in the large towns (Ashtor-Strauss 1956, 312).

In a famous passage of his *khitat*, al-Maqrizi enumerates eighty-eight non-canonical dues and taxes levied by the Fatimids and abolished by Saladin when he assumed power in Egypt. The total revenue from these *mukus*, collected in the twin cities of Cairo and Fustat, amounted to 100,000 dinars per year. Saladin's action was by no means exceptional. The caliph al-Hākim (996–1021) had made the same pious gesture before, and the ostentatious abolition of taxes not recognized by Islamic religious law became a standard practice for rulers on ascending the throne (Goitein 1967, 270).

The Fatimids, who mistrusted the orthodox Muslim population of Egypt, relied, to some extent, on the support of the Christians and the Jews. The Fatimids therefore spent money on the religious establishments of Christians and Jews, allowed them to build new churches and synagogues, and even participated in their ceremonies. All this changed when Saladin took the reins of government. The new ruler of Egypt endeavored to arouse in the Muslim masses the feeling of superiority over non-Muslims and took measures aiming at the separation of "believers" and "unbelievers" (Ashtor-Strauss 1956, 305).

The discriminatory laws against non-Muslims, which were issued by the Caliphal government in the 9th century, had fallen in abeyance for a long time. Now they were put into operation once more. According to the Egyptian historian al-Maqrizi, among the events of the month Sha'ban 564 of the Hijra [May 1169], the Sultan ordered the Christians and Jews enjoying protection under tribute to be dismissed and forbidden employment in affairs concerning the state, and in any *diwan*. Some were in fact dismissed, but not one of them left the offices of the Ghuzz. The report spread of their being driven from the country and of their dwellings being taken. During the same month, certain of their leading men were dismissed from government employment, but others remained. However, those employed in offices of the Ghuzz remained undisturbed, because their masters refused to dismiss them on the grounds that they were practiced in the management of their affairs and that if these men were discharged their interests would miscarry (Broadhurst 1980, 40–41; al-Maqrizi 1934, 47–48).

In conclusion, the reign of Saladin was a period of transition. He turned away from the tolerance which the Fatimids showed in matters of religion. But the Ayyubids were highly educated and far from being hypocrites as were their successors, the Mamluks; and the people were not yet imbued with fanaticism. Therefore social relations between Muslims and Jews continued. Al-Qadi al-Fadil paid a visit to "the physician Musa" (i.e. Maimonides) when he fell ill. In the days of Saladin, Oriental Jews were not an isolated group, like the ghetto-dwellers in Europe (Ashtor-Strauss 1956, 309).

From the days of Saladin, Jews and Christians could ride on donkeys only. Furthermore, they had to use packsaddles, as an ancient Muslim law prescribed. In previous periods those members of the non-Muslim communities who belonged to the high-ranking classes of the physicians and government officials were allowed to ride on horses; now they were subjected to the same law as other Jews and Christians (Ashtor-Strauss 1956, 307).

According to al-Maqrizi, the government proclaimed that henceforth Jews and Christians should not ride on horses and mules and that even physicians and government officials should not be exempted from this law. Al-Maqrizi mentions the promulgation of this law among the events of the year 577 of the Hijra (al-Maqrizi 1934, 77; Broadhurst 1980, 68) which corresponds to 1181/82. The ordinance of Saladin was an important step in the social degradation of the non-Muslim communities (Ashtor-Strauss 1956, 305–6).

Under the Ayyubids, Christians and Jews in Egypt had been left largely alone: so long as they paid the poll tax, they were not mistreated on the basis of their religion. Christians and Jews would serve in the government, often at high positions of power.

The German Vitztum Burkhard, the envoy of Frederick Barbarossa, who came to Egypt in 1175, judged the state of affairs quite well, when he said that, in this country, everybody could follow his creed as he liked (Ashtor-Strauss 1956, 309).

References

Arabic

Qasim, Qasim Abdu, '1979, *ahl al-dhimma fi misr, al-'usur al-wusta*. al-qahira, dar al-ma'arif, 1979.

Qasim, Qasim Abdu, 1987, *al-yahud fi misr min al-fath al-arabi hata al-ghazu al-uthmani*. al-qahira, dar al-fiqr li'ldirasat wa'l-nashr wa'l-tawzi'.

Al-Qawsi, Atiyya, 2001, *al-yahud fi zil al-hadara al-islamiyya*. al-qahira, markaz al-dirasat al-sharqiyya.

Al-Maqrizi, Taqi al-Din Ahmad Bin Ali, 1934, *kitab al-suluk lima'rifat dual al-muluk*. al-qahira, matba't dar al-kutub al-misriyya.

Wulfansun, Isra'il, 1936, *musa bin maimun-hayatahu wamusunnafatuhu*. al-qahira, lajnat al-ta'lif wa'tarjama wa'nashr.

Hebrew

Urinovski, Aharon, 1935, *Rabeinu moshe Ben Maimon (Rambam)-Hayav, Mifa'lav wusfarav*. Tel Aviv, Dvir, 1935.

Dinburg, Ben-Zion, 1935, *Rabeinu Moshe Ben Maimon (Rambam) Hayav, wusfarav,peulotav vehashqafotav*. Tel Aviv, 1935.

English

Ashtor-Strauss. E. 1956. "Saladin and the Jews," *Hebrew Union College Annual*, Vol. xxvii: 305–26.

Broadhurst, R. J. C. 1980. *A History of the Ayyubid Sultans of Egypt*. Translated from the Arabic of al-Maqrizi. With Introduction and Notes. Boston: Twayne Publishers, 1st Printing.

Cohen, Mark R. 1994. *Under Crescent and Cross – The Jews in the Middle Ages*. Princeton, New Jersey: Princeton University Press.

Ehrenkreutz, Andrew S. 1991. "Saladin's Egypt and Maimonides." In *Perspectives on Maimonides – Philosophical and Historical Studies*, ed. Joel L. Kraemer, 303–7. Oxford: Oxford University Press.

Goitein, S. D. 1967. *A Mediterranean Society*, Vol. 1: Economic Foundations. Berkeley–Los Angeles: University of California Press.

—— 1971. *A Mediterranean Society*. Vol. 2: The Community. Berkeley–Los Angeles: University of California Press.

—— 1973. "Jewish Society and Institutions Under Islam." In *Jewish Society Through the Ages*, ed. H. H. Ben Sasson and S. Ettinger, 170–84. New York.

Ibn Abi Usaibi'a. 1965. '*Uyun al-anba' fi tabaqat al-atibba'*. Beirut.

Kraemer, Joel L. (ed.) 1991. *Perspectives on Maimonides- Philosophical and Historical Studies*. Oxford: Oxford University Press.

Landshut, S. 1976. *Jewish Communities in the Muslim Countries of the Middle East*. Westport (Connecticut): Hyperion Press, Inc.

Web Sites

A critical review by Mark Cohen's, *Under Crescent & Cross* : Terry Newman's website, <http://www.terrynewman.com/LifeUnder_Crescent_and_Cross-a_criticial_review.htm>, accessed on September 9, 2007.

Al-Muhajabah's Islamic Pages, <http://www.muhajabah.com/docstorage/jewsofislam-cite.htm>, accessed on September 7, 2007.

AL-QAHIRA 969–1517 CE: Center for Middle Eastern Studies, The University of Texas at Austin, <http://menic.utexas.edu/cairo/history/qahira/qahira.html>, accessed on September 9, 2007.

Deep Field, <http://www.deepfield.com/anoot/essay/Saladin.htm>, accessed on September 7, 2007.

Encyclopædia Britannica, <http://www.britannica.com/eb/article-9011523/Ayyubid-Dynasty>, accessed on September 7, 2007.

Jews and Christians Under Islam, Dhimmi, a book written by Bat Ye'or, reviewed by Aviv Goldstein: Jewish Magazine, <http://www.jewishmag.com/57mag/dhimmi/dhimmi.htm>, accessed on September 7, 2007.

Only Connect: Reconsidering Jewish–Muslim History: <http://politicscentral.com/2006/11/10/only_connect_reconsidering_jew.php>, accessed on September 9, 2007.

The Jerusalem Post, Online Edition, <http://www.jpost.com/servlet/Satellite?cid=1143498907121&pagename=JPost%2FJPArticle%2FPrinter>, accessed on April 20, 2007.

The Relationship of Islam to Its "Dhimmi" Minorities: Peace with Realism, <http://www.peacewithrealism.org/jewarab6.htm>, accessed on 9 Sept., 2007.

Virtual International Center, <http://international.fullerton.edu/egypt/history.html>, accessed on April 20, 2007.

Notes

1 See Hamilton Gibb and Harold Bowen, *Islamic Society and the* West (London, Oxford University Press, 1960), Part II, Chapter XIV.

2 Cf. Gibb and Bowen, p. 251.

3 The first Muslim ruler to order non-Muslims expelled from government office was Umayyad caliph 'Umar ibn 'Abd al-'Aziz; see Cohen 1994, pp. 65–66.

4 A critical review of Mark Cohen's *Under Crescent & Cross*: Terry Newman's website, <http://www.terrynewman.com/Life_Under_Crescent_and_Cross-a_criticial_review.htm>.

5 Goitein 1971, p. 374; Qasim, 1987, 60.

6 Maimonides or Moses ben Maimon, Rabbi Moshe ben Maimon (Hebrew: Moshe Ben Maimon; Arabic: Mussa bin Maimun ibn Abdallah al-Kurtubi al-Israili; March 30, 1135–December 13, 1204, b. Córdoba, Spain, d. Cairo), was a Jewish rabbi, physician, and philosopher, the most influential Jewish thinker of the Middle Ages. Maimonides was a physician to the Muslim ruling elite, intellectual equal and friend of many a Muslim scholar, and head of the Egyptian Jewish community. Maimonides' coming to Egypt and his accession to the position of communal leader there corresponded with the end of Isma'ili (Shi'i) Faimid rule and the rise of the Sunni Ayyubid dynasty under Saladin. For more details, see: Cohen 1994, p. 199; Kraemer 1991, p. 8; Wulfansun, 1936, 1–25; Urinovski, 1935, 4; Dinburg, 1935, 2.

PART

II

Jerusalem: A Center for Three Civilizations

Making Jerusalem a "Holy" City for Three Faiths

HARVEY COX

How lonely sits the city that was full of people!
How like a widow she has become . . .
She weeps bitterly in the night,
Tears on her cheeks . . .
She has none to comfort her. (Lamentations I:1,2)

There is much to lament about Jerusalem. As one observer has written, Jerusalem's sadness is that so many people love her to death. It is often said that the blessing and the bane of the Holy City is that she is a city "holy to three faiths." My thesis in this essay is that the conflicting "holinesses" that have been the city's affliction for centuries could also be a source of healing.

"Holy to three faiths?" At one level this is surely true. One thinks immediately of the Western Wall, the Haram-al Sharif (Temple Mount) and the Church of the Holy Sepulcher as well as many other Jewish, Christian and Muslim "holy sites." But "holy to three faiths" also raises a number of more basic questions pertinent to the Jewish–Christian–Muslim "tri-alogue."

Does the meaning of "holiness" per se, and therefore of the holiness of Jerusalem, vary from one tradition to another? How, when and why did Jerusalem become holy to Jews? To Christians? To Muslims? Was there a time, or were there times, when the city was not holy to any of them? Has the resonance of "holiness" changed for any or all of them? If the meaning of its holiness has evolved in the past, could the meaning of the holiness of Jerusalem be changing now? If so how? Further, could all three traditions even work with each other to deepen and expand the meaning of the city's holiness?

To address these questions, I will use a historical approach, showing that the meaning of Jerusalem as a "holy city" is multivalent and mutable. The city has often been in the past holy to more than these three faiths, and at times (including now) has successfully served as a holy city for more than one faith.

The holiness of the city has waxed and waned over the centuries due in some measure to the historical circumstances of the then current relationships among the three Abrahamic traditions. The meaning of Jerusalem's holiness is neither fixed nor static. It is responsive to human influences, and it could change again.

(A) Some people think (wish?) that the name of Jerusalem means something like "city of peace." It does not. It is derived from the name of the pre-Israelite Syrian deity "Shalem." The name means "founded by Shalem," and since the founding of cities was regarded in the ancient Middle East as religious actions, Jerusalem was a "holy city" from its inception, although not within any of the three Abrahamic traditions that later made it holy.

The Bible says little about how David came to occupy Jerusalem, but he wanted the city to be called "City of David" (cf. Constantinople and Ho Chi Minh City). However, the residents still referred to it by its previous name, Jerusalem. According to the biblical account, David purchased the central religious site of the city, the "threshing floor," from the Jebusites. He then apparently allowed the Jebusite priests who had previously occupied the site to remain and to continue to use it for cultic purposes, alongside the worship of YHWH which he introduced. Jerusalem was not, under David, therefore a city marked by an exclusive monotheism. His successor, Solomon, also allowed, even welcomed other cultic practices in Jerusalem, many of them imported along with his wives. The prophets, at least some of them railed against this practice, but the fact that they railed demonstrates that it was going on.

It is vital to notice that from its first days as a "Jewish city" under David, Jerusalem was "holy" to at least two religions.

The Jewish YHWH cultus was a de-centralized one with centers in various places in Canaan. But eventually, as much for political as for religious purposes (the two can hardly be distinguished), the cultus was centered in the temple of Jerusalem, and other centers were outlawed.

During the exile of the Jewish elites in Babylon (the non-elites were left behind) Jerusalem (or its poetic equivalent "Zion") became a symbol not just of a city but of a whole way of life that had been lost and that the exiles – like exiles ever since – romanticized and longed to regain. When under the Persian ruler Cyrus the Jews were allowed to "return" (though obviously few if any of the original deportees remained alive), the city walls and the temple were rebuilt under Ezra. A strong temple-centered priestly religion closely integrated with the political ruling class was set up. When, centuries later, the Romans conquered Jerusalem, they ruled through the priestly class, centered in the Jerusalem temple, which became their collaborators. This largely puppet regime evoked a variety of protests from the Jewish people, ranging from the armed rebellion of the Zealots to the desert withdrawal of the Essenes (who gave us the Dead Sea Scrolls) to the "Jesus Movement," a non-violent but also non-withdrawalist group centered first in Galilee, whose leader was executed by the Romans when he brought his protest to Jerusalem.

After the initial success, then defeat of the Jewish rebellion against Roman rule in 68–70 CE, the temple (except for the Western Wall) was razed, the city itself destroyed. The Jews were deported from the city, thus creating a huge diaspora. But in prayer and song, for 1900 years, many still longed to "return": ("Next year in Jerusalem!"). Meanwhile, the city became holy in yet another sense, as a venue where the gods of the Roman pantheon were honored. In 130 CE, the Roman emperor Hadrian renamed it "Aelia Capitolina" after himself (his middle name was Aelius) and the temple of Jupiter on the Capitoline hill in Rome. Shrines to the other gods, in true Roman fashion, were to be built throughout the city. Both Jews and Christians at this point began to construct visions of a "heavenly Jerusalem" which could not be destroyed. (See the Jewish apocryphal book of *Enoch* and *Revelation* XXI in the New Testament.)

(B) The early Christians despised Jerusalem. Far from "holy," they saw it as the pit of death and destruction where Jesus had been crucified. They avoided it as much as they could. The bishop of nearby Caesarea was acknowledged to be more important. It was only in the 4th century, with the "conversion" of Constantine, that the city came under "Christian" rule. Then Constantine's mother Helen made her famous pilgrimage to the "Terra Sacra" and returned with the first in what developed into one of the most profitable souvenir dodges in history: the "true cross." An ugly legend claims that she discovered it where the wicked Jews had buried it only by threatening an old Jew with an unpleasant death.

Now Jerusalem became a holy city again, and this time of just one religion, Byzantine Christianity. The local bishop, Makarios, obtained Constantine's permission to tear down the Temple of Aphrodite so as to uncover the tomb of Jesus, which he claimed was buried under it. This ended the last trace of Roman holiness. The 4th century Christian historian Eusebius excitedly describes the overturning of the "lifeless idols" in this "shrine of darkness." But even he does not change his attitude toward Jerusalem itself. He still called it Aelia.

Also, Jerusalem had to compete with Byzantium, which as the seat of the Christian emperor claimed preeminent holiness, and with Rome, which as the seat of the pope was also lodging its claim. Still, after Helen, the trickle of pilgrims to Jerusalem (and to other parts of the "Terra Sacra") became a flood. The seeds of the crusades can be found in the armed guards who accompanied pilgrims, in search of blessing and relics (and adventure), along the difficult route.

During the era of Byzantine Christian rule, Jews continued to be banned from Jerusalem, but they were admitted once a year – on the Ninth of Av – to mourn at the western wall for the destroyed temple. This was, however, hardly a generous gesture. The Christian authorities of Jerusalem wanted the Jews to play an unintended role in a cruel theological drama. As the Jews wailed, the Christians watched, and were told that their sorrow was a result of God's punishment on them for refusing to recognize their messiah. By the 600s, far from despising Jerusalem, Christians now viewed it as the holiest of cities, and the tomb of Christ as the navel of the cosmos and the very source of salvation. Sophronius became patriarch of Jerusalem in 633 CE. He crafted the following tribute:

> O light-giving tomb, thou art the ocean stream of eternal life and the true river of Lethe. I would lie at full length and kiss that stone, the sacred center of the world, wherein the tree was fixed which did away with the curse of Adam's tree . . . Hail to thee Zion, splendid sun of the world for whom I long and groan by day and night.

But changes were on the way. In 637 Arab armies under Omar reached Jerusalem. Muslim rule in the city lasted, except for the Crusader Kingdom (1099–1187) and a few minor interruptions, until General Allenby led the British forces through the Jaffa Gate on December 11, 1917. Gathering the notables, Allenby promised that he would protect the holy places and preserve religious freedom for all three faiths. In seeming contradiction, however, British newspapers announced that he had completed the work of the crusaders, and that the Holy City was now a "Christmas present" and "back in Christian hands."

(C) When the earliest Muslims prayed according to the instructions of the Prophet, at first they faced Jerusalem. It was their first *qiblah* since the Prophet honored the previous revelations that had been centered there. Shortly thereafter Mecca supplanted Jerusalem as the primary *qiblah*, but Jerusalem continues to be given importance because of the Prophet's "Night Journey" (*al-isra*) during which he met Abraham, Moses and Jesus (the previous prophets) after ascending (*al mi' raj*) from the Temple Mount The stone from which he ascended is preserved under the golden Dome of the Rock, which has become a postcard trademark of Jerusalem.

With some exceptions, Jews fared better in Jerusalem under Muslim rule than they did under Christian rule. Most of the Christians in the city were of Arab descent and belonged to the Syrian Orthodox wing. They harbored little affection for Western (Roman Catholic) Christians, and when the crusader armies, about 60,000 soldiers accompanied by countless wives and pilgrims, attacked the city in 1099, the Orthodox Christians joined the Muslims in defending it against "the Franks." The defense was to no avail, and the crusaders sacked the city, killing almost all its 30,000 inhabitants – Muslims, Christians and Jews, including women and children. As soon as they took control the crusaders promulgated a law banning Jews and Muslims from the holy city. Also, because they suspected local Christians of complicity with Islam, they were banned as well. In a significant indication of the intra-Christian tension, the crusaders changed the name of the Anastasis (Resurrection) church into the Church of the Holy Sepulcher, reflecting the Western emphasis on the crucifixion and the Eastern emphasis on Resurrection in the different theologies of the two branches.

During four centuries of Ottoman rule and threes decades of British mandate, Jerusalem was open to all faiths. During the pre-state period, however, the key leaders of Zionism were not enamored of Jerusalem. Theodor Herzl only visited it once, quite briefly, and thought it old, dirty and decrepit. His vision for the capital of the Judenstaat was of a gleaming new world city where science and learning would thrive. Ben-Gurion did not warm to Jerusalem either. His ideal was Tel Aviv, a modern and very European metropolis. Jerusalem stood for what was to be discarded as a "new Jew" was born. The western section of Jerusalem became a part of the newly created state of Israel in 1948. In 1967, the Israelis captured the other half, including the old walled city. It was only after this that Jerusalem acquired the political-symbolic importance it now holds for some Israelis as the "eternal and undivided" capital of Israel. But it is important to recognize that despite the urging of some zealots to dismantle the Dome of the Rock, cooler heads prevailed, and the Israelis wisely preserved it and promised to continue the equal rights approach. Today the Haram-al-Sharif is administered by the Muslim *Waqf* under Israeli supervision. No Christians now make any claims to political sovereignty over the city. Both the Vatican and the World Council of Churches say they want the final status of the city to be determined by negotiations among the parties.

Thus, Jews consider Jerusalem holy in part because it was the site of the ancient temple, which was built there because of the belief that Abraham's binding of Isaac took place there. Catholics consider it holy as the site of the Crucifixion and Resurrection of Jesus. Some evangelical Protestants consider it holy not principally for what once happened there but or what they expect will happen there, namely the return of Christ, the climactic battle of Armageddon and the final judgment (as grotesquely documented in the popular Left Behind series of novels). Muslims consider it holy because it was the first *qiblah*, the holy site of the forerunner religions it recognizes, and the "far mosque" of the Prophet's Night Journey. Thus "holy" has overlapping but distinguishable meanings, and the history of Jerusalem shows that although it is considered holy by three faiths, what "holiness" means varies both among the three and also among wings within each of them. History also shows that while the city has been the site of horrendous violence, for significant periods the three faiths have been able to live together in relative harmony. What does this history suggest for the next phase of the Holy City's history?

I suggest that, precisely because Jerusalem is "holy to three faiths," a just final status for Jerusalem will require innovative thinking on both the theological and the political level.

First, the theological level: Islam generously provides an ample place for Judaism and Christianity as other "religions of the book," and now some Muslim scholars would like to enlarge this category to include any religion that has sacred texts. This provision is not just a dead letter. In many American inter-faith organizations the local Muslim community often supplies a disproportionate share of the support and leadership for these groups. Muslims in America want to be part of the US pluralistic religious culture.

It is not only unfortunate, it is tragic that in the tense years that have followed the attacks on the World Trade Center, the minority of Muslims who reject this inclusivist tradition have come to the fore, or at least been given the most publicity. Some scholars now even speak of a "war for the soul of Islam." I cannot be sure if they are right, but as a Christian I know about the kind of internal battles within a tradition that can breed animosity and hatred. I can only hope that somehow the generous and open tradition within Islam comes more to the fore. At least there is ample scriptural warrant for it in the Qur'an, while there are fewer such resources in the Bible, which brims with exclusivist language.

For the remainder of the 21st century we, and our children and grand-children, will undoubtedly live in a period where the two largest religions in the world, Christians, with some two billion adherents worldwide, and Muslims, with about one billion, must learn to come to terms with each other. The required reconciliation will need to take place on many levels: historical, political and cultural. But it will also necessitate some thorough re-thinking of inherited theological positions of both sides. Both communities have much work to do in the next decades to avoid a spiral of violence, a "clash" that is wholly unnecessary and fully avoidable.

As a Christian and a theologian, I think one of my tradition's most formi-dable challenges is to think anew about how the Prophet Muhammad, who has been pilloried and defamed by Christians for centuries (see Dante's Inferno), might find a place in our religious worldview. I know that task is formidable, but it is not impossible. An example from Christianity's relation-ship with another tradition helps. Half century ago, the vast majority of Christians held the conviction that Christianity had displaced or "superceded" Judaism. In the past fifty years that belief has been officially disowned by the Roman Catholic Church and by most of the Protestant churches, including many evangelicals, as well. A whole new and promising era in Jewish–Christian relations has begun. Could the same kind of things happen in relations between Christians and Muslims?

I am convinced that it could, and the future of Jerusalem could be a key. Muslims already honor Jesus, but so far Christians have no language with which to honor the Prophet. This may be because churches have often been nervous about recognizing what might be called "post-canonical" prophets, those who have appeared after the closing of the biblical canon. But if this "displacement theology," which seemed so firmly ensconced in the churches, could be re-thought and discarded by so many in such a relatively short time, might the prejudice against post-canonical prophets also be re-thought as well? If it could, this would create a religious "space" for the Prophet in Christian thinking.

There are some precedents to work with. Christians not only recognized and accepted the Hebrew prophets, but many also designated figures like Socrates and Plato as prophetic precursors of Jesus. They did this by suggesting that the same eternal logos that appeared in Jesus had also inspired these Greek philosophers. But if God could use great teachers outside the church before Christ, would that not also be possible after Christ? Mahatma Gandhi has come extremely close to being recognized as a Christian saint. His image appears in more than one stained glass window in Christian chapels. It would be a marvelous signal if some future pope canonized him officially. This may not be just a utopian fantasy. But even if it did happen, it might be much harder to make a case for the Prophet Muhammad.

Still, sainthood is not the only category that might give a status in Christian thought analogous to the position Jesus has in the Muslim spiritual tradition. In fact, Muslims might not like the use of "saint" at all for him. So why not "prophet?" In thinking about this issue Christians in western countries, in which until quite recently Islam seemed remote and ominous, have much to learn from the experience of Christians who lived for centuries within the Islamic world, especially before the more recent eruptions of animosities arising mainly from political conflicts. In those areas Christians did often ponder the religious status of the Prophet of Islam, and one Syrian Christian bishop suggested that, if not a prophet in the sense of Isaiah or Jeremiah, then Muhammad did "walk in the way of the prophets."

There have been periods in western Christian history when Islam, with its elegant simplicity, clear rules of living, straightforward doctrines and opulent fund of stories, poems and legends have had an undeniable appeal. No one who has read the Sufi poet Rumi or visited the Alhambra in Granada or the Dome of the Rock in Jerusalem can have missed the power of this attractiveness. But today the main question posed by Islam is how can Christians understand and appreciate its religious significance so that we can all live together on the one earth we share. The fact that Muslims and Christians lived together in relative harmony both in al-Andalus and in Jerusalem can be part of the religious reconstruction that is needed.

Second, the political level: Echoing the cry of *Lamentations*, Jerusalem has by and large been "abandoned" by the various negotiators who for such a long time have tried to find a solution to the larger Israeli–Palestinian conflict. True, they have often spoken of "the Jerusalem question" as a key issue. But with occasional exceptions, they have preferred to tackle first the challenges of security, borders, settlements, and refugees. They have usually chosen to postpone discussing Jerusalem until progress has been made on these questions and some confidence has been built up.

But this "Jerusalem last" strategy has obviously not succeeded. The Israeli–Palestinian standoff now seems no closer to a solution than it was a decade ago. It is time to try something new. Why not start the negotiations with Jerusalem? If the city is indeed the key, or even a key, issue, why not move its future to the top of the agenda, instead of putting it off? Jerusalem may or may not be one of the toughest knots in the tangled web. But it is a potent symbol of the whole, and if a satisfactory compromise could be found, answers to the other issues might follow.

It is within the realm of possibility that such a compromise on Jerusalem could be worked out. Contrary to popular impressions, when negotiators have occasionally broached the future status of Jerusalem, they have come at least as close to agreement as they have on the other questions, sometimes even closer. Both sides want Jerusalem to be their capital, but surveys show that most Israelis have no desire to rule the Palestinian parts of the city, and most Palestinians are prepared to compromise as well. It is true that Yasir Arafat did not accept the arrangement offered at Camp David for some kind of administrative control over Arab sections, but a few months later, even after the beginning of the second *intifada*, the diplomats at Taba in Egypt announced that they were closer than ever to major agreements. But then Barak was defeated, Clinton left office, and negotiations in effect ceased.

It now appears that genuine negotiations are beginning again. It is often said that what is needed to break the current deadlock over Jerusalem are "new ideas." But since no new ideas seem to have worked so far, it may be time to look again at some old ones. Before 1948, for example, while the UN was still discussing the nature of the partition, some countries strongly favored a three-way division of Palestine – an Arab section, a Jewish one and an internationally administered area in and around Jerusalem. Others proposed that the historic Old City, with its traditional Jewish, Muslim and Christian quarters, which is also the area where the Western Wall, the Church of the Holy Sepulcher and the Dome of the Rock are located, could be administered by a consortium of religious authorities under UN supervision. The solution that was eventually worked out for Vatican City in 1870 is sometimes recalled.

These are all "old ideas," not bad ones, but for various reasons, none of these previous schemes quite fits the situation today. Still, they do suggest hints of a possible way to proceed. If Jerusalem is the symbolic key issue, then the Old City is the symbolic key to Jerusalem, and the holy places are the symbolic key to the Old City. An overall solution must start with the Temple Mount and work outward.

Such a solution is possible. As recently as 2001 a secular Israeli scholar offered an idea that attracted considerable attention from both sides, at least at first, but is now rarely mentioned. He proposed that the Temple Mount/Noble Sanctuary/Western Wall should be placed "under the sovereignty of God." No national flags would be flown. It would then be administered by Muslim and Jewish religious authorities, with the cooperation of Israeli and Palestinian governments. The area has in fact been administered in this way since 1967, more successfully than one might imagine given the upheavals that have marked the period. But the question of sovereignty over the area remains undecided.

So why not place the Temple Mount/Noble Sanctuary/Western Wall under the sovereignty of God? Admittedly, to modern ears this suggestion sounds a bit bizarre, a genuine non-starter. But all three traditions claim to worship the same God, and given the present logjam, we need some ideas that may first appear quaint to break through the failure of the more modern and "rational" strategies that have simply not worked. Also, the idea makes even more sense when we remember that disputes over the Temple Mount have everything to do with religion.

True, it is commonly thought that religion has only made the Jerusalem question more intractable. But I do not share this view. There are of course religious die-hards on both sides. But sovereignty, as opposed to access, is a fundamentally political issue. The Muslims and the Jews who have injected religion into a political struggle represent only a fraction of either side. They are opposed both by religious moderates and by secular Israelis and Palestinians who together constitute the majority. Religious leaders and scholars – Jewish, Christian and Muslim – have often been ahead of political leaders in voicing a willingness to share the city. A few years ago 400 American rabbis issued a statement calling for just such a sharing of Jerusalem. Christian and Muslim leaders have frequently expressed a similar willingness. They all worship the same God, and they realize that, despite Jerusalem's reputation for bloodshed, there have been long periods in which adherents of the three faiths have shared the city amicably.

New ideas often lie concealed in old ones, so the history of Jerusalem can be instructive. As we have seen, when King David bought the area in Jerusalem from the Jebusite ruler in 1000 BCE, and founded his sanctuary there, he allowed the previous residents to continue their worship along with his. When Caliph Omar and his Muslim army conquered the city in 637 he allowed the Christians to continue to worship, and invited the Jews to return. Saladin, who recaptured the city from the crusaders in 1187, welcomed Christian pilgrims and Jews to the city, if they entered peaceably. One of General Allenby's first acts when he entered the city in December 1917 was to assemble the leaders of the three religions and assure them that he would guarantee access to all holy sites.

Sacred spaces can be shared. All three faiths honor the Tomb of the Patriarchs. Muslims and Christian pilgrims visit the "milk cave" outside Jerusalem where Joseph and Mary are believed to have stopped with the infant Jesus on their way as refugees to Egypt. Holy cities can also be shared. If the "key issue" is Jerusalem, let us move it to the head of the agenda instead of relegating it to an appendix. And let us enlist religious leaders, who were largely left out of the Oslo and other previous negotiations, in envisioning its future. We might be surprised to find that it is not so insoluble after all. If the Temple Mount/Noble Sanctuary can be shared under God's sovereignty, then the sharing of the rest of the Old City – which already has its separate quarters – would follow.

The blessing and curse of Jerusalem is that, like no other city on earth, three major faiths, and people from virtually every nation on the globe, have feeling of kinship and veneration for it. They also have a legitimate claim to access to the site associated with their faiths. Like no other city Jerusalem does, in some sense, "belong to the whole world." Suppose the idea of placing the old city under the "sovereignty of God" (or something like it) could be worked out, how would the actual implementation function?

Some have suggested that as the central "old city" of Jerusalem already "belongs to the world" spiritually, it should be declared a world heritage site and administered and policed by the UN in cooperation with an inter-faith council composed of representatives of Syrian Orthodox, Roman Catholic, Russian Orthodox, Protestant (Evangelical and Ecumenical), all three branches of Judaism, Shi'a and Sunni Islam. This arrangement would, of course, include everything inside the walls of the old city, including the Haram al-Sharif (Temple Mount), Western Wall and all the religious and pilgrimage sites. Within reasonable limits (stated services and prayer times, etc.), people of all faiths should be allowed to visit all sites.

The rest of the city would be divided into eastern and western sections (border to be negotiated), with the western recognized by the international community as an integral part of Israel, and the eastern section a part of a Palestinian state. Both could serve as capitals of their respective states, and the international community would recognize both as the capitals. Governing councils should be established both for the two sides and for the city as a whole. They could be constituted by neighborhood councils. The border between the two sections should be as "porous" as possible, and supervised by either joint Israeli–Palestinian teams and/or international units.

This is an arrangement polls suggest that most Jerusalemites (both Israeli and Palestinian) would welcome. Such an agreement on Jerusalem would then generate some of the trust and good will that is needed today. Building on that momentum, we might find new ways to move ahead on many of the larger issues as well. If that happens, then Jerusalem would be not just a "Christmas present for the British people," but a gift for the whole world that would last all year long, and for years to come. Then the appropriate biblical passage for the holy city might not be Lamentations but these words from the prophet Isaiah:

"Comfort ye, comfort ye, my people, Says your God.
Speak tenderly to Jerusalem, and cry to her that her warfare is ended.

The Holy Land, Jerusalem and Al-Aqsa Mosque in the Qur'an, Sunnah and Other Islamic Literary Sources

MUSTAFA ABU SWAY

Coming from the same divine source as previous revelations, Islam embodies many things that are common to them such as the special status that the Holy Land and Jerusalem enjoy.

Islam recognizes the fact that the Holy Land is sacred to the People of the Book. When Muslims say that the Holy Land is the "Land of the Prophets," certainly the prophets of the Children of Israel are included and constitute a continuum in the line of prophecy, which culminated with Prophet Muhammad (Peace be upon them all). Almost every prophet lived in the Holy Land, or had a special relationship with it, including those who were born elsewhere. An example of the latter is Prophet Abraham, the prototype iconoclast. After he destroyed and mocked the idols of his people, they planned violence against him, but he was destined to go to the Holy Land. The following verse uses inclusive language to reflect the nature of Abraham's new home:

> But We delivered him and [his nephew] Lot [and directed them] to the land which We have blessed *for the nations*. (Qur'an, 21:71)

An example of a prophet who had a special relationship with the Holy Land and Jerusalem in particular is that of Prophet Muhammad. The Qur'an stated in the chapter of the "Children of Israel" (*Banu Israel*), or the "Journey at Night" (*Al-Isra'*), that he was taken in a night journey miraculously from the Sacred Mosque to the Farthest Mosque (Al-Masjid Al-Aqsa):

> Glory be to (Allah) Who did take His Servant for a journey by night from the Sacred Mosque [*Al-Masjid Al-Haram*] to the Farthest Mosque [*Al-Masjid Al-Aqsa*] whose precincts We did bless, in order that We might show him some of Our Signs: for He is the One who hears and sees [all things]. (Qur'an, 17:1)

Scholars of *hadith*,[1] Qur'an commentators, and all of Islamic tradition take this particular verse seriously and consider the Sacred Mosque to be in Mecca and the Farthest Mosque to be in Jerusalem. No Muslim scholar challenged this position throughout the Islamic intellectual history which expands for more than fourteen centuries. The parameters of this blessed land go beyond what is between the Jordan River and the Mediterranean. Ibn Kathir (d. 774 AH/1373 CE), a medieval Muslim scholar, reported the commentary of several early Muslim scholars on verse 21:71.

According to the famous Ubayy Ibn Ka'b, the blessed land is *Al-Sham* [i.e. Greater Syria, which includes Jerusalem]. The great early commentator, Qatadah, adopted the same position.[2] A more detailed account of the Night Journey and the Ascension [*Al-Isra' and Al-Mi'raj*] and their relation to Jerusalem will follow.

In addition, there is another verse in the Qur'an with reference to this line of blessing:

> Between them and the cities on which We had poured Our blessings, We had placed cities in prominent positions, and between them We had appointed stages of journey in due proportion: "Travel therein secure, by night and by day." (Qur'an, 34:18)

According to Mujahid, Al-Hassan, Sa'id Ibn Jubayr, Malik, Qatadah, Al-Dahhak, Al-Sadiyy, Ibn Zayd and many other respected early Muslim scholars, the blessed cities are those of *Al-Sham*. Ibn 'Abbas (d. 68 AH/687 CE), the prominent early scholar of the Qur'an who was also a cousin and companion of the Prophet, maintained that the "blessed cities" is a reference to Bayt Al-Maqdis [i.e. Jerusalem].[3]

Though there are several references to *the* land, the term "Holy Land" [*Al-Ard Al-Muqaddasah*] is mentioned only once in the Qur'an:

> Remember Moses said to his people: "O my People! Call in remembrance the favor of God unto you, when He produced prophets among you, made you kings, and gave you what He had not given to any other among the peoples.
>
> "O my People! Enter the Holy Land which God has assigned unto you, and turn not back ignominiously, for then will you be overthrown, to your own ruin." (Qur'an, 5:20–21)

The context is that of Moses (peace be upon him) inviting the Children of Israel to enter the Holy Land after he delivered them miraculously from Egypt across the sea. The Children of Israel refused to enter the Holy Land, because it meant that they had to fight its people, who were known for their exceeding strength. This rejection earned them divine punishment:

> God said: "Therefore will the land be out of their reach for forty years: in distraction will they wander through the land: but sorrow you not over these rebellious people." (Qur'an, 5:26)

This verse is read in two very different ways, each one arriving at a very different meaning. The first way as shown above divides the verse into two parts, the first of which ends after "*years.*" This way of dividing the verse indicates that the Children of Israel were forbidden to enter the Land temporarily because of their disobedience.

The second reading also divides the verse into two parts, the first of which ends after "*reach.*" Some scholars interpreted this way of dividing the verse to mean that the Children of Israel were forbidden to enter the Land in an absolute sense, again as a result of their disobedience. I am personally inclined toward the first reading, which considers the prohibition temporary, and the entry to the Holy Land conditional.

Sayyed Qutb stated in *In the Shade of the Qur'an*, a contemporary exegesis of the Qur'an, that the reason for this prohibition is to allow room for a new generation of Israelites to be brought up.[4] I would add that the new generation was ready to submit to the will of God, and therefore qualified for the entry to the Holy Land as "Submitters"; those who submit their personal will entirely to the will of God. The meaning of "Muslims" is also submitters. The Qur'an states in clear terms that righteousness is a prerequisite for inheriting lands:

> Before this We wrote in the Zabur ("Psalms"!), after the Message [given to Moses]: "My servants, the righteous, shall inherit the earth." (Qur'an, 21:105)

Other verses in the Qur'an directly associate the religious state of the Children of Israel to the inheritance of the land:

> And We made a people, considered weak [in Egypt], inheritors of the East and West of the land [i.e. all of it], whereon We sent down Our blessings. The fair promise of your Lord was fulfilled for the Children of Israel, because they had patience and constancy, and We leveled to the ground the great works and fine buildings which Pharaoh and his people erected. (Qur'an, 7:137)

According to these verses, right relationship with God, which means submission to His will, is the absolute criterion for inheritance of the Land. Of critical importance to the Qur'an is the fact that genetic or biological decent is never sufficient in itself to merit such inheritance. It is a non-factor in this respect.

Jerusalem or Bayt Al-Maqdis [House of the Holy] is, by definition, a holy place. It is included in verse 17:1, either by referring to the Al-Aqsa Mosque or to its precincts about which God said: "We did bless". The great 14th century Muslim scholar, Ibn Kathir, said that Al-Aqsa Mosque is Bayt Al-Maqdis.[5] Indeed, the "Al-Aqsa Mosque" and "Bayt Al-Maqdis" are used interchangeably whereby one of them is used as a metaphor of the other, as in the following *hadith*:

> Maimuna said: "O Messenger of Allah! Inform us about Bayt Al-Maqdis!" He said: "It is the land where people will be gathered and resurrected [on the Day of Judgment]. Go (grammatically imperative!) and pray in it, for a prayer in it is the equivalent of a thousand prayers in other [mosques]." I said: "What if I couldn't reach it?" He said: "Then you send a gift of oil to it in order to be lit in its lanterns, for the one who does so is the same like the one who has been there."[6]

The *hadith* shows that it is the religious duty of Muslims all over the world to maintain Al-Aqsa Mosque both physically and spiritually. The relationship with Al-Aqsa Mosque is primarily fulfilled through acts of worship, but the physical maintenance of the Mosque is also part of the responsibility of all Muslims. The fulfillment of both duties will be impaired as long as Al-Aqsa Mosque remains under occupation! The truth of the matter is that under Israeli occupation, Muslims do not have free access to the Mosque. Those who are prevented from having freedom of worship at Al-Aqsa Mosque include, but are not restricted to, all Palestinians from the Gaza Strip, the West Bank, and occasional restrictions to Jerusalemite men younger than 45 years of age.

Since the miraculous Night Journey of Prophet Muhammad (Peace be upon him), *al-Isra' wa al-Mi'raj*, took place more than fourteen centuries ago, Muslims have established a sublime and perpetual relationship with Al-Aqsa Mosque. The Prophet was taken from Al-Masjid Al-Haram in Mecca to Al-Masjid Al-Aqsa in Jerusalem. This event marked a twining relation between the two mosques. The beginning of Surah Al-Isra' (17:1) reminds Muslims and non-Muslims of this important event.

When the Prophet (Peace be upon him) reported the event to the people of Mecca, they challenged him to prove it by describing Jerusalem to them, because they were familiar with it through their caravan trading. They used this story to undermine his credibility as a prophet; they knew that the journey from Mecca to Jerusalem would take several weeks during that time in each direction. They were considering Prophet Muhammad's abilities, not that of the Omnipotent God!

There are many references to this event in the Qur'an and the traditions of the Prophet (Peace be upon him), to the extent that it is not possible to cover all the details of the Isra' and the Mi'raj in this essay. The basic story is that Prophet Muhammad (Peace be upon him) was taken by the archangel Gabriel on a supernatural animal (Al-Buraq) from Mecca to Jerusalem and then to heaven, where he received the commandment for the five daily prayers. On his way back, the route of the journey passed through Jerusalem and there he led the other prophets in prayer. The part of the journey from Mecca to Jerusalem is called Isra' and the ascension to heaven is called Mi'raj. The journey took place during what is described as the Year of Sorrow ('Am Al-Huzn). It was during this year that the Prophet (Peace be upon him) lost two of his most important supporters: his wife Khadijah and his uncle, Abu Talib, who despite the fact that he never embraced Islam defended his nephew against the powerful tribes of Mecca.

The greatest *Hadith* scholars, Al-Bukhari and Muslim, narrated that the Prophet (Peace be upon him) said:

> When [the Meccan tribe of] Quraish did not believe me [about the Night Journey], I stood in the Hijr[7] and God revealed to me Bayt Al-Maqdis [i.e. Jerusalem] and I began describing its signs to them while I was looking at it

This *hadith* provides the setting for interpreting verse 17:1, and explains why Muslims believe that the "Farthest Mosque" is in Jerusalem.

The twinning relationship manifests itself in the fact that another term, "the Sanctuary" or Al-Haram, also refers to Al-Aqsa Mosque, deriving from the name "the Noble Sanctuary" or Al-Masjid Al-Haram in Mecca. The reference to Al-Aqsa Mosque as "Haram" is a cultural development that reflects the very close relationship between the two mosques in Islamic consciousness. In other words, strictly speaking from an Islamic *fiqh* point of view, the laws that apply to the Haram in Mecca, such as the prohibition of hunting during the time of Hajj, do not apply to Al-Aqsa Mosque.

Mujir Al-Din Al-Hanbali (d. 1522) used "Al-Masjid Al-Sharif Al-Aqsa" in the first page of his introduction to *Al-Uns Al-Jalil fi Tarikh Al-Quds wal-Khalil*. But the order of the words differed in the chapter on the description of Al-Aqsa Mosque; he used "Al-Masjid Al-Aqsa Al-Sharif".[8] Muslim scholars understood that the name 'Al-Aqsa Mosque' predates the structures, and that no one building could be called as such. It is anachronistic to call the southern-most building Al-Aqsa Mosque; Al-Hanbali called it "Al-Jami' Al-Kabir Al-Qibliyy" (The Grand Southern Friday-Mosque).[9] It is quite remarkable that Mujir Al-Din Al-Hanbali, who wrote *Al-Uns Al-Jalil fi Tarikh Al-Quds wal-Khalil* in the year 900 AH/1495, when there were no political disputes regarding Al-Aqsa Mosque, offered the following definition:

> Verily, 'Al-Aqsa' is a name for the whole mosque which is surrounded by the wall, the length and width of which are mentioned here, for the

building that exists in the southern part of the Mosque, and the other ones such as the Dome of the Rock and the corridors and other [buildings] are novel (*muhdatha*).[10]

The paragraph that preceded the definition of Al-Aqsa Mosque was dedicated to its measurement. Twice, the measurements of the Mosque were taken under the supervision of Al-Hanbali to make sure that they were accurate. He mentioned that the length of the Mosque was measured from the southern wall to the northern corridor near Bab Al-Asbat (i.e. Lions' Gate), and the width was measured from the wall overlooking the cemetery of Bab Al-Rahmah (i.e. Golden Gate) to the western corridor, beneath the Tankaziyyah School. In both cases, the width of the walls themselves was excluded.

It should be noted that the Qur'anic reference to the Al-Aqsa Mosque, as a mosque, took place years before the actual arrival of Muslims to Jerusalem. It means that part of what the Muslim believes is that Al-Aqsa Mosque was designated as a mosque by God.

Other than the three Mosques of Mecca, Medina and Jerusalem, Muslims are free to choose the site for a new mosque, but once it is established, it remains a mosque forever.

The journey by night had Jerusalem as a transit station or as a gate to the heavens. God could have taken His Prophet (Peace be upon him) directly from Mecca to heaven, but He didn't. Al-Aqsa Mosque has a very prominent place in the whole event. It was the place where the Prophet (Peace be upon him) led the other prophets and messengers in prayer. This act is interpreted, among other things, as inheriting the responsibility and becoming custodians of the mosque.

Bayt Al-Maqdis became the first *Qiblah* or direction of prayer. Al-Bara' said:

> "We have prayed with the Messenger of Allah (Peace be upon him) in the direction of Bayt Al-Maqdis for sixteen or seventeen months. Then we were directed to the Ka'bah [in Mecca]." (Narrated by Al-Bukhari and Muslim)

Despite the change of the *Qiblah*, the mere fact that Muslims prayed in the direction of Jerusalem is an indication of its prominence. According to the Qur'an, however, the mosque in Mecca was the first ever established by God for humanity, so it should not be surprising that the *Qiblah* was shifted back to it:

> The first House [of worship] appointed for men, was that at Bakkah [i.e. Mecca]: full of blessing and of guidance for all the worlds. (Qur'an, 3:96)

The same position is confirmed in a *hadith* narrated by Al-Bukhari and Muslim:

> Abu Dhar Al-Ghafari – May God be pleased with him – said: "I said: O
> Messenger of Allah: Which mosque was established first on earth?
> He said: Al-Masjid Al-Haram [in Mecca].
> I said: Then which one?
> He said: Al-Masjid Al-Aqsa [in Jerusalem].
> I said: How much time was between them?"
> He said: Forty years, and when it is time for prayer, wherever you are,
> pray, for that where the merit is.

The Qur'an teaches that, while a single system of ethics and belief should be common to the revelations and Scriptures of all peoples, the specific laws of ritual and behavior [i.e. *Shari'ah*] may vary among peoples and religions.

> . . . To each among you have We prescribed a Law and an Open Way. If
> Allah had so willed, He would have made you a single People, but (His
> plan is to test you in what He has given you: so strive as in a race in all
> virtues. (Qur'an, 5:48)

It should not be surprising, therefore, that Jews pray toward Jerusalem while Muslims pray toward Mecca. This fact does not reduce the sanctity of Jerusalem for Muslims.

The second chapter of the Qur'an (verses 142–50) addresses the change of the *Qiblah* in detail. The basic message is that both directions of prayer are from God and that:

> . . . the people of the Book know that that is Truth from their Lord.

In the area of *fiqh* (equal to the Hebrew term *halakhah*), it is prohibited to relieve oneself (e.g., urinate) in the open space in the direction of both, Al-Masjid Al-Haram in Mecca and Al-Aqsa Mosque in Jerusalem. The *hadith* that declares such prohibition refers to these two mosques as the "two *Qiblahs*."[11]

Moreover, the importance of Al-Aqsa Mosque in the life of Muslims is reflected in the many other traditions of the Prophet. One of these traditions – narrated by Al-Bukhari (#1115) and Muslim (#2475) – makes it clear that traveling in order to visit mosques for religious purposes is permitted to three mosques only: Al-Masjid Al-Haram (in Mecca), Al-Masjid Al-Nabawi (in Medina) and Al-Masjid Al-Aqsa (in Jerusalem).

The language of the above-mentioned *Hadith* in Arabic gives the impression that it is prohibited to travel to mosques other than these three. This led the prominent *Shafi'i* scholar Imam Al-Juwayni (d. 1085 CE) to have a religious ruling that it is prohibited to do so. Imam Al-Nawawi (d. 1277), who belonged to the same school of *fiqh*, rendered the position of Al-Juwayni erroneous, and that the majority of scholars (*jumhur Al-'Ulama'*) understand the *Hadith* as saying that "there is no [extra] merit in traveling to other mosques".[12]

Al-Aqsa Mosque was developed and the buildings expanded on a large scale during the reign of the two 7th and 8th century Umayyad Caliphs, Abd Al-Malik Ibn Marwan and his son Al-Walid, to the extent that it surpassed the architectural grandeur of all mosques. The magnificence of the architecture of the Dome of the Rock and the southern most building within the parameters of Al-Aqsa Mosque is witness to the importance of these holy sites in Islam.

Calligraphy is used at Al-Aqsa Mosque to reflect its status in the Islamic worldview, and to stress God's oneness and uniqueness (i.e., *tawhid*). Several chapters of the Qur'an and various other verses can be found inscribed inside and outside the buildings.

One of these inscriptions, chapter 17 (i.e. *Al-Isra'*), asserts the status of Al-Aqsa Mosque in the Islamic worldview. Like a necklace, it is inscribed on the neck of the Dome of the Rock, on the outside. The first verse of this chapter has a direct reference to Al-Aqsa Mosque, in the context of the "Night Journey". The rest of this chapter, another 110 verses, is about the story of the "*Children of Israel*", which is the second name of this chapter. The narrative shifts from talking about Prophet Muhammad and his journey to Al-Aqsa Mosque, to Prophet Moses:

> We gave unto Moses the Scripture, and We appointed it a guidance for the children of Israel, saying: Choose no guardian beside Me. (Qur'an, 17:2)

It should be noted that the same chapter is also inscribed over the niche in the southern-most building. The inscription, black on golden background mosaic with multi-colored leaves, begins immediately to the right side of the niche, facing south, and continues anti-clockwise in the direction of the east and then continues north and stops before the beginning of the two eastern "halls", the most northern of which has the rose window. The southern one has a hand-carved wood of a small part of chapter 17. It seems that most of this apparently old work of art was lost to the arson of August 21, 1969 which devastated that south-eastern corner of the building.

Some of the next verses could be considered either as a report on historical events that have taken place already, or as a prophecy that will unfold in the future, with the Children of Israel and Al-Aqsa Mosque being at the center of these events (Qur'an, 17:7).

Another chapter of the Qur'an is written on the outside of the Dome of the Rock. Like a crown, chapter 36 (i.e. *YaSeen*) covers the upper most part of the octagonal walls. There are several prophetic traditions of various strengths about the virtues of this chapter of the Qur'an. One of them, categorized as having a "weak" chain of narrators, considers it the "heart of the Qur'an".[13] *YaSeen* does begin with confirming the messengership of Prophet Muhammad, but then it moves to other topics including life, death and resurrection.

The inner side of the octagonal walls is adorned with short chapters and parts of longer ones, in addition to other non-Qur'anic inscriptions. It should be noted that the beginning and end of the following inscriptions don't always coincide with the beginning and end of the mentioned walls. Anti-clockwise, the south-eastern, eastern, northeaster, and northern walls have the following anti-Trinitarian message:

> O People of the Book! Do not exaggerate in your religion nor utter aught concerning Allah save the truth. The Messiah, Jesus son of Mary, was only a messenger of Allah, and His word which He conveyed unto Mary, and a spirit from Him. So believe in Allah and His messengers, and say not "Three" – Cease! (it is) better for you! – Allah is only One Allah. Far is it removed from His Transcendent Majesty that He should have a son. His is all that is in the heavens and all that is in the earth. And Allah is sufficient as Defender.
> The Messiah does by no means disdain that he should be a servant of Allah, nor do the angels who are near to Him, and whoever disdains His service and is proud, He will gather them all together to Himself. (Qur'an, 4:171)

Beginning with the north-western wall, we find the following verses form chapter 19 which is named after Maryam (i.e. Mary, mother of Jesus Christ), the only woman in the Qur'an to be mentioned by name:

> And peace on me on the day I was born, and on the day I die, and on the day I am raised to life. Such is 'Isa, son of Maryam; [this is] the saying of truth about which they dispute. It befits not [the Majesty of] Allah that He should take to Himself a son. Glory to be Him. When He has decreed a matter He only says to it "Be," and it is. And surely Allah is my Lord and your Lord, therefore serve Him; this is the right path. (Qur'an, 19:33–36)

The western and south-western walls have the following verses from chapter of the "Family of 'Imran":

> Allah bears witness that there is no god but He, and (so do) the angels and those possessed of knowledge, maintaining His creation with justice; there is no god but He, the Mighty, the Wise. Surely the [true] religion with Allah is Islam, and those to whom the Book had been given did not show opposition but after knowledge had come to them, out of envy among themselves; and whoever disbelieves in the revelations of Allah then surely Allah is quick in reckoning. (Qur'an, 3:18–19)

Ibn Kathir's exegesis of the Qur'an associates the dedication of Mary to the service of Al-Aqsa Mosque:

> [Remember] when the wife of 'Imran said: My Lord! I have vowed unto
> Thee that which is in my belly as a consecrated [offering]. Accept it from
> me. Lo! Thou, only Thou, art the Hearer, the Knower! And when she was
> delivered she said: My Lord! Lo! I am delivered of a female – Allah knew
> best of what she was delivered – *the male is not as the female*; and lo! I
> have named her Mary, and lo! I crave Thy protection for her and for her
> offspring from Satan the outcast. (Qur'an, 3:35–36)

Ibn Kathir interpreted the statement of Mary's mother "*the male is not as the female*" as in "strength, perseverance in worship and in serving Al-Aqsa Mosque." Chapter 20 (i.e. *Ta-Ha*) is written on the neck of the Dome of the Rock on the inside. It reflects certain similarities with chapter 17 which is written on the outside; both chapters "begin" with Prophet Muhammad and move to Prophet Moses. The Qur'an narrates, in the case of the latter, some essential stories about him including receiving revelation, his struggle against the Pharaoh, liberating the Children of Israel from servitude, the story of the golden calf, splitting the sea, and more.

Some critics of Islam have claimed that because Jerusalem was never a political center of the Islamic world, it could not have been held in high esteem by Islam. This is a false argument, for even Mecca, the most sacred religious site of the Islamic world, was never the capital of any Islamic state. This certainly does not negate the importance of sacred religious sites. One should remember that the Umayyads developed the site of Al-Aqsa Mosque before the end of the 1st century AH. They moved their capital from Medina to Damascus. Thereafter, no Muslim ruler took any of the three sacred cities – Mecca, Medina or Jerusalem – as a capital. It is rather the religious importance of these cities that led them to their decisions, not the opposite.

There are many other traditions extolling the special merits of Jerusalem, including the view that praying at Al-Aqsa Mosque is far more efficacious than prayers in other locations (with the exception of the two mosques of Mecca and Medina). In addition, Um Salamah, wife of the Prophet, said:

> I have heard the Messenger of God (Peace be upon him) saying: "He who
> initiates the minor Hajj [the 'Umrah] or Hajj at Al-Aqsa Mosque, God
> will forgive his prior sins."[14]

There is an addendum to the previous *Hadith* stating that Um Hakim, daughter of Umayyah Ibn Al-Akhnas, who reported the *Hadith* of Um Salamah, traveled from Medina all the way to Al-Aqsa Mosque and initiated the minor *Hajj* from there.

There are many other traditions that reflect the importance of Jerusalem and Al-Aqsa Mosque in Islam that for brevity I did not include in this essay. Yet, I would like to refer to two positions of 'Umar Ibn Al-Khattab, who was the second Caliph, regarding the protection of the religious space of the People of the Book, and the other regarding the endowment of the Holy Land.

Muslims conquered Jerusalem in 636 CE and 'Umar Ibn Al-Khattab concluded a treaty with Bishop Saphronius, which became known as the 'Pact of 'Umar'. This pact organized the relationship between the Muslims and the Christians, and gave assurances regarding the Christians' religious rights. Thereafter, the Bishop of Jerusalem invited 'Umar Ibn Al-Khattab to pray inside the Holy Sepulcher church. Citing his fear that future Muslim generations might claim this as a right, 'Umar declined politely and stepped outside the church to pray. 'Umar showed sensitivity, leadership and vision. His action, I believe, established a practical module for interfaith relationship, especially in relation to the religious space of the other. While this model began in Jerusalem, it does carry universal value.

'Umar Ibn Al-Khattab's name is also invoked in relation to endowing the Holy Land. One of the most important aspects of the status of land is the notion of *waqf* (i.e., endowment). This legal category is broad and can include any property endowed for the sake of the community. This may include endowing hospitals or schools . . . etc. The issue at stake here is endowing a land that became part of the Islamic state at one point its history. The most famous case is the declaration that "Palestine is a *Waqf*", as it appears in numerous contemporary Islamic theological and political writings.

There is another traditional legal option which is to divide any conquered land between the Muslim soldiers. Imam Malik Ibn Anas (d. 796 CE), founder of the Maliki school of Jurisprudence, was against the division of land amongst the Muslim soldiers. Sheikh Al-Sayyid Sabiq, a contemporary Muslim scholar, stated in *Fiqh Al-Sunnah*, after discussing 'Umar Ibn Al-Khattab's rulings vis-à-vis the conquered lands, specifically Al-Sham (i.e., Greater Syria, including Palestine), Egypt and Iraq, that "what has been established by 'Umar and the other Imams remains valid."[15]

To conclude, it should be known that the sacredness of the Holy Land does not mean that spirituality could only be achieved in such places. In a tradition narrated in Imam Malik's greatly respected *hadith* collection known as *Al-Muwatta'*, two prominent companions of the prophet had the following exchange of letters regarding Jerusalem: Abu Darda' invited Salman Al-Farisi to come to Bayt Al-Maqdis (literally, the House of the Sanctified). Salman replied by saying that the land cannot sanctify anyone. Only one's good deeds may bring one true sanctity.

Notes

This essay is a modified version of a previous one, "The Holy Land, Jerusalem and Al-Aqsa Mosque in the Islamic Sources," published by the *Journal of the Central Conference of American Rabbis* (CCAR), Fall 2000, pp. 60–68. The latter was also modified for "Where Heaven and Earth Meet," Benjamin Z. Kedar (ed.), to be published by Yad Ben Zvi Press, Jerusalem.

1   A *hadith* is a tradition of Prophet Muhammad. When the message that the *hadith* contains forms part of the Islamic worldview, it is described as *Sunnah*, or way of

the Prophet. The Sunnah constitutes, after the Qur'an, the second source of Islamic Law, *Shari'ah*.

2 Ibn Kathir, *Tafsir* (Beirut: Dar Al-Jeel, 1988), vol. 3, p. 180.

3 Ibn Kathir, vol. 3, p. 512.

4 Sayyed Qutub, *Fi Zilaal Al-Qur'an*, 12th edition (Beirut: Dar Al-Shuruq, 1986), vol. 2, p. 871.

5 Ibn Kathir, vol. 3, p. 3.

6 Abu Dawud, *Sunan* # 457; Ibn Majah, *Sunan* # 147; Ahmad Ibn Hanbal, *Musnad* # 6/463; Al-Bayhaqi, *Sunan* #2/441.

7 *Hijr Isma'il*, an area considered to be part of the Ka'bah but ended up outside it when it was rebuilt before Muhammad (Peace be upon him) became a prophet.

8 Mujir Al-Din Al-Hanbali, *Al-Uns Al-Jalil fi Tarikh Al-Quds wal-Khalil* (Beirut: Dar Al-Jil, 1973), vol.2, p. 11.

9 Al-Hanbali, vol. 2, p. 32.

10 Al-Hanbali, vol. 2, p. 24.

11 Abu Dawud, *Sunan* # 10; Ibn Majah, *Sunan* # 319; Ahmad Ibn Hanbal, *Musnad* # 4/210.

12 Al-Nawawi, *Sahih Muslim bi-Sharh Al-Nawawi* (Commentary on Hadith # 2475).

13 Al-Tirmidhi, *Sunan* # 2812.

14 Ahmad Ibn Hanbal, *Musnad* # 25347.

15 Al-Sayyid Sabiq, *Fiqh Al-Sunnah* (Beirut: Dar Al-Fikr, 1983), 4th edition, vol. 3, p. 91.

Jerusalem: From Conflict to Compromise?

MOSHE MA'OZ

The Old City of Jerusalem, about one square kilometer in size, is the only site in the universe that has always been sacred to all three Abrahamic faiths and civilizations. But rather than becoming the city of peace, it has endured for long periods of time bitter conflicts among Jews, Christians, and Muslims. Many of them have refused to share the city on an equal footing or acknowledge one another's affinity to it, but have claimed exclusivity or priority in this place. In recent times the conflict for control over the Old City and beyond has intensified between most Muslims and many Jews, whereas other Jews and Muslims, as well as most Christians, have continued to advocate for a compromise settlement to the Jerusalem issue.

Christian Attitudes

Significantly, unlike Judaism and Islam, Christianity was born in Jerusalem, through events related to the life and death of Jesus. The destruction of the Jewish Temple was regarded as a victory of Christianity over Judaism, coupled with the strong Christian objection to the earthly Jewish city in favor of the heavenly New Jerusalem. Under the first Christian empire, Byzantium (AD 326–614, 624–638), Jerusalem became an important Christian religious center, and Jews were not permitted to reside there. The Crusaders (AD 1099–1187, 1229–1244) massacred many Muslims and Jews in Jerusalem and prohibited others to reside in the city.[1]

Later on under Muslim Ottoman rule, Catholic and Orthodox Christian churches – while vying for control over the Christian holy shrines in Jerusalem and Bethlehem (the pretext for the Crimean War, 1853–1855) – rejected the Jewish claim to Jerusalem. Reportedly, the Catholic-Latin Patriarch of Jerusalem tried in 1855 to induce France to occupy the Holy Land, including Jerusalem.[2] Protestant Christians, by contrast, have acknowledged the deep Jewish affiliation to Jerusalem and, during the 19th century, British Anglicans and senior politicians even encouraged Jews to return to Palestine and revive the Jewish kingdom. For example, British Foreign Secretary Lord Palmerston wrote in 1840: "There exists at present among the Jews dispersed over Europe a strong notion that the time is approaching when their Nation is to return to Palestine." And in 1917, General Allenby, chief commander of the British forces in the region, "was told by Prime Minister Lloyd George to conquer Jerusalem as a Christmas present for the people of Britain . . . " He assured the inhabitants of "Jerusalem the Blessed" that he would protect the holy places and preserve the religious freedom of all three faiths of Abraham.[3] Subsequently the British mandate of 1920–1948 facilitated Jewish, Christian, and Muslim political activities and religious worship in Jerusalem.

During the last several decades, the Vatican and most Christian churches have changed their position on Jerusalem's status, from favoring Christian control, to an international regime (also according to the 1947 partition resolution),[4] to advocating negotiations among Jews, Christians, and Muslims for a compromise solution. In comparison, most Muslims and many Jews have claimed exclusive control or sovereignty over the Old City and beyond, although neither side has denied the right of the other to worship its faith in the holy shrines.

Muslim Traditions

Indeed, most Muslims in the world (1.3 billion population in 57 states) have intensely laid claim to control of the Temple Mount/Al-Haram Al-Sharif and the Old City. According to a major Islamic tradition, Patriarch Abraham/Ibrahim and Prophet Muhammad formed a link between Jerusalem and Mecca. Abraham, the first monotheist and first Muslim (Awwal al-Muslimin), built, with his son Ishmael/Ismail, the Ka'ba in Mecca, and subsequently the Aqsa Mosque in Jerusalem. Prophet Muhammad initially requested his followers, including Jews, to pray in the direction (qibla) of Jerusalem (Awla al-qiblatayn) and subsequently toward Mecca. The Prophet also made his nightly journey (Isra') from the Holy Mosque in Mecca to Al-Aqsa Mosque in Jerusalem, on his winged horse (Burak); and from Al-Aqsa he ascended to Heaven (Mi'raj).[5]

According to certain Islamic traditions no Jewish Temple was ever built in Jerusalem;[6] Jewish sovereignty over Jerusalem lasted only about 400 years; Jews in Jerusalem had been preceded by the Jebusites, who were Arabs; and Muslim domination of Jerusalem continued from the 7th century AD, with short intervals, to the early 20th century; but Jews were permitted for long periods to pray at the Western Wall. To be sure, these Jerusalem-centered traditions have been widely propagated by Palestinian and other Arab leaders all over the Muslim world, particularly since the Israeli occupation of East

Jerusalem in 1967, and after the arson in Aqsa Mosque in 1969 by an Australian Christian, Michael Dennis Rohan. For example, various Muslim scholars and politicians alleged in recent years that Malkitzedek, the Jebusite king who built Jerusalem, had Muslim and Palestinian roots. "the first Palestinian king in history" that the Arabs preceded Moses' period in Jerusalem by 2000 years, or that the Arab-Jebusite presence in Jerusalem is 10,000 years old.[7]

Arab leaders called for *jihad* – holy war – to liberate Jerusalem; annual commemorative days have been held for Al-Aqsa and al-Quds. The Palestinian *intifada* that started in late September 2000 after Ariel Sharon made a gross visit to the Temple Mount has been called the "Aqsa intifada." Many hundreds of books, thousands of articles, as well as audio and video cassettes have been distributed all over the Muslim world, calling on the people to liberate al-Aqsa and al-Quds.

However, there have also been other, more moderate voices and positions in the Arab and Muslim world advocating a political settlement to the conflict over Jerusalem and Palestine. For example, both in 1982 and in 2002 Saudi Arabia suggested settling the conflict through the establishment of a Palestinian state along the 1967 lines, including East Jerusalem, the Old City, and the Haram Al-Sharif. The 2002 initiative, which also involved the recognition of Israel, was accepted by the twenty-two nations of the Arab League. Similar positions were adopted by non-Arab Muslim leaders such as Pakistani President Pervez Musharraf, Indonesia's former president Abd al-Rahman Wahid, and Iran's former president Muhammad Khatemi.

Prof. Sari Nusseibeh, President of al-Quds University, wrote in 2000: "Being the earthly city that is considered in the three monotheistic religions to be closest to the divine and spiritual gateway to that world, Jerusalem must be respected by all as a city above men, not as one that is to be subjected to their domination . . . Jerusalem's political status in the Israeli and Palestinian national and cultural heritage can be enshrined through its being made the undivided capital of the two peoples . . . "[8]

Some Muslim thinkers have acknowledged the existence of the Jewish Temple in the Temple Mount, and thus the Jewish affinity to Jerusalem. But these thinkers alleged that Judaism (and Christianity) had been a first (and second) phase in the Abrahamic monotheistic message that has been incorporated in, and fulfilled, by Islam. Thus, while acknowledging Jewish traditions regarding Jerusalem, Dr. Muhammad Abd al-Hamid al-Kahbeeb wrote in 1998: "Judaism was once a form of Islam with a powerful sense and vision of universal justice. However, in becoming Judaism and in rejecting both Isa [Jesus] who was sent to them by Allah from among themselves . . . the Jews have locked themselves into a concentration camp mentality."[9]

As we know, the Jewish narrative concerning the role of Christianity and Islam and the place of Jerusalem in Judaism is quite different.

The Jewish Narrative

Thus, according to a major Jewish belief, Jerusalem has been for more than 3,000 years the only unique center of Judaism and the Jewish people, whereas Christianity and Islam, which appeared later in history, have their own centers: Rome and Constantinople, Mecca and Medina, respectively. In addition, Jews indicate that Jerusalem is not mentioned at all in the Qur'an, and was never the capital of a Muslim state. It served as the capital of the Christian Crusaders for only short periods (88 years during the 12th century, and fifteen years during the 13th century). By contrast, although the Jewish Temple in Jerusalem was destroyed twice (in 586 BC and AD 70) and Jews were exiled, they have never disengaged from Jerusalem or forgotten it. Jews continued to reside in Jerusalem for centuries, albeit in small numbers and, along with their brethren in the Diaspora, they pray toward Jerusalem three times a day. Jews would make pilgrimage to Jerusalem three times a year, chant in their prayers "Next year in Jerusalem" and would occasionally vow "If I forget thee, O Jerusalem, may my right arm wither." Indeed, Jews from the Diaspora have immigrated (or made *aliyya* – ascended) to Jerusalem throughout the centuries, notably during the Ottoman–Muslim period (1516–1917). In the year 1800 they numbered some 2,000 people (out of a population of 9,000) in Jerusalem, reaching 45,000 (out of 70,000) in 1914, thus outnumbering both Muslim and Christian communities. To be sure, those Jews were motivated merely by religious feelings, but lived in poor conditions and were oppressed by their neighbors, as Karl Marx reported at mid-19th century: "Nothing equals the misery and the suffering of the Jews of Jerusalem. Inhabiting the most filthy quarter of the town . . . the constant objects of Musselman oppression and intolerance, insulted by the Greeks, persecuted by the Latins, and living only upon the scanty alms transmitted by their European brethren . . . The Jews . . . are only attracted to Jerusalem by desire of inhabiting the Valley of Jehoshaphat and to die in the very places where the redemption is to be expected."[10]

But since the 1880s, several waves of Jewish immigrants – who were mostly secular – arrived in Palestine, driven by a new nationalist-secular ideology: Zionism.

Although the name of this nationalist movement is derived from "Zion" (another term for Jerusalem), most Zionist immigrants would not settle in Jerusalem owing to its parochial religious character. Zionist leaders had reservations regarding the city. Theodor Herzl, the founder of the Zionist movement, visited Jerusalem in 1898 and "was appalled by the musty deposit of two thousand years of inhumanity, intolerance and foulness . . . " Nahum Sokolov, the Zionist theorist, remarked: "The point of gravity has shifted from the Jerusalem of the religious schools to the farms and agricultural schools, the fields and the meadows."[11] But during the 1930s, under the British Mandate, the Zionist institutions moved from Jaffa to Jerusalem. The reasons for that move were to highlight the centrality of Jerusalem in Jewish nationalist and political aspirations and possibly combating the newly emerged Palestinian-Arab nationalist movement which made Jerusalem its political and religious center. By then, Jerusalem had expanded immensely beyond the Old City, increasing its Jewish majority population and becoming a major focus for a fierce conflict (sometimes violent) between the Jewish-Zionist and Palestinian-Arab nationalist movements. Both parties would also involve their religious sites in their struggle for Jerusalem, such as in the 1929 riots at the Western Wall, when hundreds of Jews and Arabs were killed.[12]

In November 1947 the UN tried to resolve this conflict through its partition resolution (No. 181) namely: dividing Palestine into two states – an Arab and a Jewish – while placing Jerusalem under an international regime. The Palestinian Arab leadership (as well as other Arab and Muslim nations) rejected that resolution, whereas the Jewish-Zionist *"Yishuv"* (community) accepted it. Following its victory in the 1948 war, the newly emerged Jewish state – Israel – made West Jerusalem (80 percent of the city) its official capital (1949). The Hashemite Kingdom of Jordan, which had assumed control over the Old City and East Jerusalem, would not make it even its second capital (after Amman). Jordan also refused to allow Israeli Jews to pray at the Western Wall, contrary to its Armistice Agreement with Israel (1949), and also destroyed Jewish synagogues in the Jewish Quarter of the Old City. Israel, on its part, destroyed parts of the Muslim cemetery in the western part of Jerusalem, at Mamilla Street.[13]

Israel occupied East Jerusalem (including the Old City) during the June 1967 war, annexed it, and proclaimed (in 1980) the "unified" city as an integral part of Israel and its eternal capital. It also adopted extensive steps to "Judaize" Jerusalem, including the Old City: *inter alia* evicting Palestinian Arabs from the Jewish quarter and settling Jews there. By now some 3,000 people live in this quarter, mostly American Orthodox Jews, out of a total population of 33,000 in the Old City, mostly Muslims.[14] The total number of inhabitants in "Greater Jerusalem," including new Jewish neighborhoods, is about 700,000; two-thirds are Jews and one-third Arabs.

Yet the main site of conflict between Jews and Muslims (and to some degree also Christians) is the Old City and its holy places, notably the Temple Mount /Al Haram Al-Sharif. According to a 2005 survey, 51 percent of Israeli Jews favor Israeli control over the Temple Mount (but 36 percent are for joint control). By comparison, Palestinian Arabs (90 percent) and Muslims at large request Muslim control over the Haram Al-Sharif, the Old City, and East Jerusalem.[15]

Initially in June 1967, Israel destroyed the Muslim Maghribi Quarter, adjoining the Western Wall, to make room for Jewish worshippers to pray. But at the same time, Jews were not permitted by the government to pray on the Temple Mount which has remained under Muslim *Waqf*'s control. Also, the Chief Israeli Rabbinate and many Rabbis, citing Jewish law, have prohibited Jews from praying on the Temple Mount until the arrival of the

Messiah, who would build the third Jewish Temple. By contrast, other senior Rabbis, as well as militant Jewish groups, called for the demolition of the
two Muslim mosques, Al-Aqsa and the Dome of the Rock, and instead construct there the third Jewish Temple; or at least build a new synagogue on
the Temple Mount. During the early 1980s a few Jewish fanatics conspired
to demolish the Dome of the Rock mosque and amassed a great deal of
explosives for this purpose. Another Jewish fanatic tried in 1982 to plant a
bomb in the Aqsa mosque.

These dangerous plots were aborted, but other acts of demonstration on
or near the Temple Mount by Jewish-Israeli militants provoked fierce Muslim
reactions and resulted in many dead and wounded people, mostly Palestinian
Muslims. The major events occurred in October 1990, during the first
Palestinian *intifada* (started in December 1987) when a Jewish extreme
nationalist-religious group, "The Temple Mount Faithful," held a ceremony
by the Temple Mount symbolically laying a cornerstone for the third Temple.
In September 1996, Israel's prime minister ordered the opening of an ancient
tunnel which ran alongside the Western Wall and the Haram Al-Sharif to the
Muslim Quarter. And in September Ariel Sharon, the Likud party leader,
staged a public visit (with hundreds of policemen) to the Temple
Mount/Haram Al-Sharif, thus contributing his share to the eruption of the
second *intifada*, the Aqsa Intifada.[16] In addition to these bloody events
archaeological excavations by Israeli archaeologists by the Temple Mount
alarmed many Muslims lest the foundations of the Aqsa Mosque be damaged.
By comparison, many Jews have accused the Muslim *Waqf* authorities of
digging at the northern tier of the Temple Mount in order to eliminate the
remains of the ancient Jewish Temple.

To be sure, both Jewish and Muslim militants have further hardened their
positions over the Temple Mount/Haram Al-Sharif and the Old City. For the
first time a growing number of Zionist-Jewish Rabbis have recently published
religious "halachic opinions" untying the traditional Jewish *halacha* that
prohibits Jews from praying on the Temple Mount. By comparison, a growing
number of Muslim religious leaders have called for a holy war (*jihad*) to
liberate the Haram Al-Sharif.[17]

It is evident that the Israeli government has maintained the status quo at
the Temple Mount since 1967, namely, an autonomous control by the Muslim
Waqf authorities and a prohibition on Jews to pray on the Temple
Mount/Haram Al-Sharif. Israeli governments under U.S. inducement agreed
to discuss the future status of Jerusalem in the negotiations with the
Palestinian Authority. But among Israeli (and American) Jews there has been
an increasing opposition to put the Jerusalem issue on the negotiating table.
The Israeli Sephardi-Haredi party, Shas, has recently threatened to break away
from the coalition government of Prime Minister Ehud Olmert if and when
he discusses with his Palestinian counterpart the status of Jerusalem. Apart
from their religious and nationalist motives, many Israeli Jews deeply mistrust
the Palestinians. They cannot forget and forgive the numerous terrorist

attacks and suicide bombings by Hamas and Fatah's Al-Aqsa Brigade since the mid-1990s that claimed the lives of a great many Israelis, including in Jerusalem. (The terrible Palestinian terror attack in the Merkas Harav Yeshiva on March 6, 2008 is likely to deepen these Jewish attitudes.) The ascendancy of Hamas in the Gaza Strip, its anti-Israeli, anti-Jewish ideology, as well as its recent rocket attacks on nearby Israeli towns, have significantly contributed to this Israeli-Jewish mistrust and fear. Many Muslims – Palestinians and others – equally mistrust Israeli Jews on account of their uncompromising position over the Temple Mount and East Jerusalem, as well as their mistreatment of, and military attacks, on Palestinians in Gaza and the West Bank.

By contrast, many Israeli Jews and Palestinian Arabs have sought for years a political compromise in Jerusalem and the Holy Land. Some of them have also conducted ongoing dialogues regarding a mutually agreed upon solution for Jerusalem.[18]

On May 13, 1995, Feisal Husseini, the PLO representative in Jerusalem, made a speech during a demonstration protesting against the confiscation of Arab land. Husseini said: "I dream of the day when a Palestinian will say 'Our Jerusalem'" and will mean Israelis and Palestinians. In response, seven hundred prominent Israelis, including writers, critics, artists, and former Knesset members, signed the joint statement:

> Jerusalem is ours, Israelis and Palestinians – Muslims, Christians, and Jews.
>
> Our Jerusalem is a mosaic of all the cultures, all the religions, and all the periods that enriched the city, from the earliest antiquity to this very day – Canaanites and Jebusites and Israelites, Jews and Hellenes, Romans and Byzantines, Christians and Muslims, Arabs and Mameluks, Ottomans and Britons, Palestinians and Israelis. They and all the others who made their contribution to the city have a place in the spiritual and physical landscape of Jerusalem.
>
> Our Jerusalem must be united, open to all and belonging to all its inhabitants, without borders and barbed wire in its midst.
>
> Our Jerusalem must be the capital of the two states that will live side by side in this country – West Jerusalem the capital of the State of Israel and East Jerusalem the capital of the State of Palestine.
>
> Our Jerusalem must be the Capital of Peace.[19]

Summary

Can a compromise be reached to this deep conflict over Jerusalem's Old City and the Temple Mount/Haram Al-Sharif, a conflict that is likely to stir a new religious Islamic–Jewish war, in the worst-case scenario?

By contrast, a mutually accepted solution to this conflict may significantly improve relations among children of Abraham, notably Muslims and Jews, and help isolate the militant elements on each side. Such a solution should be based on the following Talmudic case and its verdict:

> Two are holding a garment . . . one says it wholly belongs to me; the other says it wholly belongs to me . . . They should partition it.[20]

Apparently, this principle was the gist of President Clinton's blueprint of 2000. He suggested dividing the Temple Mount vertically and the Old City horizontally between Palestinian Arabs and Israeli Jews, in addition to having two capitals in Jerusalem and two states in Palestine. Such a compromise solution is now the highest mission and historic challenge of the current US President, the Israeli and Palestinian leaders, as well as Muslim, Christian and Jewish religious authorities.

Pray for the peace of Jerusalem; May they prosper that love thee.[21]

Notes

1 Cf. Karen Armstrong, *A History of Jerusalem. One City, Three Faiths* (London, HarperCollins Publishers, 1996), pp. 171ff; 272ff.

2 Moshe Ma'oz, *Ottoman Reform in Syria and Palestine, 1840–1861* (Oxford, The Clarenden Press, 1968), p. 219.

3 See respectively, British Public Records Office, FO 78 (390 No. 134, August 11, 1840); Armstrong, p. 370.

4 *The Israel–Arab Reader*, edited by Walter Laqueur and Barry Rubin (New York, Penguin Books, 1995), pp. 92ff.

5 Cf. Chapter 6, by Mustafa Abu-Sway; see also A. L. Tibawi, *Jerusalem: Its Place in Islam and Arab History* (Beirut, The Institute of Palestine Studies, 1969).

6 Armstrong, p. xv.

7 Yitzhak Reiter, *From Jerusalem to Mecca and Back. The Islamic Consolidation of Jerusalem* (in Hebrew, Jerusalem, The Jerusalem Institute for Israel Studies, 2005), pp. 31ff; 51ff. Cf. Arif al-Arif, *Ta'rikh al-Quds* (The History of Jerusalem, Dar Ma'arif, Egypt, 1951), pp. 11ff.

8 *Jerusalem: Points of Friction – and Beyond*, edited by Moshe Ma'oz and Sari Nusseibeh (The Hague, Kluwer Law International, 2000), p. 9. Cf. Khatemi's interview with Sever Plotzker, *Yediot Ahronot*, January 26, 2007.

9 Reiter, pp. 46–47.

10 Quoted in Roger Friedland and Richard Hecht, *To Rule Jerusalem* (Berkeley, University of California Press, 2000), p. 17.

11 Quoted in Armstrong, pp. 366–67.

12 See for example Benny Morris, *Righteous Victims* (New York, Vintage Books, 1999), pp. 112ff; *Jerusalem in the Modern Period*, ed. E. Shaltiel (in Hebrew, Jerusalem, Yad Ben-Zvi, 1981), pp. 302–54.

13 See respectively, Moshe Ma'oz, *Palestinian Leadership on the West Bank* (London, Frank Cass, 1984), p. 30; Armstrong, p. 389.

14 *The Status of Jerusalem*, The United Nations, N.Y. 1997, pp. 19ff; Wasfi Kailani, *Identities in the Jewish Quarter of the Old City of Jerusalem: American Orthodox Jews Between Holy and Mundane* (Ph.D. thesis, Hebrew University, Jerusalem, 2007), pp. 52ff.

15 Reiter, p. 85. At the end of 2007, 66% of Israeli Jews opposed any "concessions" in Jerusalem, Uzi Benziman, *Ha'aretz*, March 16, 2008.

16 See respectively, Armstrong, pp. 389ff; Reiter, pp. 84ff; "Rival Claims on Jerusalem Lie at Heart of Palestinian–Israeli Hostility," by Serge Schmeman, *New York Times*, October 27, 1996.

17 See respectively Nadav Shragai, *Ha'aretz*, 2, July 30, 2007; Reiter, p. 102.

18 See for example a special issue on Jerusalem, *Palestine–Israel Journal*, Vol. VIII, no. 1, 2001.

19 *Ha'aretz*, June 16, 1995.

20 *The Talmud*, Baba Metzia A, 1.

21 The Book of Psalms, 122:6.

Divergent Epistemologies in the Search for Co-existence: The Jerusalem 2050 Project

DIANE E. DAVIS

As war and armed struggle continue to create turmoil in the greater Middle East, as the Israeli–Palestinian conflict simmers relentlessly in an environment where Palestinians are fighting each other as much as Israel, and as threats of escalated conflict still hang like a specter over the entire region, it is time to re-assert the importance of peacemaking if Israel and its surrounds are going to survive without suffering more instability and the sustained threat of future bloodshed. The recent meeting convened in Annapolis by President Bush, after several years of relative US administrative neglect of Palestinian-Israeli discord, is testament to this realization. But even more important are the continual and renewed efforts* by citizens and academics to place peace and co-existence at the center of discussion and activity. The recent conference organized by Moshe Ma'oz and his colleagues at Harvard University's Weatherhead Center is yet another example of these heroic efforts.

---

* *Just Jerusalem: Vision for a Place of Peace* is an interdisciplinary initiative sponsored by MIT's Center for International Studies (CIS) and Department of Urban Studies and Planning (DUSP). The competition began on March 2, 2007 and concluded on December 31, 2007. Winners will be announced on March 19, 2008. The competition has four entry tracks: physical, economic, civic, and symbolic infrastructure. An international panel of nine jurists from a variety of disciplines and professional backgrounds will award five prizes and five honorable mentions. This reflects our belief that there is no single answer, no panacea. Jerusalem is multifaceted; the conflict is multifaceted; therefore, peace must be multifaceted. Winners will spend up to three months at MIT as fellows during the Fall 2008 semester, in order to continue developing their proposals and to participate in ongoing dialogues, exchanges, and conferences. For more information on the competition guidelines, winners, upcoming events, the International Jury, and other relevant documents, please check our websites: <http://www.justjerusalem.org and http://web.mit.edu/CIS/jerusalem2050>.

In considering what it would take to generate peaceful co-existence among all the "children of Abraham," Christians, Jews, and Muslims alike, the question at hand is not merely how to accomplish such goals, but where and how, exactly, to begin? Scholars from divergent disciplinary vantage points will no doubt answer this question differently. Historians will focus on the past, and debate among themselves whose past must be remembered, and how it is known or knowable. Religious scholars will focus on texts and principles embedded in these defining narratives of peoples and their religions, and use this as a starting or ending point for harmony or conflict. Political scientists and economists will examine the defining contracts that give order to society, whether between rules and ruled, producers and consumers, citizens and others. Anthropologists, sociologists, and psychologists will focus on the everyday interactions of peoples in given locales, and the ways that identities, customs, and rituals may generate inclusion or exclusion, conflict or co-existence, or just mere tolerance. Then, of course, there are the geographers, who might debate about where these disciplinary perspectives most be applied, and with what implications for those from the three great religions who have histories and connections all over the world.

The Promise of the City

As a scholar who has studied cities and the relations between cities and nations for decades, I would like to propose yet another disciplinary perspective, one that draws on all the above social sciences, but focuses on their interactions in space. In conceptual terms, I consider this disciplinary vantage point to be that of **urbanism**, a field built on both normative and analytical preoccupation with the urban experience and the so-called "promise of city."[1] In this tradition, cities are not merely hosts for certain forms of architecture, the locus of population density, or the source of economic innovation and productivity. Cities also are key sites of tolerance, diversity, cosmopolitanism, expansive citizenship, and democratic inclusion. Such claims about the city not only have a grand lineage dating to Max Weber, among others, they still flower in many contemporary writings on the city. From Marshall Berman's notion that the city offers perhaps the only kind of environment in which modern values [of tolerance, freedom, and so on] can be realized"[2] to Andy Merrifield's view of the city as host for "togetherness *in difference*"[3] to Ira Katznelson's sense that "the compound of liberalism and the city promote a liberalism of depth and complexity"[4] to Richard Sennett's idea that the city is a place where strangers meet and his attendant proposition that "people grow only by processes of encountering the unknown"[5] (a view prefiguring the political theorist Iris Young's views on the togetherness of strangers in cities), scholars have long celebrated the humanistic potential and endowments of the city. As David Harvey further reminds us, the "figures of 'the city' and of 'Utopia' have long been intertwined," as have the notions of city and citizenship, such that "[p]rojects concerning what we want our cities to be are, therefore, projects concerning human possibilities, who we want, or perhaps even more pertinently, who we do not want to become."[6]

Many of these same hopes and ideals sustain Henri Lefebvre's seminal writings as well, especially his notion of "the right to the city," a proposition which holds great resonance to those living in divided cities like Jerusalem, where mobility and access to everyday activities and the urban built environment are hindered or strongly curtailed. It is worth remembering that Lefebvre conceives of the city as "gathering the interests of the whole society" as much as those who physically inhabit it.[7] But what may be most significant about Lefebvre's formulation is his use of society – not the state or nation – as the conceptual reference point for the city's humanitarian promise. Moreover, for Lefebvre a city's "inhabitants" are not necessarily bounded in space or in the formal confines of the city proper. Arbitrary territorial boundaries coercively imposed by national or other state authorities are antithetical to this proposition, and would violate Lefebvre's notion of the right to the city if they also restricted the flows, the "place(s) of encounter," the "priority of use value," and the natural spaces in and surrounding formally-drawn city borders.[8] In this sense, Lefebvre is highlighting "the right to urban life" as much as to the city itself, a presupposition that sustains a desire to place the notion of urbanism as central to any emancipatory political vision.

Lefebvre's views of urbanism rest not merely on a recognition of the importance of individual access to a wide range of places and spaces, on the exposure to social and class diversity, or on myriad other ways to 'rightfully' partake of the city. They also build heavily on a specific understanding of the relations between cities and nation-states in a way that is particularly relevant for understanding the problems of Jerusalem. Not unlike the classical arguments formulated by Max Weber and paralleled more recently in work by Manuel Castells,[9] Lefebvre suggests that where cities are dominated by or fused with states one is likely to see violence and a "vacillat[ion] between democracy and tyranny."[10] The assumption here is that in order to eliminate violence and tyranny, and restore the possibilities for democracy in both city and society at large, this fusion must be challenged. Of course, given the nature of this challenge and the fact that states are not about to disappear, any progress in disarticulating city and state (national or otherwise) must be best measured in degrees rather than as a total break. Still, Lefebvre is not alone in advocating for a conception of the city as operating on its own terms in order to sustain a society's greatest potential; nor is he alone in seeing cities as the territorial location most likely to generate democratic institutions and practices.

Writing about an entirely different time and place, urban legal theorist Gerald Frug comes to similar conclusions about the challenges to democracy and social justice that arise when cities are dominated by states or not allowed to flower as autonomous domains of decision-making that "gather" – to use Lefebvre's notion – the multiple localities and social collectivities that constitute society. Taking the US as his focus for study, Frug argues that overbearing "state control has reduced the importance of cities as instruments of public policy and thereby diminished the opportunity for widespread participation in public decision making" in a way that challenges basic fundamentals of liberal democracy. But in a departure from many other urban democratic theorists, especially those who build on the Tocquevillian tradition of reifying neighborhoods, communities, and other smaller-scale territorial units as the bedrock of democracy, Frug is clear in advocating for empowerment and autonomy on the level of the city – understood as a jurisdictional, legal, and spatial entity larger than the neighborhood but smaller than the nation and sub-national states. In fact, Frug goes so far as to suggest that the legal contours of overly localized power, which in the US rest on the asserted superiority of private interests, both individual and corporate, prevent cities from fulfilling their democratic and civil society function by turning them into "vehicles for separating and dividing different kinds of people rather than bringing them together, withdrawal from public life rather than engagement with others, and the multiplication of private spaces instead of walkable streets and public parks "[11] And the reason for this, he argues, is that this legal context of localism "treats autonomous individuals and the nation-state . . . as interested in pursuing their own self-interest" in ways that challenge the independent capacity of cities to guarantee the collective urban interest.[12]

To be sure, given his focus on the US, what Frug has in mind when he uses the notion of city is the metropolitan area, not so much a given city's formally cast political boundaries – many of which trace to earlier historical moments when transportation technology and other political requisites kept cities relatively circumscribed in size. One of his main concerns is that the divisions between central cities and their suburbs help reinforce fragmentation and spatial separation on the basis of race, income, or other forms of privilege that together undermine democratic deliberation in the urban area as whole. But such concerns – in addition to replicating Lefebvre's intent to envision cities as reflections of society in all its diversity – merely underscore the importance of thinking of how and on what basis to define the urban unit of analysis around which claims for the right to the city might be forged. They also are relevant to all cities where questions and concerns about the distinction between the city and the metropolitan area now dominate the urban, social, and political agenda.

Jerusalem as Promised Land, or "The Promise" of Jerusalem?

In the case of longstanding and virulent conflicts among Muslims, Christians, and Jews, it is not difficult to see how the theoretical and normative path of urbanism could lead directly to the gates of Jerusalem, an important spiritual center for all. Jerusalem is not only a city where the question of boundaries remains politically and socially contested, and where claims of cultural or religious "ownership" have led to conflict; it is also a city whose historical diversity, tolerance, and cosmopolitanism are as famous as its more recent division and persistent instances of intolerance. In this sense, it may be the single most important key to peace among the "children of Abraham," not to mention the larger region as a whole. It is often said that the future of the Israeli–Palestinian conflict depends in large part on Jerusalem, and this clearly is the impression left in the wake of prior peace dialogues and attempted diplomatic settlements, most recently the Oslo Accords. If this is true, then the city of Jerusalem is a natural starting point for peace-building. But can change and improvements in Jerusalem be achieved independent of a final Israeli–Palestinian peace agreement? Are there issues to be addressed that are important to the local residents and could also contribute to a politically negotiated agreement between Israel and the Palestinian Authority?

As an urban locale, Jerusalem has modern infrastructure, spectacular new housing complexes, historic beauty, and deep religious meaning. But it also is a site of resource scarcity, ecological degradation, segmented areas of built space, social tensions, fear, and insecurity. The local economy lags behind those of neighboring cities, particularly Tel Aviv and Haifa. Jerusalem is one of the poorest cities in Israel, with the per capita income being one-third that of the Israeli national average. Within the municipal city, 42 percent of Palestinian and 22 percent of Israeli households live under the poverty line. This is in part due to the fact that 30 percent of its Jewish population are Haredi, ultra-orthodox Jews, who are not economically active, in the formal definition of the term, and tend to be poor, while 41 percent of the Palestinian population is under the age of 15.[13] Additionally, the city has an economy based predominantly on services (tourism and commerce) rather than manufacturing. Meanwhile, many middle and upper class families are moving out of municipal Jerusalem and relocating to the metropolitan area or to other cities.

Socially, the city is divided ethnically and economically; housing is increasingly unaffordable. The desire for security and freedom from terror and the nature of occupation, combined with a fragmented transportation system, have slowed, if not prohibited, free movement within the city for all its residents. Many live in constant fear of violence, whether by suicide bombers or by military and police forces. Though some of these qualities could describe many other cities in the region, Jerusalem's location and the historical struggles of Palestinians to claim the city as their capital have created unique and unavoidable tensions over the city's built environment and among its peoples.

For all these reasons, one possible way to make progress on peaceful co-existence is to think about new ways to make the city of Jerusalem a more livable, sustainable, and harmonious place for all its residents. If quality of life in this contested locale could improve, and the city could show itself to be a model for future generations who seek to live together in peace and harmony, then some progress in the current national and regional conflict just might accrue. In many ways, the challenge here is to make a city claimed by two nations and central to three religions 'just' a city, albeit a dynamic, historically unique, and prosperous one, a place of difference and diversity in which contending ideas and citizenries could co-exist in benign yet creative ways.

While the nationalist politics of the greater Israeli–Palestinian conflict certainly cannot be completely ignored, Jerusalem's political or sovereignty status is not the only factor to be considered. We must remember that this city is also a place in which people live, work, shop, worship, and play. Far more than being merely the contested terrain upon which seemingly irreconcilable nation-states struggle for power, the city of Jerusalem[14] has produced its own unique mix of urban cultures, spatial practices, physical connections, economic activities, and political institutions, many of which existed long before 20th century efforts to classify its peoples in terms of particular national identities. During the Ottoman period, in fact, long before struggles for the creation of a single sovereign national state in this territory, a multiplicity of institutional arrangements governed servicing and representation in the city, and they operated in ways that led to relatively peacefully co-existence among the city's Jews, Muslims, and Christians. It is this undeniable historical fact and the promise that it holds for re-envisioning the city that offers some hope for Jerusalem's future – and hopefully in ways that can help ease the Palestinian-Israeli conflict more generally.

By no means is this to suggest that scholars or citizens consider an uncritical return to frameworks generated under a period of imperialism. At the end of the Ottoman rule the city was suffering from lack of basic services and most of its residents had neither civil rights nor economic autonomy. However, in this early period the binary – or even tripartite – understanding of space and identity that now generates so much controversy was almost completely absent.[15] This is said not in order to diminish what has happened in the Jerusalem during the last several decades, but to suggest that the linking of land, people, and nationality – which now serves as the unquestioned basis for almost all negotiations – is just one of the many possible ways the city could and has been organized. In fact, as a blueprint for current and future actions, it has very little grounding in Jerusalem's own long history. Such observations suggest the importance of thinking about alternative models for organizing and managing the city, including those that disappeared when competing nation-states hijacked the discourses and practices of urban organization.

In particular, would it be possible for contending protagonists in the search for harmony in Jerusalem to recast their understanding of conflicts or tensions, and possible solutions to these problems, not in light of questions about competing nations, but in light of questions about what might make Jerusalem a vibrant, democratic, and peaceful city? What if they cast their eyes towards the types of urban institutions and built environmental patterns that would host a vibrant metropolis, rather than the types of political arrangements that sustain a certain form of state legitimacy and sovereignty? Rather than always being hamstrung by the "national question," might there be constructs of *urban* place and city meaning to be imagined that could lead to peace, and by so doing, perhaps even help reconcile seemingly intractable national claims?

The point here is to seek a new vantage point for entering into a decades-old conflict, one that may lie between – or across – the conventional points of entry used to address the conflict. Rather than thinking about Jerusalem in terms of the real or symbolic role it will play in the struggle over national sovereignty, why not think more seriously about the city in and of itself? If the superimposition of nationalist projects and aspirations on ethnically or religiously-diverse urban locales like Jerusalem has fanned the flames of aggression and violent conflict, could concerted efforts to think about what social, political, economic, or spatial practices would free this city from nationalist blueprints possibly serve as the solution, or, at minimum, help lay a partial foundation for greater tolerance and perhaps even peace? While utopian in conception, this question requires a new way of thinking, which is precisely our aim here. To paraphrase Arjun Appadurai in his reflection on Benedict Anderson's claim that the nation is an imagined thing, "we must be prepared to recognize the critical reciprocal of [Anderson's] insight, that it is the imagination that will have to carry us beyond the nation."[16]

From Jerusalem 2050 to Just Jerusalem and Back: Questioning Boundaries in Time and Space

Armed with these reflections, a group of MIT faculty, trained in political science, sociology, history, architecture, and urbanism transformed these epistemological premises into a scholarly, university-based project *Jerusalem 2050* aimed at finding new paths toward peace.[17] Rather than promoting the standard route of negotiation between "representative" peoples, we as a group have turned instead to the liberating potential of imagination, vision, and design. Rather than aiming for unity or synthesis among competing parties, we encourage the production of bold and 'non-negotiated' visions for Jerusalem, with the assumption that through such methods there might potentially emerge a shared understanding of the basic urban livability conditions necessary for a tolerant, peaceful, just, and culturally vibrant urban public sphere to flower, independent of ethnic or religious partisanship. A second but related aim is to promote the use of creative imaginings of space as techniques for arriving at a more positive social, political and economic organization of the city, which we see as a location where publicity and democracy find most elective affinity.

A key feature that defines us as a collectivity is optimism that daily living conditions for the city's inhabitants could get better in the future if enough creative and innovative thinking could be marshaled on behalf of this goal. This not only means that we are not engaged in efforts to rehash the past; nor are we allowing ourselves to become overly paralyzed by the terrible situation on the ground, whether it be fear of further occupation and isolation, fear of further terrorist attacks, or unwillingness to "sanction" the *status quo* that has generated these conditions.[18] We feel one of the best and most effective ways forward is for those who care about Jerusalem and how its residents live to offer views of its potential as *just a city*, and about its foreseeable future.

It is essential that these points be clarified and spelled out systematically in terms of two basic principles that underlay this initiative. The *first* is that we want to address and understand problems in Jerusalem from the vantage point of the city and urban livability, and not necessarily from the nation – or the actions of competing nations – and their objectives. This does not mean that we intend to blind ourselves to the nationalistic, religious, and political debates over the city or the real power of nation-states (in the region and outside) to determine the fate of the city and its citizens. Nor does it mean that we give up the importance of thinking about concepts, like citizenship and meaning, that are often seen as the purview of the nation or religion. But it does underscore a desire to question the epistemologies and conventional ways of seeing or understanding the city that have taken as their vantage point the nation or religion, while treating Jerusalem primarily as the blueprint upon which these identities or struggles are fought or enacted.

As such, we think it is important to start from the point of view of the city and its resident. How might they live their lives in the near future; how could quality of life and urban conditions be better on a quotidian scale; and what might full urban citizenship look like, independent of other scales or references points of identity? We have coined the nomenclature *Just Jerusalem* for the international, juried competition that that Jerusalem 2050 project is hosting as in order to encourage and enable this envisioning process. With this competition, we ask ourselves and the world whether a focus on Jerusalem "just" as a city, rather than primarily as a space where nation-states fight their battles, might open up new windows of opportunity for peace. That is, we want to think about what might make Jerusalem a peaceful, prosperous, culturally vibrant, just and diverse cosmopolitan locale that people would want to live in, thereby giving testimony to its history as one of the world's most spiritual and humanist locations. In this sense, the competition's title is a *double entendre*: just as in justice, and just, as in solely, or only, the city.

The *second* key principle that informs and sustains this project is a focus on the future, as much as on the present. Stated another way, we would like competition entrants to try to understand what the city and urban citizenship might look like in the future (or by the year 2050), if justice, peace, and sustainability were the framing device for its functioning. The year 2050 is not as some arbitrary point in time, so much as metaphoric construct that suggests enough distance from the presence to allow a sense of optimism that things can change, and enough closeness to the presence that it will host the next generation of residents, whose lives will be most damaged if peace, justice, and sustainability are not achieved. In many ways, like other contributors to this volume, we are concerned with and oriented toward the Children of Abraham, with the emphasis being *children* themselves, and their future.

One could ask why not focus on the present rather than the future, since conditions today also demand serious attention. The answer is that we do not consider these two time frames to be in opposition to each other, but rather, intricately connected. The hope is that an analytical focus on the future will generate ideas, materials, and a sense of common purpose that can be translated into action right now – almost a working backwards from the future to the present, in inverse order of the way the "road map" to peace is often conceptualized. We ask ourselves and competition entrants: what does peace look like; and once that is clear, the next steps are to determine how to get there.

We selected this strategy purposefully, and with much deliberation. Our sense as a group was that the present situation of Jerusalem is perceived to be so dire, so conflicted, so fraught with global and local power imbalances and militarized responses, that trying to get people to think about an alternative vision for Jerusalem today might be impossible if not foolhardy. It would too easily be dismissed as a utopian dream or even a heartless game, especially because change takes time, and because cities are comprised of bricks and mortar, and not merely people and institutions. Moreover, with a history of failed peace negotiations (from Oslo to Geneva), not to mention the problems of getting divergent "sides" to be able to sit down and negotiate over the present, we found ourselves looking for an alternative way of giving hope and a new vehicle for new, creative, out-of-the-box ideas about how to improves the situation for all the city's residents.

With all these challenges in mind, we have opted to solicit ideas – through a global competition open to all – for a peaceful Jerusalem by the year 2050. One could think of this as a Rawlsian experiment,[19] where those thinking about what would make a just city would not know in advance their own particular position, role, or power position, and would thus be encouraged to conceptualize the most equitable, fair, and inclusive arrangements for all.

Different "Ways of Seeing" Jerusalem and the Search for Defining Principles

Two key elements of this project are its focus on the *city*, or urban livability, and *the future*. We arrived at these "innovations" based on our own recognition that conventional ways of understanding the city – as the contested space over and in which nations competed; as the repository of the historical past, be it imperial, national, or religious; and as the conflicted cauldron of the present struggle between nation-states and/or religions over future sovereignty and identity claims – were precisely the problems that lay at the heart of violence and injustice in Jerusalem. Recognizing the difficulties inherent in the "old ways of seeing" the city pushed us to think about new conceptualizations as an epistemological counter-weight.

Among the conventional ways of seeing Jerusalem that have led to sustained conflict, most build on assumptions about the most appropriate spatial (or territorial) boundaries of influence, about the most appropriate political boundaries or sovereignties, and the most appropriate symbolic content for the city (i.e. whose religion, culture, or law should prevail, how, when, or where). Our aim is not to negate these defining epistemologies, but to examine each of them critically, and assess their limitations as much as their value in laying the foundations for peace and co-existence.

Physical boundaries are perhaps the third rail of the Arab–Israeli conflict, and for this reason any examination of the formal boundaries of the city is bound to be as controversial as are efforts to discuss sovereignty or symbolic content.[20] But the purpose of doing so is to demonstrate that there are not any "natural" or uncontested manner in which boundaries have been drawn around Jerusalem, be they political or spatial. Indeed, a simple survey of maps from various time periods over the centuries clearly highlights the varying and changing identities of Jerusalem. Depending on who is the ruling government, what is dominant religion, who is portraying the city, whether it was done retrospectively or for the present, the boundaries have expanded and contracted; the prominent and identity-defining sites and buildings have changed, despite many of the buildings and monuments remaining. What maps also show, however, and indeed help us visualize, is the fact that many of the conflicts over the city derive from questions or competing assumptions about "what IS the city," or *what constitutes Jerusalem* in spatial, political, or symbolic terms. As different persons and powers have answered this question differently over time; maps too have changed in their representation as Jerusalem grows, becomes more divided, and more religiously identified and complicated.[21]

For example, a Christian map of Jerusalem during the Crusades frequently shows churches, hospitals with Christian names, and Biblical sites, particularly those relating to the New Testament. A 1790 drawing of Biblical Jerusalem highlights David's palace, the city walls and the temple, with space instead of resident housing. The famous 6th century Madaba mosaic map shows the walled city with lots of housing, and the Church of the Holy Sepulcher. The mosaic also includes other cities in the region but Jerusalem is disproportionately large.[22] It is clear that the boundaries (or in ancient times, the actual walls) of the city and the maps more generally always denoted religious and symbolic content, but that the city itself was much larger than either of these aspects. Primarily starting at the end of the 19th century, we find boundaries and walls extend beyond the purely religious and symbolic. This has been largely the result of economic and political developments associated first with the Ottoman Empire, and then with British colonial rule. The story of Jerusalem's boundaries in the 20th century is all too well known, with its division in 1948, and its "reunification" and redefinition since 1967, such that today, many people talk of three "Jerusalems." But even these boundaries and the content of the city are ever changing as a result of globalization, immigration, urbanization, expanded settlements, the building of the wall, and the ongoing Arab–Israeli conflict, including the internal tensions within the Palestinian Authority.

These shifting and changing "Jerusalems" manifest themselves in political and social rhetoric as well as civic practice and identity, and are as evident in shifts in population within the bounds of the city as without. Municipal Jerusalem is often divided into East and West.[23] Of the municipal city's 680,000 residents, 60 percent live in East Jerusalem, of which more than half (232,000) are Palestinian. Meanwhile, almost all of West Jerusalem's residents are Israeli. These ethno-national and religious demographics, which speak to differences within the city, all too frequently influence one's perception of the city as a whole. Additionally, there is metropolitan Jerusalem which has 1,020,000 residents, 66 percent living in the municipal and 33 percent living in the metropolitan area. As a growing number residents move out of the city, 50 percent are choosing to live in the metropolitan area.[24] This is changing not only the physical, economic, and political landscape, it also is transforming the meaning of the city and challenging longstanding perceptions of Jerusalem's identity both from within and outside, including from the point of view of other cities in Israel.[25]

While there is still contention and discussion about what constitutes Jerusalem, either in terms of its outer boundaries or its "inner" populations and activities, one thing is clear: the territorial boundaries of the city today go far beyond the religious and the symbolic core that was evident so many centuries ago. And within its new expanse, new demographic patterns and other symbolic identities or sovereignty concerns continue to materialize. Many of these changes, including the shifted meaning of old and new spaces, inspired Meron Benvenisti, former deputy mayor of Jerusalem, to remark that the city of Jerusalem was "dead," in urbanistic terms at least, and all that remained was an isolated, tourist-oriented old city surrounded by a declining urban fabric, fueled in part by the outmigration of younger generations to places like Tel Aviv.[26] While this perhaps seems like a bleak assessment of the situation, the point remains, as Salim Tamari recently noted, that over the course of just the past 100 years, Jerusalem has changed in form and content way beyond anyone's imagination.[27] The Jerusalem of 1922 is very different from Jerusalem 1948 and Jerusalem of 1967 is very different from the Jerusalem of 2007, even with just several decades of time separating these data points.

From Liability to Opportunity?

The above cited statistics and demographics do not give a comprehensive or complete picture of Jerusalem, its boundaries, residents or their identity.[28] But they do call attention to the city's complexity and the myriad ways in which it has been and continues to be presented and conceived. They also show that

Jerusalem means many things to many people. The Jerusalem 2050 project has tried to incorporate these shifting and competing views, and to design a project that recognizes the multiplicity of ways that people will see and experience Jerusalem.

For some critics, the fact that what defines or constitutes Jerusalem is a constantly moving target, whose form and symbolic content are up for continual re-interpretation if not renewed efforts at "resolution" through negotiation, war, or other forms of violent struggle, might pose a non-trivial barrier to efforts to generate new and peaceful visions for the city. If there is no consensus on what exactly constitutes the city, how can progress be made? And if to address this concern one were to select one of the many maps, definitions, or interpretations, would they not be privileging a particular interpretation of who was there first, or of who did or did not, does or does not, have the right to rule and to draw the boundaries, or of what Jerusalem is supposed to symbolize? Rather than finding ourselves intellectually paralyzed by these dilemmas, we have chosen to treat the multiplicity of boundaries, identities, and meanings that have comprised Jerusalem over the years as an opportunity, rather than a liability. That is, we openly recognize that Jerusalem means many things to many people, both in the region and around the world. And to give life to these different views, we have launched the *Just Jerusalem Competition*, so as to solicit and document as large a number of views as possible.

Through the competition we encourage all who care about the city, and peace in the region, to offer innovative definitions of Jerusalem in physical, symbolic, and even sovereignty terms, asking participants from anywhere in the world to define "their Jerusalem 2050" and to specify how this particular mapping (or understanding) of the city works with their proposal to enable peace, justice, and sustainability. We seek to reverse the conventional order of causality used to define and make plans for the city, encouraging a more interactive or dialectic way of establishing the relationship between physical, symbolic, and sovereignty boundaries and peace in the city. Likewise, in this competition we have opened the discussion of Jerusalem to the world, or global civil society as we prefer to call it, in order to unfetter the peace process – a process often hamstrung by the limited inclusion of a narrowly defined set actors via pre-ordained representatives who are frequently constrained by political allegiances or formal diplomatic relationships.[29] Finally, the competition addresses the belief that the nature of the city, and the way out of its conflicts, cannot be reduced to a single, negotiated agreement or top-down master plan. In the case of Jerusalem, imposed blueprints and forced consensus-building strategies have often been part of the problem, leading to conflict over the terms and outcomes. By engaging global civil society in a bottom-up approach, our competition sidesteps the standard route of negotiation between small numbers of high level representatives and turns instead to the liberating and regenerative potential of individual imagination and vision. Our hope is that the competition results will serve as a platform from which a new dialogue on change in Jerusalem can occur and where world-wide support can help sustain local efforts for change.

Mindful of the current political implications of any project focused on Jerusalem, we have tread carefully in this project, protecting its scholarly and intellectual origins, building into its contours a critical examination of conventional epistemology, and offering transparency in our composition and aims. Our intent has and continues to be simple: to inspire and generate innovative ideas and new discussions about Jerusalem as it might be in the future – a just city shared in peace by its residents, whether Muslim, Christian or Jewish, Palestinian or Israeli. The descendants of the children of Abraham will be the beneficiaries of these ideas and this project, whether they live in Jerusalem or not, but residents of Jerusalem 2050 will be the direct inheritors of any changes produced as a result of our efforts. We at the Jerusalem 2050 project believe that positive change can occur by transcending the socially constructed frames that individuals have long used to interpret or understand the city, by recognizing the existence of a multiplicity of images, meanings, and understandings of the city, and by focusing on the future.

In the end, Jerusalemites will be the ultimate agents of their self-chosen and self-directed change. But to aid in this endeavor, the Jerusalem 2050 project through the *Just Jerusalem Competition* seeks to empower and inspire civil society and local government officials and planners through an inclusive global dialogue based on creative innovative ideas on all aspects of urban life, in the spirit of academic study and a shared common humanity.

Notes

This essay is a revised version of a public presentation given by Diane Davis and Leila Farsakh, co-directors of the Jerusalem 2050 project, at the Children of Abraham conference. Materials related to mapping, demographics, and general political and economic statistics were compiled by Leila Farsakh, drawing partly on her own research, and have been modified for inclusion here. Special thanks to Leila for these and other contributions to the structure and content of this essay, as well as to Amy Spelz for considerable editorial modification, conceptual elaboration, and overall assistance in the preparation of this text.

1   For a synthetic view of this promise, and more discussion of differences, democracy, and the city, see Kian Tajkbakhsh, *The Promise of the City: Space, Identity, and Politics in Contemporary Social Thought* (University of California, 2001).

2   Marshall Berman, *All that is Solid Melts into the Air: The Experience of Modernity* (Penguin Press, 1988), p. 318.

3   Italics in original. Andy Merrifield, "Social Justice and Communities of Difference: a Snapshot from Liverpool" in Andrew Merrifield and Eric Swyngedouw, *The Urbanization of Injustice* (New York University Press, 1997), p. 201.

4   Ira Katznelson, "Social Justice, Liberalism, and the City: Considerations on David Harvey, John Rawls, and Karl Polanyi" in Andrew Merrifield and Eric Swyngedouw, *The Urbanization of Injustice* (New York University Press, 1997),

p. 49. Katznelson defines liberalism as the divide between public and private; guarantee of individual and group rights; moral pluralism.

5 Richard Sennett, *The Fall of Public Man* (Alfred A. Knopf, 1977), p. 295.

6 Harvey, *Spaces of Hope*, pp. 157, 158.

7 Henri Lefebvre, "The Right to the City," p. 158 in H. Lefebvre, *Writing on Cities* (Blackwell Publishers, 1996).

8 Ibid., p. 158.

9 See Manuel Castells' discussion of the comunidades de Castilla in *The City and the Grassroots: A Cross-Cultural Theory of Urban Social Movements* (University of California, 1983).

10 "Rhythmanalysis of Mediterranean Cities," in ibid., p. 232. This formulation comes from Lefebvre's analysis of Mediterranean cities. He further notes that in city-states, or places were there is a fusion of city and state, "the State, whether it be inside or outside the city, always remains brutal and powerless, violent but weak, unified by always undermined, under threat." Ibid., p. 233.

11 Frug, *City Making: Building Communities without Building Walls*, pp. 8–9. Again, it is worth emphasizing that when Frug uses the word city in contradistinction to locality he has in mind the idea of cities as metropolitan bodies which extend in space to include a variety of (fragmented) localities where some form of deliberative power rests.

12 Ibid., p. 9.

13 ICBS, *Statistical Abstract of Jerusalem*.

14 In this text I purposively employ the term Jerusalem, and not Al-Quds (Arabic) or Jerushalayim (Hebrew), because I seek to move beyond binary identity claims that have torn the city apart, and to rediscover the primarily "urban" identities that peoples of different religions, ethnicities, and nationalities can share together.

15 The people of Jerusalem at the beginning of the 20th century did not identify themselves simply as Christians, Muslims or Jewish; they constructed their religious identity with a zealousness and specificity that entailed drawing very circumscribed sub-boundaries within larger ecclesiastical groupings. Folks identified themselves as Latins, Franciscans, Greek Orthodox, Russian Orthodox, Armenians, Syrians, Jacobites, Copts, Abyssinians, Anglicans, Presbyterians, Arabs, Muslims, Sunnis, Turks, Bedouins, Ashkenazis, Yemenites, Bagdadim, Persians, Karaim and Sephardims, among others, and acted as distinctive groups in their daily demands for Jerusalem spaces. In addition, their religious identity was crisscrossed by different nationalities. Holy City residents responded to different earthly laws, using the legal codes of Turkey, France, Britain, Germany, Greece, Russia, Italy or United States to judge their actions. For more on the city under Ottoman rule, see Nora Libertun de Duren, "Jerusalem at the Beginning of the Twentieth Century," unpublished manuscript, Department of Urban Studies and Planning, MIT, 2004. For more on the city in the key transition between imperial (Ottoman) and colonial (British) rule, see Amy Dockser Marcus, *Jerusalem 1913* (New York: Penguin Press, 2007).

16 Arjun Appadurai, "Sovereignty without Territoriality: Notes for a Post-national Geography" in Setha Low and Denise Lawrence-Zuñiga (eds.), *The Anthropology of Space and Place – Locating Culture* (Oxford University Press, 2003), p. 337. Appadurai is engaging the work of Benedict Anderson, author of a seminal work on nationalism titled *Imagined Communities*.

17 For more information on the specific faculty involved, the history of this project,

and the academic seminars we have hosted over the past several years, please see our website: <http://web.mit.edu/CIS/jerusalem2050/index.html>.

18 It is this same logic that often prevents Palestinians from exercising their demo-cratic rights at the ballot box in the city, or from attending community meetings about housing or transportation policies. It is not that they do not care about the city; but rather, this response is seen as an act of protest at the larger sovereignty aims under which planning decisions for Jerusalem are being made.

19 In reference to the great political theorist, John Rawls, and his seminal book, *A Theory of Justice* (Oxford University Press, 1999).

20 Even when restrictive boundaries persist, it is still worth considering whether and how the power of design can be harnessed to a more positive vision of the city. An analogous situation, echoing our project, could be found in the Hauptstadt Berlin competition of the late 1950s, when the West Germans attempted to envision what a unified city would look like in the future. The plan was never implemented, of course, since the East Germans would have nothing to do with its originating premises. Instead, not long afterwards, they erected the Berlin Wall. Even so, one can certainly argue that there was considerable value to the effort to conceptualize a future unified city, and that this kind of forward-looking thinking may well have been useful when, more than three decades later, the city was actu-ally re-unified. Perhaps the Hauptstadt Berlin competition would have been more powerful had it been explicitly visionary and had attempted to project a "Berlin 1990" future, as we seek to do with Jerusalem. Is there not some value in offering the vision – if not the tools – for a city's rebirth just at the moment it seems to have been irreparably torn apart?

21 Some of these complexities involve thinking about the nested boundaries of different "iterations of the city," starting with the smallest but oldest unit, the old city, and moving up through municipal boundaries and into the greater metro-politan area, etc. But many of these "locales" have more or less significance in symbolic or sovereignty terms, ranging from seeing parts of Jerusalem as a reli-gious center for all three major world faiths, to seeing parts or all of the city as the capital of one state, two states, no states, etc.

22 For pictures of Jerusalem maps, including the mosaic map, see <http://jeru.huji.ac.il/jeru/maps_index.html> or Hebrew University's online collection of Jerusalem maps (<http://maps-of-jerusalem.huji.ac.il>).

23 There are also many maps portraying Jerusalem in terms of East and West, and Municipal and Metropolitan. For some examples, please see the Foundation for Middle East Peace website (<http://www.fmep.org/maps/overview.html>).

24 ICBS, *Statistical Abstract of Jerusalem.*

25 Uri Ram, "Jerusalem, Tel Aviv and the Bifurcation of Israel," *International Journal of Politics, Culture and Society*, online version, July 3, 2007.

26 Meron Benvenisti speaking at "The Jerusalem Visionaries Conference" hosted at MIT, April 8, 2005.

27 Salim Tamari, speaking at the formal launch of the Just Jerusalem Competition, March 2007, MIT.

28 For a more thorough listing of maps, demographics, statistics and histories, please see the registered webpages of the Just Jerusalem website (<www.just-jerusalem.org>), *Palestinian Labour Migration to Israel* by Leila Farsakh, *Jerusalem: The Contested City* by Menachem Klein, or publication from the International Peace and Cooperation Center .

29 Given Jerusalem's global emotional, spiritual, and political importance, its universality, and the fact that people from all over the world have personal connections to the city, we have not confined our competition only to "locals," that is only Palestinians and Israelis. It is not just that people around the world have an interest in peace in this city.. Having physical separation from Jerusalem allows citizens in and from other countries a certain amount of distance from the emotional and political tensions that can sometimes blind individuals from seeing new, alternative, and creative solutions. For all these reasons, the competition is open not just to Israeli and Palestinian civil society but to global civil society.

PART
III

Education and Textbooks

CHAPTER 9

Teaching Interfaith Initiatives: Jews and Christians in Muslim Educational Institutions (Focus on Pakistan)

MUHAMMAD SHAFIQ

When we consider Islam's approaches to interfaith relations, especially about Judaism and Christianity, we see that Muslims have a rich and a long history of living in multi-religious and multi-cultural neighborhoods and societies. Islam recognizes a plurality of religions and asks Muslims to respect other religions and followers of those religions.

The Qur'an could be rightly called a book of dialogue, a dialogue between Abrahamic faiths. The Qur'an not only recognized the essence of Judaism and Christianity, but also used the words *Ahl al Kitab* (People of the Book), and laid down the rules of dialogue with respect and tolerance for all. Jews and Christians rejected each other before Islam. The Qur'an's unique contribution to world civilization is the recognition of the presence of other religions and its emphasis on the need to live in peace with religious freedom. This recognition is not a courtesy but an acknowledgment of their religious truth, as Isma'il R. al Faruqi would say.[1]

Muhammad (peace be upon him) claimed himself from the heirs of Abraham and a prophet from the Biblical line. He called other prophets as brothers in the same faith. He grieved with Christians when the Zoroastrian Persians defeated the Byzantine Christians. When he migrated to Medina, he signed a treaty with its Jewish tribes, a pledge to live together in peace and cooperation. The Jewish tribes were called an *Ummah* (a religious community) – the same word was applied to the Muslim community. Muhammad had some good Jewish friends till his death and whenever he needed financial help he turned to them.[2]

But something has seriously gone wrong with Muslim communities around the world. Today, Muslims are far behind in intra- and interfaith dialogue to the extent that the *Interfaith Dialogue: A Guide for Muslims* could be considered as the first Muslim publication in the field of modern interfaith dialogue. Muslims in Europe and America have made some headway in intra- and interfaith dialogue, but many in Muslim countries are held up in bitterness, anger, hatred, and intolerance towards fellow Muslims and others as well.

The Qur'anic stance on interfaith dialogue, appreciation of pluralistic society and freedom of religious belief and expression has become questionable today. Muslims are divided over the interpretation of some of its verses. There are some who have taken an extreme view of interpretation and there are many who listen to them. Listening to pro-al Qaeda tapes, many in the West today believe that Islam is not a religion of *Salam* (peace).

Without understanding that most of the al-Qaeda type of attitude is a by-product of the Afghan *jihad* during the USSR occupation, the Iraq war and the continuing Israel–Palestine conflict have further fueled the anger. Most of the literature preaching Muslim exclusivism and hatred against others was produced during this period from 1970 to 2000. It does not mean that there was no classical literature where such interpretations could be found, but those books had lost significance for Muslims.

Education plays a key role in molding human character. What we teach to the next generation and how we train them have a deep impact on them and on their character. This essay examines the teaching of interfaith dialogue, with reference to Jews and Christians in Muslim educational institutions, especially in Pakistan; it also deals with the Muslim controversy over the issue of contemporary interfaith dialogue by discussing some of the controversial verses of the Qur'an relating to interfaith dialogue as they are taught in some Muslim traditional (*Madrassah*) and modern educational institutions. The essay will focus particularly on the Qur'anic use of *Ahl al Kitab*, the words *Kufr* (disbelief or hiding the truth) and *Wali* (friend/master), including the concept of religious exclusivity.

Teaching of Interfaith Dialogue (Jews and Christians) in Pakistan Educational Institutions

Pakistani schools, colleges and many of its modern universities do not have departments teaching world religions. The schools and colleges curriculum have courses on Islam, Islamic faith and history. Most of the Qur'anic citations in the courses are about character building and belief, including verses about *jihad*, struggling in the path of Allah, including warfare if necessary. Recently, some of the Islamic Studies texts taught in schools were modified in reference to *jihad* and its explanation.

Most Pakistan universities have postgraduate departments of Islamic Studies. A course on world religions – Hinduism, Buddhism, Judaism and

Christianity – are part of the curriculum. But the course is no more than an introduction.[3] Pakistani universities do not as yet have a department of world religions compared with those in many Western universities. The International Islamic University, Islamabad has a department of world religions in the Faculty of Usul al Din but lacks academic experts in each discipline.[4]

The traditional religious institutions are called *Madrassah* (pl. *Madaris*) in Pakistan. Different religious schools have their own *Madaris*. The dominant schools are Deobandi, Barelvi[5] and 'Shi'a *Madaris*. Besides these Jama'at-i-Islami[6] and Ahl al Hadith[7] have *Madaris* too. The texts taught in each school of thought of these *Madaris* emphasize their understanding of the religion; opposing views are emphasized, as their view is the most correct and the other wrong, and therefore rejected after comparison. For example, Tafsir (Qur'an exegesis) in the Deobandi *Madaris* are mostly of those explained by the Deoband School of Thought. Similarly the Tafsir taught in Braveli *Madaris* is from Raza Khan, the founder of the school; *Madaris* run by Jama'at-i-Islam teach Tafhim al Qur'an by Maududi; and the same is true about other *Madaris*. Most students of these different *Madaris* graduate with opposing views and with little respect for the schools of thought.[8]

In 1970s, the conflict between the Sipah Sahaba (the soldiers of the companions of the Prophet), a group from Ahl al Hadith, and the Sipah Muhammad (the soldiers of the Prophet),[9] a group from the Shi'a school of thought, resulted in religious riots, killings and bomb explosions against one another. They openly called one another *Kafir*s (disbelievers) and brought the intra-Muslim relations to its lowest ebb. This militancy between the two groups was a product of an ideological warfare that took place during and after the Iran–Iraq war. Much literature was translated and printed in all Pakistani languages. The pro-Ahl al Hadith literature openly called the Shi'a *Kafir*s (non-Muslims)[10] and similar harsh words were used in the literature supported by the Shi'a.

Recently relations have been improved through the MMA (Mutahidda Majlis-e-Amal) organization in which all five major schools of thought are members, but the schools' radical wings stay out and are opposed to such dialogue. The MMA organization is weak, and religious relations between different parties have not improved much. It can be said that the organization is held together more by political interests rather than religious reconciliation. It goes without saying that intra-faith dialogue is very essential between these different groups to restore respect and civility in their relations, and in Pakistan well.

Most of these *Madaris* are a product of the post-independence period and reflect the opposing views with reference to independence and religious thought. The curriculum in each of these different schools of thought have little to do with interfaith relations, especially about Judaism and Christianity, because this aspect is not a pertinent issue to these *Madaris* as far as their religious and political interests are concerned.

Christine Fair, in *Islamic Education in Pakistan*,[11] is right to say that the curriculum taught in these Madaris is simple and many texts are centuries old. The students spend the first few years in Sarf and Nahw learning Arabic grammar and memorizing the Qur'an. Such Madaris are everywhere; they are also called *Maktab* (Islamic School). Then the students are taught Tajweed and Qira'at (how to pronounce the Qur'an correctly and recite better), and are then exposed to elementary *Fiqh* (legal school of thought, mostly of their own). In the next few years the students are taught Qur'anic exegesis, *Hadith* and *Fiqh*, and they might opt for specialization in one or the other field.[12]

It was during 1973 that the degrees of the Madaris were first made equivalent to college degrees in North West Frontier province when Mufti Mahmood, a graduate of Deoband School of Thought, became the Chief Minister of the Province. The Madaris degree of Mutawassita was made equivalent to 8th grade, Sanaviya equal to 10th, 'Aliya equal to BA and 'Alamiya equal to MA in Islamic Studies and Arabic language.[13] The recognition give a boost to Madaris' graduates in the North West Frontier Province and later all Pakistan Madaris' graduates were made equivalents to college degrees in Islamic Studies and Arabic during the regime of Zia al Haq. The graduates also had to pass English and some other subjects at different levels if they were to compete in other fields. The Madaris also received substantial financial support from the Zakat Fund that the government of Zia al Haq had established. The Madaris further received financial boost during the *jihad* in Afghanistan against Russian occupation. It was during that time that many Afghan youngsters were enrolled in Pakistani Madaris, mostly in the Deobandi School of Thought, as many Afghans are Deobandi.[14]

The Afghan *jihad* made Pakistanis, and especially the Pashtuns, exposed to all sorts of ideologies – Kalashnikov culture, and political and moral bankruptcy. The Pashtuns had their own tradition and most were Deobandi, but were barely educated. The tribes were encouraged and were used as freedom fighters in Kashmir, even before the partition of the Subcontinent. But the Afghan *jihad* was very different and brought more challenges.

First, the Pashtuns were exposed to Wahhabism[15] and, second, the Pashtuns were ideologically groomed, and encouraged to fight for the liberation of Palestine and destruction of Israel. The Afghan *jihad* in the beginning was a *jihad* against the Russian infidels; under these circumstances the Abrahamic faiths joined together to fight the war. The slogan was to save Asia from the red and keep it green. The red color stood for communism and green represented people of faith. But when the *Jihad* heated up, it took a new turn – to liberate Palestine and then Saudi Arabia from foreign occupation after the liberation of Afghanistan.[16] With the collapse of USSR, the western nations pressured the Pakistan government about the activities of *Mujahidin* (the freedom fighters), and the government tried to engage them for *jihad* in occupied Indian Kashmir. This brought India and Pakistan close to the brink of another war.

It was during this period that force not dialogue became commonly accepted. Many Arabs and non-Arab *Mujahidin* had stayed for long in the tribal built of Afghanistan and Pakistan. They had made it their homes for they were not safe back in their home countries. Many had married women from the Pashtuns or had adopted tribal Pashtun life-style. With the defeat of Taliban government after 9/11, they had no place other than the mountains. When they found themselves not safe even in the mountains, they resorted to terrorist activities in Afghanistan and Pakistan. The West was their enemy and the two governments of Afghanistan and Pakistan and many other Muslim heads of states were the agents of the West and thus their enemies too. Pashtuns are believed to be the descendants of the lost tribes of Israel, but now the Jews were disliked and many blamed the Jews for all that had taken place. It was not unusual to hear processions chanting, "Israel and America *Murdabad*" (death to Israel and America). This made any interfaith dialogue almost impossible. The prevailing situation has resulted in distrust, hatred and enmity among the Abrahamic religions.

Muslim Controversy over Interfaith Dialogue

Indeed, any interfaith dialogue with Jews and Christians became an act of *Kufr* (disbelief). Pamphlets and posters were circulated calling interfaith dialogue a "*bid'ah*," an innovation in Islam not practiced by the Prophet. The literature written and published including some Qur'an exegesis between 1970–2000, emphasized more on *Jihad*[17] and puritanical[18] Islamic faith leaving no or little room for dialogue.

The views of <www.muttaqun.com>, representing the extreme Salafi views of the Wahhabi style are interesting to note. Hizb al Tahrir[19] shares similar views in reference to interfaith dialogue. They quote verses from the Qur'an and quote some *hadith* in their support. In their opposition to the interfaith dialogue, they stated

- That interfaith dialogue is part of ecumenism and ecumenism is Christian.
- That the purpose of interfaith dialogue is to create one religion for all.
- That to say "Your faith is mine and there is no difference" is *haram* (forbidden) in Islam.
- That interfaith dialogue is committed to creating new, blended, diluted worship services common to all and that Muslims are already participating in these worship services.

Those Muslims who oppose interfaith dialogue commonly quote the following verse from the Qur'an.[20]

> Never will the Jews or the Christians be satisfied with thee unless thou follow their form of religion. Say: "The Guidance of Allah that is the (only) Guidance. Wert thou to follow their desires after the knowledge

which hath reached thee, then wouldst thou find neither Protector nor
helper against Allah. (2:120)

While some Muslims understand this verse as condemning any dialogue
with Jews or Christians, a scientific, historical approach to this verse reveals
that it refers to the controversy that emerged after the Prophet (SAAS) was
asked to change the *Qibla* (worship direction) from Jerusalem towards
Ka'bah at Makkah [Mecca]. The Jews were certainly unhappy with the decision. The Prophet (SAAS) did his best to explain his position on the change
of *Qibla* and to maintain his good relations with the Jews. It is in this context
that the Prophet was told that the Jews and Christians of that time would not
be pleased with him in spite of his utmost efforts until he followed the teachings of their religions with respect to the centrality of Jerusalem. The verse did
not ask him to break his relation with Jews and Christians, but was indicative that total satisfaction was impossible.[21]

Here is another verse, in Surat Al-Saff, which some Muslims say condemns
dialogue with those of other faiths:

> It is He Who has sent His Messenger with Guidance and the Religion of
> Truth, that he may proclaim it over all religions, even though the Pagans
> may detest [it]. (61:9)

Analyzing this verse within a wider Islamic context, we realize that, first,
Islam is the message of Truth and that Muslims have to do their best to spread
the message throughout the world. Second, that when the truth spreads, there
will always be resistance. And third, that Muslims must be ready to face the
consequences of this resistance and discover positive solutions to it. For
Muslims remember that truth cannot be spread in hostility, but rather with
graciousness and patience. One has to do his/her best to create a peaceful environment of trust. The Prophet (SAAS) provided us with a model of peaceful
behavior in situations of hostility when he signed the agreement of *Hudaibiya*
with those who opposed him, and had expelled him and his followers from
his hometown, Makkah. He could see that that the treaty would lead to peace
and that by his signing it Muslims would be able to move freely in a peaceful
atmosphere to spread the message of Islam. This verse demands that Muslims
build good relations with others for the service of Islam.

As for the *hadith* often quoted by those opposing interfaith dialogue, the
following may serve as an example: "Everyone will be with those on the Day
of Judgment whom he loves."[22]

Those Muslims who oppose interfaith dialogue quote this *hadith*
frequently. Once there was a Jewish–Muslim dialogue. After the dialogue was
over, the next day a Muslim who opposed dialogue with Jews was quoting
this *hadith* and was saying to others, "Those who favor dialogue with Jews
would be with Jews on the Day of Judgment because dialoguing with them is
to love them." Yet interfaith dialogue is not about loving the "other" in the

sense of becoming "one" with him. It is about respecting the "other's" views and by that means paving the way for a peaceful society. Yet many of those who oppose dialogue take this and other *hadith* out of context and use them to frighten those Muslims who participate in dialogue by accusing them of having thereby committed a sin. The dialogical process itself forces Muslims to examine and reconfirm their own religion and identity. It causes them to strengthen their own *iman* (faith) while respecting the "others" with patience, tolerance, and good *adab*. In fact, this particular *hadith* does not pertain to dialogue or bridge building at all; it actually calls on Muslims to love Allah and His Messenger, to stand firmly behind Muslim causes, and not to mix Islamic beliefs and practices with other faiths, keeping their *iman* in its authentic form.

Generalizing mistakenly from verse and *hadith* like those above, Muslims who oppose interfaith dialogue claim such interaction is actually designed to:

- Expand the Western political, military, economic, and cultural influence
- Westernize Muslims and Muslim countries
- Make Muslims lose political, economic and cultural independence
- Eradicate Islam and the Islamic way of life from the world
- Convert all people to Christianity

We acknowledge these fears; however, progressive post-colonial societies have developed the capacity to address such concerns and issues openly, with equality and with respect. Fear of interfaith dialogue actually reveals a lack of faith, of confidence and of spiritual endurance. These deficiencies lead to the loss of the opportunity to introduce Islam to a diversity of people.

But even more positively, interaction with the West and its pluralistic society through dialogue can directly and indirectly expand non-Muslims' knowledge and understanding of Islam. Fear can be replaced with confidence in one's Islamic faith and used for positive understanding of Islam through networking and involvement with others on common projects. Muslims engaging in such interaction have a golden opportunity of representing Islam as what it actually is: the truthful and peaceful religion given in the Qur'an. Numerous people who have not met a Muslim or come in contact with Islam on an interpersonal level, desire the opportunity to do so. By offering this opportunity with good intentions rather than keeping closed in on ourselves in fear, Muslims encourage their dialogue partners by their good experience and may bring others to seek similar encouraging interaction.

Muslims have other fears about interfaith dialogue. One is that the non-Muslim participants are actually missionaries looking for additional information and insight to better aid their evangelization and conversion of Muslims. While this motive may characterize some missionaries, it can backfire. There is an instance where a missionary, having gained an in-depth knowledge of Islam and then having ventured forth to convert Muslims to Christianity, soon found that he himself was the one converted to Islam!

Does Interfaith Dialogue Aim to Create a Civil Religion?

Still another fear of interfaith dialogue is that emerging from it will be a new, diluted "Abrahamic" religion, something resembling Akbar's *Dini-Ilahi* (Divine Faith). Akbar (1542-1605) was the third Mughal emperor of India (1556-1605).[23] To create unity and reach out to many religions, he created a new faith, the *Dini-Ilahi* (Divine Faith), which was a combination of Islam, Brahmanism, Christianity, and Zoroastrianism. Though Akbar had strong relationships with scholars of all faiths, this new religion failed to establish itself with the people. This fear of creating Akbar's type of *Dini-Ilahi* is why some Muslims, especially Muslims from South Asia, sincerely oppose interfaith work. They support building good and friendly relations with people of other faiths without being involved in interfaith dialogue.

The key point is that interfaith dialogue does not aim to unify the religions. Muslim participants need to be aware of this. When the Prophet (SAAS) was approached by the Makkans to let them worship their gods for a year and then worship his God the next year, Qur'an in Surat Al Kafirun rejected their request. The Qur'an told Muhammad to tell the Makkans, (Meccans): " . . . for you is your religion and for me is my religion" (109:6). The Qur'an stands for freedom of religion and religious worship and rejects compromise on idol worship.

From all that has been said it is evident that imams should not hesitate to participate in interfaith dialogue. On the contrary, their participation will help their congregations overcome their fears and consider the advantages of contemporary interfaith dialogue. Interfaith dialogue is about freedom and respect for every religion. It is a bridge-building movement to ease tension and hatred between followers of different religions. Religions are God's gift to bring peace to humanity, not hatred. Religions can live together in peace only through organized efforts of understanding, mutual appreciation, and the building of good relations.

Some Issues that are Debated Between Pro and Con Interfaith Muslim Groups

The Concept of Kufr (disbelief)

The Qur'an has used this word – generally translated in English as " disbelief" – to mean different things. Its basic meaning is being ungrateful, hiding or covering truth, rejecting truth and not believing in God; other meanings could also be derived. The meaning "being ungrateful" is clear from this example from the Qur'an: *Said one who had knowledge of the Book: "I will bring it to thee within the twinkling of an eye!" Then when (Solomon) saw it placed firmly before him, he said: "This is by the Grace of my Lord! – to test me whether I am grateful or ungrateful! and if any is grateful, truly his gratitude is (a gain) for his own soul; but if any is ungrateful, truly my Lord is Free of all Needs, Supreme in Honour!"* (27:40) Here the word *Kufr* is used in opposite to the word *Shukr* (grateful).

The meaning of the word *Kufr* depends on the historical context of its use. Note, for example, that in the following verse *Kufr* is used of a specific situation where Allah asks the Jews to believe in the Qur'an as a revelation from God. *Allah says, And believe in what I reveal, confirming the revelation which is with you, and be not the first to reject Faith therein, nor sell My Signs for a small price; and fear Me, and Me alone* (2:41). Here the word *Kafir*, derivative of *Kufr*, is used meaning rejection. It does not mean that the Jews in general are not believers in God, but is used for those Jews who were rejecting Muhammad (SAWS) and the Qur'an at that period.

Similarly those are other verses of the Qur'an where the word *Kufr* in the Qur'an is used in reference to the Jews and the Christians (2:41 and also in other places the word *Kafara* or *Kufr* is used). The interpretation of those verses relating to Jews or Christians does not mean that Jews and Christians do not believe in God. The Qur'an makes it clear that the God of the Jews, Christians and Muslims is the One and same God (29:46).

Jews and Christians are not infidels, which means people who do not believe in God, but the Qur'an does ask Jews and Christians to believe in Muhammad and the Qur'an as the last revelation from God along with their belief in the Biblical prophets (peace be upon them) and the scriptures that were revealed to them. *The Qur'an says: But those who believe and work deeds of righteousness, and believe in the (Revelation) sent down to Muhammad – for it is the Truth from their Lord, – He will remove from them their ills and improve their condition* (47:2).

Furthermore, the Qur'an asks Christians to give up their concept of the Trinity and adopt the true concept of Oneness of God.

The Qur'an uses the word *Kafara* (covering up, hiding the truth or even of committing disbelief) for calling Jesus the Son of God or for saying that Allah is one of three in a Trinity. The Qur'an asks Christians to reject these false concepts (5:72. 73).[24]

When Isma'il R. Al Faruqi was asked this question whether Jews and Christians should be called 'infidels' in Islam, he explained that the term 'infidel' is applied to a person who does not recognize God at all. It should not, he said, be applied to the adherent of another religion who believes in God. Al Faruqi further said that no Jews and Christian may be called 'infidel' a priori. However, if he or she denies God or God's unity and His transcendence, he/she may be called so.[25]

Muhammad Asad's *The Message of the Qur'an* has a good discussion on the word *kufr* and its derivatives in reference to Ayahs 2:6 and 74:10. He translates the word *Kafir* as generally meaning *"denying the truth,"* with the exception of 57:20, where the word is used for farmers covering the seeds. He feels the translation of the word *kufr* as unbelievers and particularly "infidels" would generally be inappropriate.

It is helpful to explain that the Qur'an, carefully distinguishing among people's allegiances to God, divides humanity into five religious categories. They are:

1 **Al Mu'minun wa al Muttaqun.** True believers and the righteous people. These are those who believe in One God, in all Biblical prophets (peace be upon them) including Muhammad (SAWS) as the seal of the prophets; on all revelations including the Qur'an as God's last revelation to humanity and the Day of Judgment (Qur'an, 2:2-5).

2 **The Kuffar** (the disbelievers in God) or those who do not accept the existence of God. The frequent use of the word in the Qur'an is always precise (The Qur'an, 2:6 & 7). Regrettably, however, the word *Kuffar* has been used as a blanket term of reproach and rejection of all those felt to be enemies. Such usage is incorrect and inapplicable to most people. It has been used as a term of insult against Christians and Jews, blocking rather then opening dialogue and the possibility of peaceful relations.

3 **Al Munafiqun** (the hypocrites). "Those who say that they believe in God but their actions do not confirm their belief" (Qur'an, 2:8–18). When Muhammad (SAWS) migrated to Medina, some pretended to be Muslims, but in their hearts were not. The Qur'an has addressed these people almost in every Sura revealed in Medina.

4 **Al Mushrikun** (the Associationists, those who worship idols). These are Makkans before Islam who were idol worshippers. It is in reference to their idol worship that the Qur'an says: "Allah forgiveth not that partners should be set up with Him; But He forgiveth any thing else, to whom He pleaseth; to set up partners with Allah is to devise a sin most heinous indeed" (4:48 and also 4:116).

5 **Ahl al Kitab** (people of the Book, Jews and Christians). These are believers in God, but disbelievers in Muhammad (SAWS) and the Qur'an as the last revelation of God, the Qur'an, 2:105, 3:64; the words *Ahl al Kitab* are repeated in many places.

The point of all these examples is that the Qur'an, the *Hadith*, and the *Sunna* all emphasize Islam's respect for people's rights and for their humanity. Everyone from the companion to the wayfarer has the right to be respected, to be treated fairly, and to be protected from harm and indignity (4:36).

Will Christian and Jews end in Hell Fire?

Another sensitive topic in interfaith dialogue is whether Muslims believe Jews and Christians will inevitably end up in Hell. For example, in one recent public dialogue between Christians and Muslims, the first question was how Christians can possibly dialogue with Muslims since Muslims believe Christians are damned. In return, the Muslim speaker asked the Christian who had asked the question what he believed about Muslims' chances of escaping Hell. Didn't Christians believe that the way to heaven is through Jesus alone? The Muslim speaker added, "We are not here to send people to heaven or hell, but to find ways of building good relations with each other and to serve the cause of suffering humanity."

Yet the question of who will end up in heaven or hell is a crucial issue in interfaith dialogue.

Every religion believes that their 'God' will place them in heaven ahead of others. Jews and Christians also believe this of themselves. No faith is ready to share the same place in heaven with another faith. At the same time the sense of exclusiveness that each faith brings to its understanding of heaven and hell gives believers energy and the motivation to do well in their own belief systems. It brings competition which the Qur'an calls *Liyabluwakum Ayyukum Ahsanu 'Amala* (To try you who is best in deeds, 67:2). This belief resembles the concept of nationalism yet without nationalism's violence. For just as each nation-state today proclaims itself to be superior to all others, so too does each religion seek to outgain the others in converts and to become dominant, not only on earth but in heaven. But the Qur'an's concept of *Istabiqul Khairat* (excel and compete in doing well) reveals that this competition should be in the area of achieving works of peace, not of war. So while nothing is wrong with this competitive spirit, the most important thing is how to live in peace with others. It is not who wins or loses but "how the game is played." Islam instructs its believers to adopt *adab*, compassion and respect towards all others whose religions have likewise told them to strive to do well.

Interfaith dialogue does not seek to send all people to heaven; its concern lies in encouraging people to avoid violence and hatred and to cultivate peace and solidarity with all humanity. Interfaith dialogue says that the positive claims each religion makes about itself should be made forthrightly without reliance on invidious comparisons. Consider the difference between the following two approaches. On the one hand, there is the imam who was giving a *Khutba* (sermon) on Friday and saying that Jews and Christians are bound to hell unless they accept Islam. On the other hand, there is the imam who says that Islam is the chosen path of Allah. That those who believe in Allah, the One and the only God, in the angels, in all the prophets (AS) including the Prophet Muhammad (SAWS) as seal of Prophets (AS), in all holy scriptures including the Qur'an as the last and final message of Allah to humanity, in the hereafter, in the resurrection, and in the day of judgment – that such as these Allah in His mercy and forgiveness will bless in heaven. Can you tell the difference in approach between these two imams? Which of these imams more truly represents the spirit of interfaith dialogue?

Muslims would most certainly oppose and reject others when they say that

Muslims are bound to hell or that Islam is an evil religion. In the same manner, Muslims should avoid saying that Jews, Christians, Hindus, Buddhists or others will end in hell. Allah has gifted people with intellect; they understand what is meant by saying that God will reward Muslims. Direct criticism of other faith practices and beliefs is unhealthy in any setting, especially in a dialogical context. Such behavior may easily escalate into further animosity and even hatred.

Yet it is true that Muslims are divided on the criteria for judging whether a person will go to heaven or to hell. Some assert that the criterion for entering is fairly inclusive. They say that the criterion consists in belief in one God along with belief in the Day of Judgment and in good deeds, as well as in the belief that the prophets and the Holy Scriptures were sent to guide people towards that goal. Authoritative works upholding this broad view include *Tafsir Tarjuman Al-Qur'an* by Abu'l Kalam Azad, *Al Manar* by Rashid Rida, *Al Mizan fi al Tafsir Al-Qur'an* by Muhammad Hussain Al Tabataba'i as well as certain writings influenced by Sufi writers. Fazlur Rahman in his *Major Themes of the Qur'an*, Appendix 11, expounds on this understanding of the criterion for entering heaven. Farid Esack in his book *Qur'an: Liberation and Pluralism* (Oxford, 1998) develops F. Rahman's thesis, basing his conclusions on an elaborate study of the Qur'an's approach to other faiths. Among modern commentators, Maududi in his *Tafhim al Qur'an* in reference to verse 2:62 says that the Jews believe that they will enter alone to heaven. But the Qur'an rejects their concept of being chosen by saying that criteria for heaven is belief in one God, the Hereafter and good deeds. The opportunity to enter Heaven is open to all. Wahidudin Khan in his *Tadhkir al Qur'an* supports Maududi's point of view on this verse.[26]

But the majority of Tafasir in both the classical and modern periods argue for a more exclusive criterion. These Tafasir, while listing belief in God, in the Day of Judgment, in good deeds, in all the prophets and in all the Holy Scriptures as essential, also include belief in Muhammad as the seal of Prophets and in the Qur'an as the last and perfect message of God to humanity. The majority of Muslims endorse this interpretation of the Qur'an.

The same Qur'anic verse can sometimes support both sides of the debate. Those Muslim scholars taking the inclusive position in support of religious pluralism and of the universality of Islamic values have buttressed their belief that some Jews and Christians will go to heaven on verses like the following: *"Those who believe (in the Qur'an) and those who follow the Jewish (scriptures), and the Christians, and the Sabians, and who believe in Allah and the Last day, and work righteous, shall have their reward with their Lord; on them shall be no fear, nor shall they grieve"* (2:62).

Those who oppose this inclusive interpretation argue that this verse and others like it refer only to those Jews and Christians alive during the time of their respective prophets and before the appointment of Prophet Muhammad (SAWS). They point out that when the Prophet was asked what would be the fate of those who died before his Prophet-hood, he replied that they would be treated according to the standards of their own faith.[27] The Noble Qur'an commentary quoting Al Tabari argues that this verse was abrogated by the verse 3:85, meaning whosoever seeks religion other than Islam is not acceptable.[28] They argue that many other verses confirm that belief in Muhammad and that the Qur'an is essential for people to enter heaven.[29]

But perhaps too much consideration of these questions is unproductive. After all, many Muslims do not ponder the criterion of who will enter heaven or hell issue too much. They say it is for Allah alone to make this judgment. And in interfaith dialogue, debating this criterion is not an issue either. The real issue of interfaith dialogue is how one expresses oneself and builds peaceful relationships while participating in dialogue. Islam is an earth-bound religion. It is very concerned about peace on earth. While belief in the hereafter is a very significant part of the Islamic faith, this belief must not be disfigured by harsh, provocative language but should be explained gently and modestly. For the truth is that no one knows who will enter Heaven but Allah. Yes, the criteria for heaven and hell are given in the Qur'an, but they should be explained in a gentle tone. It would be best to say when finding oneself involved in such a discussion: *"I do not know what my fate will be in the hereafter. Allah knows best who will end in hell and heaven."* The Qur'an, describing the Judgment vividly, makes clear that to Allah alone belongs the criterion:

> *"And the trumpet is blown, and all who are in the heavens and the earth swoon away, save Him whom Allah willeth. Then it is blown a second time, and behold them standing waiting. And the earth shineth with the light of God, and the book is set up, and the prophets and the witnesses are brought, it is judged between them with truth, and they are not wronged. And each soul is paid in full for what it did. And He is best aware of what they do."* (39:68–70)

Yet while it is important on certain occasions to adopt a more inclusive stance towards other religions, it would be a serious error to adopt this stance on all occasions. It is misleading for Muslim scholars sitting in a dialogic context to claim that a universal set of beliefs is valid for all religions or to claim that Islam includes all religions. Such an assumption of inclusiveness denies Islam its unique message. It also denies the specific historical and religious traditions that distinguish Islam and which make it appealing.

Of course, on the opposite side, there are those Muslims who believe that interfaith dialogue is *Haram* (forbidden). They wrathfully assert their belief in the damnation of non-Muslims. Muslim participation in interfaith dialogue calls for those on the extremes to adopt a middle way to avoid sharp divisions among Muslims and thus to preserve the *Ummah*'s unity. This is particularly important for Muslim communities in Europe and America experiencing difficult times. Imams and the Muslim scholars of Islamic Studies should make joint efforts to guide the community toward moderation. By easing the pressure on them, they will enable them to follow the ways of the Prophet (SAWS) more faithfully.

Conclusion

The major issue before Muslims is the interpretation of some Qur'anic verses. The Qur'an was revealed piece by piece over 22 years and a few months. Many times the revelation came responding to a particular situation at Makkah and then in Medina. The present format of the Qur'an is in 114 *Suras* (chapter) from longer to small. Muslims believe that the arrangement came from God. This arrangement makes it difficult to understand the relevance and application of some verses in our contemporary context. It is hard to determine which verse came before the other and which takes preference. Therefore people turn to different verses to justify their own agenda.

The Afghan war encouraged the extremists. In their zeal for *jihad* and with the support of oil-rich countries and the Western powers, much literature was published from 1970 to 2000 urging Muslims to fight against the USSR. Most of the literature carried the Salafi stamp of the Wahhabi branch. These books were printed on fine paper and were made available in all languages. Libraries were filled with them and the books were distributed mostly free of cost, very much like today anti-Islam and anti-Muslims literature swamps Western markets and is mostly distributed free of cost.

The Afghan Taliban and the students in many Pakistani *Madaris* had little connection with Wahhabism before the war. Pro-Wahhabi people in Pakistan were known as *Ahl al Hadith*; they were in confrontation with people of the Deoband School of Thought. Today Wahhabism influences many *Madaris*.

To reverse this process and restore moderation in Muslim thought, literature with a moderate, intellectual interpretation of the Qur'an and Islamic tradition is desperately needed.

Religious extremism and fundamentalism cannot be controlled without a pluralistic approach of teaching to different *Madhahib* (schools of thought, including the *Shi'a*) in the case of Islam for intra-faith understanding and world religions for interfaith understanding. Most of the Sunni *Madaris*, including the Medina Islamic University in Saudi Arabia, do teach the four schools of thought but they prefer to promote their own teachings and reject others, with little or no appreciation of the rival teachings. In some *Madaris*, other schools of thought are even ridiculed (personal observation). The *Shi'a* are taught as *Kafirs* (disbelievers) in some *Madaris*. Teaching of world religions is mostly non-existent. It even receives little attention in the secular universities too.

Some of the people who fought the Afghan war were from the Middle East, and they had great sympathy for the people of Palestine. Before his assassination, Abdullah Azam was heard frequently at Peshawar, Pakistan that they would fight against Israel after defeating the Russians. From this observation alone it is clear that it would be near impossible to bring a positive change through curriculum and teaching alone without just and peaceful resolution of the Palestine and Israel conflict.

The 21st century is the century of religious revival. Inter-faith and intra-faith dialogue are the only ways to keep the revival on the path of moderation. Supporting and promoting both intra- and inter-faith dialogue is a religious duty, a sacred task to fulfill our obligation to God and humanity. Failure in this dialogue will result in a bigger mess and yet more suffering than People of the Book have endured so far. To date the Abrahamic faiths can be held responsible for most of the distress in our present world.

Notes

1 Isma'il R. al-Faruqi, *Islam and Other Faiths*, ed. by Ataullah Siddiqui (UK: Islamic Foundation, 1998) p.74.

2 For details on Prophet treatment of other Prophets see: Muhammad Shafiq and Mohammed Abu-Nimer, *Interfaith Dialogue: A Guide for Muslims* (VA: The International Institute of Islamic Thought, 2007), chapter 4, treating non-Muslims in the light of the Prophet Sirah and Muslim history.

3 This writer himself was head of the Department of Islamic Studies at Peshawar University and taught the course on world religions for several years before he moved to the United Statues permanently in 1997. He was also a member of National Educational Committee on Islamic Studies.

4 For details about the courses on Usul al Din and the Department of Religion go to the International Islamic University website: http://www.iiu.edu.pk/

5 Deoband is a name of a town in India where the first Madrassah was founded soon after the 1857 freedom war known as Mutiny in British history of India. The graduates of this school went back to their homelands and opened schools on the same pattern. The Brelvi system of Madaris is known after Raza Khan of Brelvi in India who disagreed with some of the teachings of the Deoband Madrassah, particularly in reference to the status of the Prophet Muhammad, Sufi Saints and visiting graves etc.

6 Jama'at-i-Islami was founded by Mawlana Abul A'la Maududi just before the partition of the sub-continent into India and Pakistan in 1947. He followed the Deoband School of thought, but differed with it on some religious interpretations. His thoughts influenced college graduates, attracted students and people from the middle class.

7 Ahl al Hadith emphasized the practice of Sunnah of the Prophet and rejected the Madhahib (legal schools of thought like Hanafi, Shafi'i, Maliki and others. The Ahl al Hadith Madaris promoted the Salafi method of teaching by criticizing other schools of thought as deviating from the Sunnah.

8 The writer himself studied in a Madrassah run by the Deoband school of thought and remembers when the teacher would use the word *Daal* (gone astray) and *Mudil* (make others to go astray) for other schools of thought. Once in late 60s a member from the other school of thought led the prayer in our town mosque: when the Imam from the Deobandi school of thought came, he told the people that their prayers had to be repeated because they prayed under instruction from the wrong person.

9 The two groups – Sipah-e-Sahaba and Sipah-e-Muhammad – are banned in

Pakistan today, but the bitterness created by the two groups continues and will take time to heal.

10 Ihsan Ilahi Zaheer was the leader of Ahl al Hadith in Lahore, Pakistan. He published many books against Shi'as calling them as *Kafirs* (disbelievers). He created great controversy and finally he was assassinated. Many believed that he was killed by the Shi'a.

11 Christine Fair, *Islamic Education in Pakistan,* research submitted to the United States Institute of Peace, see <www.usip.org>.

12 The writer himself studied in the Madrassah system of the Deobandi school.

13 This writer was an MA student at the Department of Islamiyat at Peshawar University. We were told that if the graduates of these Madaris were made equivalent to MA in Islamic Studies then most of the jobs would be taken by the Madaris graduates and the university graduates of Islamic Studies would face unemployment. Although I was a Madrassah graduate, I participated in the protests to prevent the Madaris graduates to be recognized as equal.

14 The writer became lecturer in Islamics at Peshawar University in November 1974 after graduation and came to the US in September 1976 for higher education. I returned to Peshawar University in March 1982. Peshawar was the Center of Jihad activities and all forces – Western, Middle Eastern and others – were playing their role.

15 The Movement of Imam Syed Ahmad Shaihid and Isma'il Shahid in the 19th century exposed them to the Wahhabi style of ideology, but the Pashtun rejected it.

16 Abdullah 'Azzam was the key leader of this movement, with Bin Laden supporting him. Bin Laden became known internationally after 'Azzam's assassination.

17 See *The Noble Qur'an*, by Muhammad T al-Hilali and Muhammad Muhsin Khan, published by the King Fahd Complex for the Printing of the Holy Qur'an at Medina, Saudi Arabia and many other such publications.

18 The Arabic word *Muttaqi* (pl. *Muttaqun*) means pity, purity and righteousness. The Muslims love this word and is very attractive to them. Anything that would be against *Taqwa* (purity), good Muslims would resist it. The opponents of interfaith and intra-faith dialogue use such catchy words that appeal to Muslim psyche. No Muslim would like to be labeled as *Shaitan* (Satan), *Kafir* (disbeliever) or to be accused committing a *Bid'ah* (innovation).

19 For Hizb al Tahrir views see its website: <www.hizb-at-tahrir.org>.

20 For details see: <www.muttaqun.com> in reference to interfaith dialogue to understand their point of view.

21 For detailed commentary on this verse, see *Tafsir Ma'arif Al-Qur'an* of Mawlana Mufti Muhammad Shafi' (Karachi: Idara Ma'arif, 1997) or others that present the background of the verse.

22 Bukhari, *Kitab Al-Adab*, hadith number 6169.

23 "As the son of Emperor Humayun, he was born in Umarkot, Sind (now in Pakistan), and succeeded to the throne at the age of 13. He first ruled under a regent, Bairam Khan, who recaptured for the young emperor much of the territory usurped at the death of his father. In 1560, however, Akbar took the government into his own hands. Realizing that Hindu acceptance and cooperation were essential to the successful rule of any Indian empire worthy of that name, he won the allegiance of the Rajputs, the most belligerent Hindus, by a shrewd blend of tolerance, generosity, and force; he himself married two Rajput

princesses. Having thus secured the Hindus, he further enlarged his realm by conquest until it extended from Afghanistan to the Bay of Bengal and from the Himalayas to the Godavari River. Akbar's supreme achievement, however, was the establishment of an efficient administrative system that held the empire together and stimulated trade and economic development." (For reference see: "Akbar," Microsoft(R) Encarta(R) 97 Encyclopedia. © 1993–1996 Microsoft Corporation).

24 For more details on this issue, see Jamal Badawi's article on: "Muslim and Non-Muslim relations: Reflection on Some Qur'anic Texts," <www.islamonline.com>.
25 Isma'il R. Al Faruqi, *Islam and other Faiths*, see Discussion on page 93.
26 Maulana Wahidudin Khan, *Tadhkir al Qur'an* (New Delhi: Maktaba al Risala, 2002).
27 See Tafsir Al Zamakhshari, Tafsir Al Tabari and Tafsir Ibn Kathir in reference to the verse, 2:62.
28 Al-Hilali and Khan, *The Noble Qur'an*, see reference to the verse, 2:62
29 Those who believe that belief on Muhammad commonly quote these and many verses; Al-Qur'an is also essential for all people, they are: 3:19, 3:84, 85, 5:3, and 33:40

Bibliography

Ali, AbdullahYusuf, *The Meaning of the Holy Qur'an* (Maryland: Amana Publication, 1998).
Al Faruqi, Isma'il R., *Islam and other Faiths* (London: Islamic Foundation, 1998).
Al Hilalai, Muhammad T. and Muhammad Muhsin Khan, *The Noble Qur'an* (Riyadh: Darussalam, 1997) .
Al Qardawi Yusuf, *Halal and Haram* (Kuala Lumpur: Islamic Book Trust).
Khan, Maulana Wahidudin, *Tadhkir al Qur'an* (New Delhi: Maktaba al Risala, 2002).
Haykal, The Life of Muhammad, translated by Isma'il R. Al Faruqi (American Trust publications, 1976).
Ismaeel, Saeed, *Muslim and Non-Muslim Relations* (Toronto, Ontario, Canada: Al-Attique International Islamic Publications, 2003).
Maududi, Abu al A'la, *Tafhim al Qur'an* (Lahore: Idara Tarjuman al Qur'an, 1997).
Shafi', Mawlana Mufti Muhammad, *Tafsir Ma'arif Al-Qur'an* (Karachi: Idara Ma'arif, 1997).
Shafiq, Muhammad and Abu Nimer, Mohamed *Interfaith Dialogue: a Guide For Muslims* (Herndon, VA: International Institute of Islamic Thought, 2007).

10

Teaching Islam and Christianity in the Jewish Education System in Israel

ELIE PODEH

This study aims to examine the depiction of Islam and Christianity in Jewish textbooks in Israel. The analysis does not follow a chronological historical sequence, as presented in the textbooks, but rather focuses on certain topics, which deal or engage with Jewish–Muslim and Jewish–Christian encounters throughout history. The research is based on the hermeneutic or descriptive-analytical method, focusing on the disclosure of explicit biases and prejudices found in the text.[1]

Current Israeli history textbooks belong, according to my findings, to the third generation of books. The first two generations contained many biases, distortions and omissions in relation to the presentation of the Other; these were largely eliminated in the third generation. This improvement reflects changes that have recently taken place in Jewish society in general and in the education system in particular.[2]

According to the history curriculum, the history of Islam and Christianity are taught in various stages of history classes both in the secular school system (in Hebrew: "the state school") and in the religious school system (in Hebrew: "the state-religious school") in junior and senior high school. The textbooks also deal with the topic of the "stranger" (in Hebrew: ger) in the context of Bible and oral Torah classes taught in both systems albeit with different emphasis. The textbooks of the ultra-orthodox stream have not been examined as they are not under state supervision.[3]

The term for "other" in Jewish tradition (ger) appears in the Bible 36 times. At each mention, the Jews are commanded to treat the stranger with dignity, wherever he is to be found.[4] Similarly, the teachers' guidance accompanying the textbooks on Bible study points to an interpretation in this spirit. For example, the explanation for the verse "And you shall love the stranger" (Deuteronomy) appears in the teacher's guide to the religious school textbook thus: "Apparently, this should be interpreted that if the Lord of Hosts loves the stranger, then we are obliged all the more to do likewise. Or, as Rabbi Hirsch comments: We must imitate the qualities of the Holy One."[5] The teacher's guide emphasizes that the pupils should draw two main conclusions from the text: "First, that the Torah repeatedly forbids deceiving the stranger. Second, that there is a connection between fear of G-d and the commandment to love the stranger: inasmuch as everything belongs to the Holy One, His commandments are binding."[6] The attitude of Judaism toward strangers is also reflected in the teacher's guide to the textbook on the study of oral Torah in secular high schools. In discussing this theme, the teacher's guide recommends "positioning the commandment to love the stranger, and the pronounced emphasis of the Torah on it, as the focus of the lesson on the Torah verses [dealing with the stranger]."[7]

The attitude to the stranger in Bible and oral Torah classes, therefore, is not biased or distorted, either in the secular or the religious educational approach. However, when the discussion of the "other" shifts from the realm of the abstract to the concrete, the image reflected in the textbooks is far more complex. A good example is the depiction of Abraham in Bible and History classes. Since Abraham is the first Patriarch of the Jewish people and the person to whom God made the promises of giving the land of Cna'an ("the Promised Land"), it is hardly a surprise that his biblical stories (in the book of *Genesis*, chapters 12–25) are extensively studied in various educational stages.[8] Yet, the fact that Abraham plays also an important role in the Islamic and Christian religions has been completely ignored in the textbooks. Thus, the Jewish textbooks convey the message that Abraham "belongs" only to the Jewish religion. Though the reluctance of the Jewish education system to share Abraham with other religions is intelligible, it may be considered as a missed opportunity for discussing the commonalities between what is called "the three Abrahamic religions."

A. The Jewish View of Islam

History textbooks are the main source for the study of the pillars and history of Islam in the Jewish education system. The current textbooks, which belong to the third generation of textbooks in use since the establishment of the state of Israel, date back to the mid-1990s when a revised history curriculum for junior and senior high schools was adopted. The history and the fundamentals of Islam are studied both in secular and religious junior high schools (seventh grade). It is taught in greater depth in senior high school but only in classes for matriculation majors in the subject "History of Islam and the Arabs."

War and Peace in Islam

A textbook for the religious system presents the Islamic religion, *inter alia*, as the "religion of the sword." The following text is quoted by way of illustration:

> A widespread story among Arabs concerns a caliph who declared a jihad against the emperor of Byzantium. The emperor, fearing the Muslims and weary of war, called for the caliph and made him three proposals on the condition that he annul the threat of war: (1) He would pay the caliph all the costs that he had incurred in the war; (2) He would free all the Muslims taken into captivity, without ransom; and (3) He would use imperial funds to reconstruct a Muslim city destroyed by the war. The caliph, unable to decide, bowed down and requested guidance from Allah. At the end of the prayer he replied to the emperor: "Remember what the Qur'an replies in the name of the loyal slave Suleiman to Malakhi Bulkish the queen of Yemen (the reference is to King Solomon and the Queen of Sheba): No matter what you possess, I possess more . . . for if money, gold and every treasure of the realm were held in one hand, and pure faith in God of the heavens were held in the other, the latter would be decisive. And as for your proposal to redeem the captives, the captives in your jail, if their souls and hearts are directed toward heaven and their eyes toward the goodness awaiting them in the next world – they are freed even while in captivity. And if their thoughts are directed toward greed for money and the pleasures of this world – they will be slaves even in their freedom. Thus, there is no reason to redeem them. As for your third proposal, know that that which is built by strangers is destruction. Only Muslims will build their city and only the sword shall decide between us." When the caliph finished speaking, he faced the army and said: "Arise, for Allah has put the enemy in your hands." And indeed the Muslims were victorious over the Christians.[9]

At the end of the story, the pupil is asked to reply to this question: "Examine Chapter 20 of Deuteronomy and write: How must we behave toward a nation that seeks to reach a peace agreement with us?" The selection of this story, and the depiction of it as widespread "among Arabs," imbues it with an importance and centrality beyond its role in Islamic-Arab culture. The text itself conveys an unequivocal message to the pupil regarding the close affinity between war and its role in Islam: Muslim rulers prefer fighting by Allah's command to arriving at peace agreements with an enemy prepared to surrender. The question presented at the end of the text harbors a particularly negative message. Deuteronomy 20:10–13 says:

> When thou drawest nigh unto a city to fight against it, then proclaim peace unto it. And it shall be, if it make thee answer of peace, and open

unto thee, then it shall be, that all the people that are found therein shall become tributary unto thee, and shall serve thee. And if it will make no peace with thee, but will make war against thee, then thou shalt besiege it. And when the Lord thy God delivereth it into thy hand, thou shalt smite every male thereof with the edge of the sword.

Thus, Judaism teaches that if the enemy accepts the conditions of surrender ("if it makes thee answer of peace"), all hostile activity against it must be canceled. If the enemy rejects the conditions, war must be waged and the men must be killed. In other words, while Islam is presented as a religion in which war (*jihad*) is preferable to peace, Judaism is presented as a religion that prefers peace to war.[10]

Muhammad and the Jews

One of the central issues in the depiction of the rise of Islam is Muhammad's attitude toward the Jewish tribes in the Arabian Peninsula. A textbook for religious junior high schools approaches the issue thus:

> Muhammad hoped that belief in Allah would spread from the city of Yathrib [the former name of Medina], for Jewish tribes lived there as well and they would help him spread the belief in one god. However, the Jews of Yathrib distanced themselves from Muhammad and were therefore persecuted by him. In one clash, Muhammad's followers killed all the men in one of the Jewish tribes and sold the women and children into slavery. Muhammad divided the property of the Jewish tribes among his followers.
> Three Jewish tribes lived in Medina, the Prophet's city. Under orders from Muhammad, his followers expelled two tribes [the reference is to the Qaynuqa' and Nadir tribes]. The members of the third tribe [the reference is to the Qurayza tribe] were killed by the sword. Muhammad also accused the Jews of straying from the path of God. According to him, the Jews adulterated the holy books and inserted errors in them. Muhammad distanced himself from the Jews and altered customs that imitated Jewish customs. . . . Yet, after Muhammad established himself in Medina and managed to disseminate his faith in the Arabian Peninsula, he changed his attitude toward the Jews. Muhammad promised them that he would protect their lives and property on condition that they recognize his rule and pay taxes to him.[11]

The following two passages are taken from two other textbooks, which are used in secular junior high schools:

> Up until the rise of Islam, the status of the Jews in the Arabian Peninsula

was reasonably good. . . . When Muhammad began to spread his doctrine, he sought support for it from the Jews as well, but they rejected the new message and ridiculed its messenger. Once he acquired enough power and took control of Medina, Muhammad demanded that the Jews convert to Islam. When they refused, he accused them of falsifying God's Torah and making additions to it. Gradually, certain Jews whom Muhammad and his followers hated were murdered, and eventually two of the Jewish tribes (the Qaynuqa' and the Nadir) were expelled. The third tribe (the Qurayza) was massacred. Both in the Qur'an and in later tradition the attitude toward the Jew was alienating and contemptuous, reflecting the desire to block any Jewish influence on faithful Muslims.[12]

Muhammad, in his pronouncements, claimed that he was not establishing a new religion and that his mission as a prophet coalesced with and completed that of Moses and Jesus. In his view, the Jews and the Christians had not properly preserved the holy book that was given to them by God and he was therefore bringing another holy book from God, in Arabic. At first, Muhammad allowed the Jewish tribes in Medina to practice the commandments of their religion and promised to protect them. Muhammad anticipated that the Jews, too, would join Islam and expected them to use them in spreading his religion. . . . When the Jews did not join him, he altered some of the commandments he had laid down: he instructed Muslims to pray facing Mecca, to fast for one month each year, and to pray communally every Friday at noon. Muhammad also changed his attitude to the Jews and began fighting the Jewish tribes living in Medina. As a result, two tribes were forced to leave the city, abandoning all their property. Some of the tribespeople who left Medina settled in Khaybar; others migrated to Syria, Babylonia and the Jericho area. The fate of the third tribe, the Quraytha, which waged war against Muhammad, was different: the men of the tribe were murdered, while the women and children were sold as slaves. Thereafter, Muhammad set out to fight the Jewish tribes in Khaybar. They surrendered and were ordered to hand over half their produce to the Muslims. The Jews of Khaybar continued to keep the customs of their religion.[13]

The attitude of Islam and of Muhammad to the Jews is presented ambiguously in the religious school textbook referred to above (*From Generation to Generation*, II). Two sources are quoted at the end of the chapter dealing with the attitude of Islam to Judaism. One is the Qur'an: "Make war against those who will not believe in God and his messenger . . . those to whom the book was given, until they bring the tax in their hand and become humbled." (Qur'an 9:29) The second is a writ sent by Muhammad to the Jews: "And it shall come to pass when this letter reaches you you shall live securely, God's patronage and the patronage if His messenger (Muhammad) will be extended to you . . . for God's messenger will protect you . . . " (taken from B. Z. Dinur, "Israel in the Diaspora," 19, Hebrew).[14]

The description of Muhammad's attitude to the Jewish tribes is fairly similar in all three textbooks referred to above. It is presented factually, even dryly, and therefore ostensibly without biases. The first two books deal with the "expulsion" of the tribes, while the third book claims that two tribes "were forced to leave the city."[15] With this, a pronounced bias in this context seems to be the absence of a comprehensive explanation of Muhammad's behavior toward the Jews. Muhammad first approached the Jews in the expectation of assistance from them in light of their wealth and their religious proclivity toward him in his fight against the infidels of the Qurayish tribe. When the Jews refused to convert to Islam, Muhammad expelled or exiled two Jewish tribes with the intention of taking over their assets, which enabled him to mount a war against the infidels in the Arabia Peninsula and establish a homogeneous Muslim community. The destruction of the Quraytha was undoubtedly an exceptional act. Goitein, in attempting to assess the event historically, wrote that "It was the simple law of war: the enemy is condemned to death and the women and children to slavery. This rule was accepted in the Jewish and Muslim formal legal tradition."[16]

French historian Claude Cahen wrote in this connection that "there was a basis for Muhammad's hope that he could gain the support of Medina's Jews. However, when this expectation was disappointed, he acted against them, alternating between attacks and diplomacy, until the Jews were removed from the city, whether by the sword or through emigration."[17] Another analysis holds that "Muhammad's wars against the Jews were not a goal in themselves but a part of his wars against the population of Mecca. Every time a war against the Meccans ended – whether successfully or in failure – the Jews fell victim to exile . . . or slaughter."[18]

In the absence of these explanations, which provide the historical context for Muhammad's activity, his behavior is perceived as particularly anti-Jewish. Notably, in light of the good neighborly relations that were the norm between Jews and Arabs before the appearance of Muhammad, many Arabs expressed regret at the exodus of the Jews.[19] Lastly, the ambiguous presentation of the attitude of Islam toward the Jews, as it appears in the religious school textbook discussed above, obscure the position of Islam toward Judaism by attaching the same importance to two conflicting sources that it quotes.

The Sanctity of Jerusalem in Islam

The sensitive, politically significant topic of the status and role of Jerusalem in Islam is in fact presented in a reasonably balanced fashion. Following are two treatments of the subject in the junior high school textbooks for the religious and the secular school systems, respectively:

> In the course of time, Jerusalem became the holy city for Muslims, too. According to Muslim tradition, Muhammad flew from Mecca to

Jerusalem on a magic horse named *Al-Buraq*. Muhammad tied the horse to one of the stones of the Western Wall and ascended on foot to the top of the Temple Mount. From there he rose up to heaven and brought the Qur'an back to earth. After the Arabs conquered Eretz Yisrael, they built the dome of the Rock (popularly called the Mosque of Omar) on the spot from which Muhammad rose to heaven, according to their tradition, and on a spot further away, where Muhammad alighted on the Temple Mount, they built the outer mosque – the al-Aqsa Mosque. [The pupil is questioned on this segment thus: "Jews call the sole remnant of our Temple the Western Wall. Christians call it the Wailing Wall, and Muslims – Al-Buraq. What is the explanation for each of these names?"][20]

According to Muslim tradition, Muhammad at first instructed Muslims to pray facing Jerusalem and only later decided that they should pray facing Mecca. Jerusalem is not mentioned by name in the Qur'an [a note adds: A hint of Jerusalem is to be found in Sura 17:1: "Blessed be His name whose servant was flown by night from the Holy Mosque (in Mecca) to the mosque at the furthest extreme." Muslim exegetes explain that the words "the mosque at the furthest extreme" signify the al-Aqsa Mosque in Jerusalem, but what is recounted is that Muhammad flew from Mecca on his magic beast *Al-Burak* – who had a human head, the body of a horse and wings. . . . Toward the end of the 7th century, Caliph Abd al-Malik built the dome of the Rock structure in Jerusalem [called the Mosque of Omar]. Abd al-Malik hoped that Jerusalem would replace Mecca, which was controlled by his opponents, and would become a center for Muslims. He saw many grand churches in Jerusalem and apparently wanted to build a structure that was more beautiful than the churches and that would serve as a source of pride for the Muslim faithful. His son, al-Walid, built the al-Aqsa Mosque south of the Dome of the Rock. The construction of the al-Aqsa Mosque enhanced the holiness of Jerusalem in the eyes of the Muslims. . . . The construction of the Dome of the Rock and the al-Aqsa Mosque did not prevent the Jews from praying at the Western Wall and the Temple Mount. Muslim sources testify that Abd al-Malik appointed ten Jewish families as custodians of the Dome of the Rock, including craftsmen who produced goblets, candles, lamps and wicks for the use of the Muslims. In return, these Jews and their children were exempt from the payment of all taxes.[21]

The formulation of the historical narrative above obliquely conveys a sense of the superiority of Jerusalem in Judaism as compared to its role in Islam, in that Jerusalem's holiness is not directly mentioned in Islamic sources but is referred to only indirectly, by means of Muslim exegesis for the Qur'anic verse "the mosque at the furthest extreme." It would have been more appropriate to add that regardless of the historic facts, Jerusalem is perceived as holy by Muslims. Hava Lazarus-Yaffe has written, in this connection, that "in the course of generations, [Muhammad's] legendary voyage has been accepted as historic fact and not as a dream or a vision." Therefore, she continues, "there is no longer any reason to question the holiness of Jerusalem in Islam, for the religious legend struck the deepest possible roots in it, and surely the force of religious truths is not necessarily nurtured by historic truths but by the extent of the belief they elicit. Thus, the holiness of Jerusalem to Islam is undoubtedly fact."[22]

Jewish–Muslim Relations ("The Covenant of Omar")

The main issue dealt with by the textbooks in this context is the regulations of Caliph Omar II, which determined the status of protected persons under the rule of Islam. It is worded thus in the junior high school textbook for the religious school system:

> These laws forbade protected persons to bear arms, ride horses, conduct religious ceremonies in public and build new houses of worship. Protected persons were required to wear special clothing to distinguish them from Muslims, and were forbidden to serve in offices that would give them control over Muslims. These regulations imposed severe limitations on the Jews, although most rulers did not implement them strictly. They would rather be aided by the Jews and make use of their talents for their own and their kingdom's benefit.[23]

Another volume of this textbook states that "the status of the Jews in the Islamic lands was also determined by Omar's laws. These were laws compiled in a single document, apparently at the beginning of the 8th century. Their intent was to elevate the Muslims and denigrate the protected persons – the Jews and Christians."[24] The junior high school textbook for the secular school system words this as follows:

> Following the conquest of the northern Arabian Peninsula and southern Eretz Yisrael (632), the conquerors designated the status of the Jews (as well as of the Christians) for generations to come as part of the *conditions of surrender* [emphasis mine]: The status of the Jews and the Christians was indeed inferior, yet in exchange for a head tax (*jizya*) which they were obliged to pay, the Jews became persons protected against all harm (*dhimmi*). These conditions were established as a tradition with the validity of a religious commandment in Islam.[25]

These passages teach the pupil, whether obliquely or directly, that "conditions" were imposed by the Muslims on the protected persons. The textbook for secular schools terms these rules "conditions of surrender." In contrast, Muslims view this document as a kind of "alliance" or "contract" (this is also the translation of the term used in Arabic, *'ahd*) – an arrangement that anchors relations between the Muslim ruler and minority groups in a legal framework, with the use of the term "protected persons" designed to preserve the dignity of such groups. Furthermore, the material in the textbooks implies that the Jews were a primary factor in the fixing of the regulations, although they were intended for the benefit of all the non-Muslim monotheistic religions generally and in this context were applied to the Jews as well. The textbook for the secular schools minimizes this fact in particular, implying that these regulations were directed first and foremost against the Jews. Additionally, this textbook, in contrast to the textbook for religious schools, neglects to point out that in many cases the Muslim rulers did not implement these regulations.

The fact that Muslim commentary on the Covenant of Omar differs from Jewish (or Christian) commentary is not surprising.[26] However, the textbook should have mentioned the contradiction between the Muslim perception, which views the document as an expression of Islam's manifold tolerance for the stranger, and the Jewish perception, which views it at least partially as a reflection of discrimination and arrogance. Moreover, since the implementation of the regulations was largely dependent on the ruler, broad generalizations regarding the attitude of "Islam" toward the Jews cannot be made. Rather, each aspect of the issue should be considered on its merits – whether in the geographic or the chronological realm. In this context, Lazarus-Yaffe observed that "much has been written about their discriminatory laws, but occasionally the fact has been emphasized that even though the 'contract' was a kind of corpus of governmental regulations imposed on 'protected persons,' the Muslims, for their part, did obligate themselves to discharge their part of the 'alliance.'"[27] Furthermore, in her view, the document does not reflect the true reality of the status of the Christians and the Jews under Muslim rule so much as it reflects the "ideal" of their inferior and degraded status.[28]

In addition to the above, the textbooks are singularly lacking in any reference to the inadvisability of judging the past through the conceptual prism of the present. Since Islamic society did not pretend to be egalitarian, Jewish society did not expect, and could not have expected, such treatment under Islamic rule.[29]

Judaism between Islam and Christianity

The Jews passed under Christian and Muslim rule intermittently during various periods. These conditions inevitably led to comparisons between their situation under both these types of governance, invariably portraying Islam as more tolerant than Christianity. The textbook for the secular junior high schools states: "Generally, Islam was more tolerant than Christianity. Muslim rulers protected the autonomy of the monotheistic religious groups, and persecution based on religion was unusual."[30] Elsewhere, the text states: "The Muslim conquest greatly eased the situation of the Jews wherever they lived.

Following a short period of uncertainty regarding the status of the non-Muslims, the new rulers adopted a policy of religious tolerance. For the Jews, the conquest ushered in a period of unprecedented prosperity."[31]

Another textbook for the secular school system also describes the condition of the Jews both in Jerusalem and in Spain under the Muslim conquest in a more positive light than that during the period of Christian rule.[32] The teacher's guide for this book presents a comparative table depicting Jewish life in Spain under Muslim and under Christian rule. Two items appear under the heading "Confrontation and Struggle" during the period of Muslim rule: the al-Muwahhidun Affair and the murder of Jehoseph (see below), while under Christian rule the list cites "religious disputations, the massacres of 1391, the Inquisition, forced converts and Marranos, expulsion from cities, expulsion from the country" (see also the analysis of Christianity in the textbooks, below).[33] When manifestations of hatred and violence did appear in Muslim-controlled Spain, they are portrayed as the exception, e.g.:

> Between the tenth and the end of the eleventh centuries, the Jews of Muslim Spain enjoyed a period of prosperity. . . . The Jews attained wealth, but their success evoked envy and hatred, which erupted on occasion (albeit rarely) in bloody riots. For example, hostility toward Samuel Hanagid broke out during the time of his son Jehoseph, and a great massacre of the Jews of Granada occurred.[34]

The situation changes in depicting the reasons for the departure of the Jews from Andulasia, namely that the Golden Age came to an end with the invasion (in 1146) of the Muwahhidun, a "fanatic Muslim sect from North Africa [who] instituted religious coercion in the areas under their rule and ordered the annihilation of non-Muslims."[35] Indeed, the accepted premise regarding the history of the Jews of the Maghrib is that there was only one case of "mass organized persecution." Notably, moreover, the toll among the Jews was less severe than among the Christians, while the Muwahhidun also killed many Muslims who were suspected of deviating from pure Islam. In any case, there is no resemblance between this example of persecution and expulsion and such acts ordered under Christian rule in Europe (see below).[36] This issue, then, appears to be presented in a balanced fashion in the textbooks.

The Jews under Islamic Rule

The textbooks deal with three issues that fall under this category: the condition of the Jews in the Ottoman Empire; the condition of the Jews in Eretz Yisrael under Mamluk and Ottoman rule; and the condition of the Jews in Morocco, Persia and Yemen.

In the first case, all the textbooks (both for the secular and the religious school systems) emphasize the tolerance displayed by the Ottoman rulers toward the conquered peoples generally and the Jews in particular. For example, the junior high school textbook for religious schools states that "the sultan issued an order permitting the exiles [from Spain] to enter and reside in his country. Moreover, he warned the inhabitants of his country that 'no governors of his towns would be allowed to mistreat the Jews or expel them; but rather all were to welcome them properly and, should they fail to do so, they should be executed.'"[37]

The other two topics appear primarily in the textbook for religious schools, which is not surprising in light of the emphasis in this book on the study of Jewish history and Eretz Yisrael. The situation in Eretz Yisrael at the start of the Mamluk period, a short while after the termination of the Crusader Kingdom, is described by means of an extract from a letter by Maimonides to his son written in 1267 after the father settled in the city of Acre: "The desolation and barrenness [of the country] is great and, to sum up, he who is more blessed than his friends destroys more than his friend."[38] Another, more detailed description of Mamluk rule is also provided:

> For the Mamluks, Eretz Yisrael was a land beyond Egypt in the Syrian territories under their control, and they did not therefore bother to reha-bilitate or develop it. Neglect and desolation were evident, especially along the coastal plain, which in the past had been heavily populated and in their day was deserted. Even great port cities such as Jaffa and Acre were reduced to ruins or had become impoverished villages. Destruction and desolation were apparent in Jerusalem, too. The city had no walls, and a livelihood was hard to come by. Only a handful of tenacious Jews resided there. However, when Rabbi Ovadiah from Bartinuro in northern Italy, known as Rabbi Ovadiah of Bartinuro, immigrated to the land (1488), a certain revival occurred in the city. The synagogues in the city filled with worshippers [and] study at the city's yeshiva was renewed. . . . Still, despite his efforts to restore the city to its past glory, he did not succeed in turning it into a major Jewish center. Jerusalem, which was holy to other religions too, attracted many believers, and riots and neigh-bors' quarrels broke out between them. The Muslim rulers of the city even limited the number of Jews permitted to live in Jerusalem.[39]

In contrast to the desolation described during the Mamluk period, the Ottomans were portrayed as "investing great effort in developing the country." However, this aspect is overshadowed by a long description of developments in the Jewish community during the Ottoman period, such as the emergence of Safed and Tiberius as important religious centers and the attempt to revive the Sanhedrin (the ancient juridical–legislative assembly of 71 ordained scholars).[40] Furthermore, Eretz Yisrael had become a destination for the forced converts from Spain:

In their view, the Ottomans' successes and the Christians' failures were signs from heaven of the impending arrival of the Messiah. They believed that whoever settled in Eretz Yisrael would be privileged to be among the first to welcome the Messiah. This faith impelled many to leave their homes in the Diaspora and settle in the land. They were certain that dwelling in Eretz Yisrael would help them purify themselves from the defilement of the Diaspora, especially from the years of forced conversion when they pretended to be Christians.[41]

The negative tone in the depiction of the Mamluk period, side by side with the disregard of the role of the Muslims in Eretz Yisrael during the entire Ottoman period, are meant to emphasize that in contrast to the various Muslim conquerors, who treated Eretz Yisrael with a measure of contempt, the Jews consistently viewed it as the center of their world and made strenuous efforts to settle and develop it throughout their history.

The third topic concerning the Jews under Islamic rule relates to a description of the conditions of the Jews in three countries not part of the Ottoman Empire – Morocco, Persia and Yemen. Following are passages from the textbook for religious schools:

> Beginning in the 16th century, the rulers of Morocco, influenced by the religious leadership, adopted measures designed to degrade heretics. For example, the Jews of Morocco were obliged to remove their shoes each time they passed a mosque or the home of a Muslim dignitary. A Jew was obliged to bow to a Muslim who passed in the street, bless him and give him the right of way. The French consul in Morocco described the condition of the Jews in the country thus: "The lowest of Muslims believes that he is permitted to mistreat Jews, and no Jew dares defend himself because the Qur'an and the judge always justify the Muslim." An English priest who visited Morocco wrote in the same spirit: "The present condition [of the Jews] under Muslim rule is nothing but a refined version of slavery . . . "
>
> The rulers of Morocco isolated the city Jews from their Muslim neighbors. They settled them in special neighborhoods surrounded by a wall. At night, the gates of the neighborhood were locked, with no possibility of leaving or entering. Living conditions in the closed neighborhood – the *mallah* – were harsh and crowding was extensive. The water supply was poor and fires broke out periodically, destroying all the dilapidated buildings. A Jewish writer described the mallah thus: "The dimensions of the *mallah* were minimal, approximately a kilometer long by a kilometer wide. Not a single public park was to be found in it. . . . The sun's rays would penetrate most of the narrow, dark alleys for only a few moments of the day." Sometimes, an incited crowd would burst into the *mallah* and attack and loot the Jews who lived there.[42]

The fate of the Jews of Yemen and Persia was even more difficult than that of their brethren in Morocco. Both these countries were ruled by the Shi'a. They believed that heretics were contaminated (najis) and therefore imposed degrading restrictions on them. For example, Jews in Persia were forbidden to walk about in the rain lest they step in a puddle and splash Muslim passers-by, thereby contaminating them. In Yemen, the Jews were forbidden to wear [proper] headgear but could only cover their head with a piece of cloth of a color different from that of their Muslim neighbors.

The event carved in the memory of the Jews of Yemen above all others occurred in 1648. In that year, the governor of the city of San'a in Yemen ordered all the Jews in the city to convert to Islam or leave their homes. The Jews of San'a refused to convert and were expelled to Muzah, a barren, blazingly hot plain along the Red Sea. Many of the San'a Jews died on the way to exile or once they arrived in Muzah, but those who survived were recalled to the city. The Arabs in San'a had pressured the governor to annul the expulsion order, for they found it difficult to live in the city without the Jewish craftsmen.[43]

The discussion of the condition of the Jews in Morocco, Persia and Yemen supports the recommendation (made above) to present the complex position of the Jews under Islamic rule not in broad generalization but by means of concrete historic examples. Moreover, the long description of the condition of the Jews in these three countries, side by side with the brief description of the "harmony" that prevailed throughout the Ottoman Empire, is distinctly disproportionate.[44] A reverse disproportion exists in the texts for the secular school system, which present the Ottoman period in a positive light but do not deal with the condition of the Jews in the Islamic countries outside the Ottoman Empire.[45]

B. The Jewish View of Christianity

As is the case for the study of Islam, history textbooks constitute a primary source for learning about Christianity in the Jewish school system. These books were published during the mid-1990s in tandem with the new history curriculum established for junior and senior high schools. The historic and religious principles of Christianity are taught in both the secular and religious junior high schools at seventh and eighth grades. In contrast to the method of teaching about Islam, however, the method of teaching about Christianity in the Jewish school system has never been examined academically. Yet, it would not seem an exaggeration to contend that the older-generation textbooks were laden with biases, distortions and omissions in the presentation of Christianity – as was the case in the presentation of Islam – in comparison with the improved situation of today's textbooks.[46] Seven topics illustrating how Christianity is learned in the Jewish school system are discussed below.

Jesus and the Early Christianity

The founding of the Christian religion is described in the textbook in a factual and balanced fashion.[47] However, the discussion in the textbook for religious schools is presented as part of the ancient dispute between Christianity and Judaism. Jesus is presented as someone who was "born Jewish and during his entire lifetime felt himself to be a Jew and apparently did not think of establishing a new religion." By contrast, Paul, "although born a Jew, deviated from Judaism. He believed that after the appearance of Jesus there was no longer any need to observe the practical commandments, for faith in Jesus was the essence."[48] In order to prove that the Christians drew their inspiration from the Jews, the pupil is given an exercise titled "From Whom Did the Christians Learn?" as follows:

> Persecution by the Roman caesars created a dilemma for the Christians: should they deny their religion, or sacrifice their lives for it? They responded to this through drawings. Here are pictures of Daniel in the lions' den, and Hananya, Mishael and Azarya in the furnace. Answer these questions: (1) Why did the Christians often draw these particular characters? (2) Read Chapter 3 of the Book of Daniel. What was the reason that Hananya, Mishael and Azarya were thrown into the furnace? (3) Read Chapter 6 of the Book of Daniel. How was Daniel saved from the lions' den? (4) List the names of other figures from our history who could have served as a shining example of the sanctification of the Lord to Christians.[49]

By reading from the Book of Daniel, the pupil is expected to understand that these Jewish figures, who were thrown into the furnace for their unwillingness to bow down to the image of Nebuchadnezzar, constitute a shining example for Christians. Daniel, who was saved from the lions' den after praying to God continuously, constitutes a particular example to Christians because many of them were thrown into lions' dens in Roman times. The pupil is then asked:

> The heretics (the Christians) say of the length of our exile that (it is because) we do not believe in Jesus' Torah. We answer them: "Why was there an exile before Jesus was born? Additionally: . . . that G-d ordered us to be scattered in the lands of the Gentiles because we abandoned the Torah of our Lord, his commandments and his laws, and not because of Jesus' sin or any other reason." (a) How do the Christians explain the exile of Israel? (b) How do Jews negate the Christians' arguments? (c) Find explanations for Israel's exile in the Bible or in sayings by our Sages of Blessed Memory.

This passage, too, is part of the religio-historic disputation between the Jews and Christians. The pupil learns the Christian argument, but in tandem he/she is guided as to how to respond to it and, with the help of the teacher, to locate additional explanations for Israel's exile in the Bible and the Sages literature.[50]

The textbook for the secular system offers a balanced account of the adoption of Christianity by the Roman Empire.[51] The textbook for the religious system, however, emphasized the various discriminatory measures were implemented toward the Jews. The textbook for the religious school system writes in this context:

> The Jewish religion alone merited a special attitude in the empire. The
> Jews were not pagans and were also not Christians who had deviated
> from the path. . . . The Jews' crime, in the Christian perception, was that
> they did not understand that the time had come to change their customs
> and give up their religion. The church, therefore, did not prohibit the Jews
> from observing the commandments of their religion, and the ceasars even
> reaffirmed that Judaism was a permissible religion in the empire. . . .
> Nevertheless, discriminatory laws were issued against them. The Church
> fathers wrote that due to the refusal of the Jews to believe in Jesus, the
> Jews of every generation are partners in the crime of the killing of Jesus
> and for this they must bear punishment. Like Cain, who was sentenced to
> wander forever because of his sin of killing Abel, all the Jews, who sinned
> by killing Jesus, must wander. One of the Church fathers quoted the verse:
> "Slay them not, lest my people forget, make them wander to and fro by
> Thy power, and bring them down . . . " (Psalms 59:12), explaining: killing
> the Jews is forbidden, but they must be made to wander, so that the
> Christians will see their degraded condition and will understand that their
> Christian religion is the true religion. In this spirit, the Church determined
> that the Jews must be degraded and depressed, ruled and not rulers, the
> subjects of commands and not the commanders. Thus, Jews may not hold
> public office or governmental posts, or serve in the Roman army. The
> harsh attitude of the Christian Church toward the Jews also influenced the
> rulers, and the prohibitions issued by church synods were approved by the
> caesars and quickly became law.[52]

In an effort to underscore the power of the Church, the text explains that "even what was permitted to the Jews by law was not always protected" by the caesars. This issue is illustrated by a story about a caesar permitting the reconstruction of a synagogue destroyed by Christian ruffians. The bishop reacted thus, according to the story:

> The honor of the Lord is offended by Caesar's order to rebuild the Jewish
> synagogue. For soon the Jews will rejoice over the downfall that they
> caused the Christian people and they will engrave this inscription on their
> synagogue: The Temple of Heresy Built From Christian Spoils. And should
> you say that you cannot rescind – on the contrary, rise up, go out, and

annul your decision! The bishop's words impressed the caesar so deeply, that he was filled with remorse and confessed his sins. The bishop gave him a penance and forgave him his sins. The great Roman Empire had surrendered to the Christian Church![53]

The condition of the Jews under Christian rule during the early centuries AD is described slightly differently in three passages in the textbook for the secular schools:

> The attitude of Christianity toward the Jews is complex. The Church claims that in the past the Jews were indeed God's chosen people, but because they rejected Jesus, this chosen status passed to the Christians. The Jews must be punished for their attitude toward Jesus, yet the fact of their existence as a people testifies to the truth of the prophecies that appear in the Old Testament. The Jews, thus, are a witness people and therefore may not be killed. Side by side with this attitude, however, there was great hostility and even hatred. The Jews, too, for their part, hated the Christians as well and ridiculed them . . .
>
> This view of the Jews as a witness people – i.e., a people that by its very existence bears witness to the veracity of Christianity – is what allowed the Jews to continue to exist among the Christians in the West despite the grave indictment of them – the murder of God. Yet, Christian "tolerance" was accompanied by great hostility and even hatred toward the Jews. The Jews, too, for their part, hated the Christians and ridiculed them. The story of Jewish history under Christian rule is a story of a complex and difficult relationship between the "elder brother" (the Jews) and the "younger brother" (the Christians). . . .
>
> The Jews [in the Ashkenaz lands, i.e., in Germany] comprised one grouping in the mosaic of groups and classes of Middle Ages society. Up until the first Crusade, and perhaps for a certain period thereafter, their condition was good and their social status secure.[54]

The main problem that stems from all these descriptions relates not so much to the information contained in the textbook but to that which was omitted. Several issues should have been emphasized. First, the laws issued by the caesars were not aimed at the Jews alone but against various other minorities, including pagans. Second, the main reason that prompted Christianity to issue these laws related to its desire to protect itself from foreign competition and influence by means of undermining the character of rival religions. Judaism was perceived as especially threatening to Christianity because of the complex interrelationship that existed between the two religions during the early period of the spread of Christianity.[55] On the opposite side, Judaism, too, attempted to protect itself, for example by incorporating the prayer composed by Rabbi Gamliel de-legitimizing apostates and slanderers so as to "distance Jews who converted to Christianity from the synagogue."[56] Third, despite the existence of discriminatory laws against the Jews, the many gaps between Christian doctrine and reality should be highlighted, namely, a substantial proportion of Church prohibitions were not implemented by the secular rulers. Generally, the condition of the Jews in Christian society until the crusaders was good, especially in comparison with other minorities.[57] This fact is not mentioned in the textbook for religious schools and is insufficiently emphasized in the textbook for secular schools. Lastly, the interrelationship between the Jews and the Christians should be analyzed through the prism of the early centuries – i.e., during a period when injustice and violence were permanent features of society. Even so, the Church tended to attain the baptism of Jews by persuasion rather than force or violence.

The Jews and the Crusades

The description in the textbooks of the condition of the Jews during the crusader period is exemplified by the events known as the "Massacres of 1096." The textbook for religious schools portrays the Jewish community in France as "facing the choice of conversion or death. Some [were] converted by force but most stood fast and were killed as martyrs at the hands of the rioters."[58] The massacre that took place in Worms, Germany, is depicted thus:

> The rioters shouted at every Jew who was caught: "Christianity or death." One by one, the Jews chose death. The bodies of those killed were thrown out of windows into the street. Torah scrolls were burned to shreds. The crusaders competed amongst each other over who could kill more Jews. A widespread rumor had it that the Pope promised the pardon of sins to anyone who killed even a single Jew. . . . The number of fatalities mounted. But not all the Jews were killed by the crusaders. The rioters snatched Jewish children, brought them to the church and baptized them.[59]

The textbook also quotes from sources in *The Book of Edicts Against the Jewish Communities of Ashkenaz and France* (A. M. Haberman, 1946, Hebrew): "Then they justified their judgment and trusted their instinct . . . and took their children and slaughtered them as martyrs to the revered and awesome G-d . . . and all . . . blessed G-d with all their heart and with a willing mind slaughtered one another, young boys and virgins, old men and old women."[60] The textbook also presents the legend that grew up around the writer of the liturgical hymn *Oonetanneh Tokef* ("Let us tell the mighty holiness of this day"), written by Rabbi Amnon of Mainz, which became part of the Ashkenazi High Holiday prayer service. Amnon was tortured by the local bishop for resisting baptism. "When they began amputating his legs at the joints, they would ask him before cutting into each joint whether he wanted to convert, and he would reply 'no.' At the end, the bishop ordered that Rabbi

Amnon be laid on a bed with all the joints of his legs placed next to him, and thus they sent him to his home.[61] At the end of the chapter, the pupil is asked: "It may be argued that the brave death of the Jews triumphed over the crusaders. What is your opinion?"[62]

A similar description of the condition of the Jews is given in the textbook for the secular schools:

> The preachers called upon the crusaders to force the Jews to be baptized, and if they refused – to kill them. They argued: What is the point of going to war with the defilers of the Messiah's grave in the East, when the murderers of the Messiah live amidst the Christians in the West? And the crusaders indeed attacked the [Jewish] communities and massacred those who refused to convert.[63]

This textbook, too, quotes a passage from a historical source taken from *The Book of Edicts Against the Jewish Communities of Ashkenaz and France*:

> And the enemies rose up against them and killed children and women, boys and old men, in a single day, they did not favor *kohanim* (priests), they did not spare old people, they took no pity on infants, they showed no mercy for pregnant women, they left no survivor. . . . For all of them called for martyrdom, and even when the enemy was upon them they all shouted loudly with one heart and one voice: "Hear, o Israel, the Lord our God the Lord is one."[64]

In contrast to the textbook for religious schools, however, the textbook for the secular system emphasizes that

> the Jew-hatred that burst out during the First Crusade was a new phenomenon, as was the popular Crusade itself. . . . The crusaders viewed the Jews of their time as murderers of Jesus. The death of the Christian Messiah was not a remote matter a thousand years old but a terrible injustice against which it was not too late to erase. This was the first time that the Jews in the West were subjected to large-scale massacres.[65]

The description of the capture of Jerusalem by the crusaders relates to the condition of the Jews in the city, both directly and indirectly. The textbook for the secular schools quotes the following passage from a source written by an anonymous crusader who depicts the conquest in emotional terms:

> Our men pursued them [the defenders of the city] until Solomon's Temple and did much killing of them. The slaughter here was so great, that our men waded in blood up to their ankles. . . . Our men spread out throughout the whole city, looted gold and silver, horses and donkeys, conquering houses filled with all manner of good things. [Afterward] they

all hurried, with tears of joy in their eyes, to the grave of our Redeemer
Jesus, to honor Him and avenge the main debt. . . . A massacre of heretics
such as this had never been heard of or seen heretofore.[66]

At the end of the passage, the pupil is asked: "What impressed you most about
the testimony in this document?" At the end of the chapter, the pupil is asked
additionally: "Jerusalem was captured by Muslims in the seventh century and
by Christians in the eleventh century. Compare the attitude of the Muslims
toward the residents of Jerusalem with that of the Christians."[67] Both these
questions are clearly biased, as they lead the pupil to emphasize the intensity
of the hatred and violence of the Christians in comparison with the behavior
of the Muslims. By contrast, another textbook for secular schools notes that
"during the conquest of Jerusalem Jews were massacred not because of their
religion but because they took part in defending the city . . . The Jews had the
benefit of autonomy and were not subjected to persecution."[68]

The Expulsion of the Jews from England, France and Germany

The expulsion of the Jews from England (1290), France (1306) and Germany
(the fifteenth and early sixteenth centuries), side by side with the legislation
by the Church of laws designed to discriminate against the Jews, constitute
the climax of a period of Jewish suffering under Christian rule that began in
the late Middle Ages and lasted until the start of the Renaissance. The textbooks written for the secular school system describe this period in detail:

> Incitement, a satanic image and horror stories – all these contributed to
> the growing isolation of the Jews in Christian society. . . . Jewish history in
> the West in the fourteenth century is a tragic story of calamities. . .
>   The disturbances of the First Crusade did not have a lasting impact.
> The massacres were perceived as an exceptional outburst by an inflamed
> mob and not as a significant change in Christian policy. . . .
>   In the wake of the religious revival in Christian society, the faithful
> resumed reading the New Testament, highlighting the suffering and death
> of Jesus. The Jews, they claimed, were responsible, which called for more
> concerted efforts at isolating and degrading them . . .
>   The Church helped fan the hatred and denounced money-lending for
> interest as an obscenity. . . .
>   Apostates familiarized the Christians with the existence of the Talmud
> and translated passages for them that described, for example, Jesus
> burning in hell in boiling excrement. . . . The first reaction of the educated
> [Christians] was surprise and hostility . . . [and] the burning of the Talmud
> in France. . . .
>   Highly negative images of the Jews were widespread in all strata of
> society. From the twelfth century onward, the Jews were accused of the

ritual murder of Christian children and the use of their blood for various purposes. . . . Stories about the stench emitted by Jews were widely circulated among the people. The concept of the "Jewish nose" emerged, along with the image of the Jew as a Satan-worshipper. The Jew became a scapegoat. . . . Incitement, satanic image and horror stories – all contributed to the growing isolation of the Jews in Christian society.[69]

One of the textbooks for secular schools lays particular emphasis on the subject of blood libels:

> Side by side with the development of closer relations between Jews and their neighbors, the libeling of Jews intensified. This slander stemmed from ignorance, popular superstition and incitement by priests and monks. . . . The libels entrenched the tendency by Christians to view the Jews as linked with Satan. Jews were depicted in distorted images with a tail and a goat's beard – as Satan was sometimes portrayed. . . . The most widespread libel amongst the Christians was the blood libel, according to which the Jews were accused of kidnapping Christian children before Passover and using their blood in the baking of matza. Believers in the blood libels claimed that in so doing the Jews were re-enacting the murder of Jesus, who, according to their faith, was crucified during Passover by the Jews, and in this way they disparaged the Christians. . . . The popes issued decrees denouncing the blood libels, and the libels were not widespread in the areas under papal control. However, the masses were receptive to them. Another anti-Jewish libel was that of the holy bread – bread present in Catholic churches which, according to Christian faith, becomes transfigured into the body of Christ in a special ceremony. In this libel, the Jews steal the holy bread from the churches, abuse it, and thus harm Jesus.[70]

Within the context of blood libels, the textbooks mention the attribution by Christians of the smallpox plague (the "Black Plague") to the Jews. According to the textbook for the religious school system, "the spread of the plague throughout Europe evoked terrible rioting targeting Jews. Scenes of horror reminiscent of the massacres of 1096 recurred, and the lists of martyrs in commemorative books lengthened. Whole communities were wiped out and in many places were never re-established. Many Jews who managed to escape the rioters migrated in search of a new place to live."[71]

The textbook for the secular school system, too, emphasizes that the plague heightened hatred: "The Jews were also stricken by the plague, yet they were still accused of poisoning wells and causing the plague with the aim of killing the Christians. This accusation was sufficient cause for the masses to vent their fury on the Jews and run riot among them. In some cases the city councils came to the aid of the Jews; the Pope called for an end to the rioting, arguing that the plague came from heaven, but these pleas were disregarded."[72]

Although emotional writing characterizes the narrative in these textbooks, they seem in general to portray these harsh events in Jewish history in a reasonably balanced fashion. However, perhaps here, too, the spirit of the times should have been emphasized as an explanation for the killing by Christians of non-Christians.[73] Similarly, all the textbooks should have noted, as did one for the secular school system, that "blood-libel trials of Jews resembled the witchcraft trials that were widespread in Europe during that time."[74]

The Jews in Christian Spain

The Jewish–Christian relationship in Spain constitutes one of the main topics in the textbooks for the Jewish school system in light of its tragic conclusion with the expulsion of the Jews from Spain in 1492. All of the texts make comparisons, both obliquely and directly, between the condition of the Jews in Spain under Christian rule and under Muslim rule. According to the textbook for the religious schools, with the conquest of northern Spain by the Christians, many Jews fled southward to the area under Muslim control, as "despite [Muslim] religious fanaticism, they preferred living in the shadow of the advanced Muslim culture rather than the Christian culture."[75] With this, Jews held important positions in Christian Spain, for the Christians "relied on the Jews more than on the Muslims." The turn for the worse in their attitude toward the Jews occurred in the thirteenth century, when "fanatic monks filled with hatred of the Jews" arrived in Spain. At the same time, the nobility and the mercantile class were not favorably disposed to the economic success of the Jews. The first sign of change was the public disputation on religion and faith held between Maimonides and a Jewish apostate in the presence of King of Aragon (1263). A passage from Maimonides' argument during the disputation appears in the textbook for the religious school system:

> And I said to the king . . . and I read them the portion from Deuteronomy . . . And it shall come to pass that all these things shall befall you. . . . And the Lord your God will bring down all these cudgels on your enemies and on those who hate you and have persecuted you. And I explained to them that your enemies [are] the Christians, and those who hate you [are] the Ishmaelites, the two nations who have persecuted us. And they did not reply. . . . [76]

This passage is obviously meant to praise Maimonides (the text indicates that he won the disputation), yet it also entrenches the perception that both the Christians and the Muslims constitute enemies and haters of the Jews, an approach that contradicts the differentiation made in the textbooks between the conduct of the Muslims toward the Jews and that of the Christians.

The textbooks emphasize the massacres of 1391 in light of the deteriorating Jewish–Christian relationship. The textbook for religious schools writes:

> Jew-hatred, which had always existed in secret, erupted in 1391. That year, the king of Castille died, leaving an heir who was a child. The masses took advantage of the weakness of the government and attacked the Jews. Rioters passed from city to city and, as in the massacres of 1061, demanded that Jews convert or die. Many thousands died a martyr's death at the hands of the rioters, although there were many who converted.[77]

Similar descriptions appear in the two secular-school textbooks:

> The social, economic and religious causes of hostility toward the Jews coalesced in a terrible outburst of violence in 1391 (known in Jewish history as the massacres of 1391). The rioting began with the death of the king of Castille and spread to Aragon. In some instances, the rioters allowed the Jews to convert to save their lives, but many were murdered on the spot.[78]
>
> Commercial and labor tension served as fertile ground for the buildup of a wave of violence that began in Seville and spread throughout Spain, during which many Jews were killed. These events are termed the Massacres of 1391. Sometimes during the events of 1391, a governor or nobleman would agree to protect a certain community and they were not harmed, but with the exception of such cases, many communities were destroyed, such as the Jewish community of Barcelona. In the wake of the rioting, many Jews left Spain. . . . In contrast, some Jews converted. . . . The converted Jews were referred to derogatorily as Marranos, or pigs. Acts of violence were perpetrated against the converts, such as the Toledo Massacres (1449), as well as violent rioting between "new Christians" and "old Christians" in cities in southern Spain.[79]

The textbooks also devote considerable attention to the fate of the Jews who decided to convert – the forced converts. Labeled by the Christians with the degrading term "Marranos," these converts "displayed supreme courage in the face of torture perpetrated in the dungeons of the Inquisition courts and did not reveal anything of their own or other converts' practices."[80] Another textbook recounts that "in 1491 the Inquisition in La Guardia sentenced several Jews and new Christians to death on charges of the ritual murder of a Christian child and of plotting to take control of Spain and to convert it [to Judaism]. The child was declared a saint, and the fabricated story of his torture by the Jews was circulated throughout Spain."[81]

A particularly emotional description of the story of the expulsion from Spain appears in the religious-school textbook:

> The expulsion decree was a shock to the Jews. They had lived in Spain for

hundreds of years and had shared all the vicissitudes that had befallen it. They remembered the Golden Age as well as the harsh periods of persecution and anti-Jewish edicts. Even so, it was their homeland and the land of their fathers, and now – they were obliged to leave it within a few weeks. Could it be that after years of toil they would be forced to leave all their possessions behind and abandon their country naked and stripped of everything? For they could take only vital necessities! And the most pressing question was – where would they go? Who would accept them and where would they rebuild their lives?[82]

A less emotional description is given in the secular-school textbook:

> The Jews of Spain experienced a severe trauma. . . . Many of them sold their property cheaply and left the state; others did not manage to sell and abandoned their possessions. Many in the wealthy class converted and remained in Spain. Some Jews left during the expulsion but, encountering difficulties, returned to Spain and then converted. The authorities expropriated synagogues, cemeteries and community property. Some of the synagogues were turned into churches. We do not have accurate statistics about the number of emigrants; historians estimate the figure to be between 70,000 and 130,000.[83]

This textbook emphasizes the differences between the condition of the Jews in Spain under Muslim rule (relatively good) and under Christian rule (relatively difficult). The teacher's guide contains a table showing the extent of the integration of the Jews into society vis-à-vis processes of confrontation and contention. Under Christian rule, the listing for confrontation and contention includes "religious disputations, the riots of 1391, the Inquisition, apostates and forced converts, expulsion from cities and from the state." In contrast, examples of the integration of the Jews in Islamic society are numerous, while confrontational examples are limited to two – the al-Muwahhidun affair and the murder of Jehoseph[84] (see the analysis of Islam as presented in the textbooks, above).

In summary, although the expulsion of the Jews from Spain is one of the bitterest chapters in Jewish history, the textbooks present this event in a relatively balanced fashion, even if some of the descriptions are emotional in style (at least in the narrative of the religious-school textbooks). Notably, the textbooks also provide the social and religious context in which the Inquisition network operated, which allows the pupil to evaluate the events in the spirit of the time rather than in contemporary terms.

The Jewish Community of Poland

The condition of Polish Jewry during the fifteenth century is given prominence in the religious-school textbook. In explaining the background for the eruption of massacres in Poland at that time, the text notes that "the cultural and intellectual level of the Jews widened the [economic] gap between them and the Christians. This gap heightened tension and hatred between them."[85] A chapter titled "The Massacres of 1448–1449," relates that the peasants "called the Jews heartless enslavers [because they served as lessees, or administrators] and greedy robbers. In the words of a folk song from that period: 'While the peasant sings at the inn, the Jew robs him of all his money.'"[86] The book devotes considerable space to the Cossack uprising (1648) led by Bogdan Chmielnicki, whom the Jews branded "Chmiel the Wicked":

> The Ukrainian peasants were eager to do battle, murdering noblemen and slaughtering the Jewish lessees with great pleasure. Anyone not caught by them fled in panic westward and all their possessions were set on fire. . . . A large Jewish community existed in the city of Nemirov, and the [aristocratic] escapees hid with the local Jews in the town fort. . . . When the Jews in the fort opened the gates [having been tricked], the Cossacks cried: "Christianity or death." Most of the Jews refused to convert and died as martyrs. The Cossacks massacred some six thousand souls in the town . . . and they drowned several hundred in the water and by all kinds of cruel torments; and they slaughtered [Jews] in the synagogue, before the Holy Ark . . . and afterward they destroyed the synagogue a bit [sic] and took out all the Torah scrolls and tore them apart . . . and they also made sandals of them" (Rabbi Shabtai ben Meir Ha-Cohen, *Megillat Afah*). In the city of Tulchin Jews and Poles joined forces and formed a unit that volunteered to guard the city, but when the Cossacks approached the city, the Poles betrayed their partners and handed them over to the Cossacks. The Jews of Tulchin, too, refused to convert and died as martyrs. . . . Tens of thousands of Jews were killed and slaughtered with horrible cruelty. One of Chmielnicki's assistants boasted that he "skinned all the Jews alive," and a Jew who witnessed the terrible outbreak wrote: "There was no weird death in the world that they (the rioters) did not inflict . . . " (Rabbi Nathan Hannover, *Yavan Metsulah*). Hundreds of communities were destroyed totally and others were severely damaged and atrophied. Thousands of Jews were seized by the Tatars and sold as slaves.[87]

In contrast, the secular-school textbook merely cites the fact that "the peasant masses hated the Jews, both because they were in positions of authority as lessees on behalf of the nobility and because of their religion." In reference to the Chmielnicki uprising it states: "The uprising left a path of murder and destruction in the Jewish communities. Dozens of communities were destroyed, thousands of Jews were slaughtered. Many other Jews fled in every direction."[88]

The focus by the textbooks on the fate of the Jews is justified, yet this focus blurs the fact that the Ukrainian Revolt, as it is termed in the literature,[89] was aimed not only against Jews but against all outsiders, including Christians who were not Greek-Orthodox.

The Reformation and the Jews

The Christian Reformation movement does not appear at all in the textbook for the religious school system, while the following passages appear in the textbooks for the secular school system:

> Luther was perceived [by the Jews] as having returned in practice to Judaism but as not yet admitting it. . . . Indeed, at first, Luther himself justified these illusions: he wrote a treatise in which he mentioned that Jesus the Christian was a Jew and insisted on treating Jews with grace so as to bring them to Christianity. However, when he realized that the Jews had no intention of abandoning their faith, he changed course and became fanatically and venomously anti-Jewish. Most of the other reformers, with a few exceptions, were also hostile to the Jews.[90]
>
> At first, Luther hoped that his preaching for a different kind of Christianity would lead the Jews to convert. . . . However, when the Jews did not convert as he expected, he changed his attitude toward them and began attacking them. In one of his treatises he proposed destroying synagogues, taking the Jews' holy books and their property away from them, forbidding them to deal in money-lending for interest, and even expelling them from the state (1543). During the religious wars, Jews were victimized as well. Many cities, especially Protestant cities, expelled the Jews because the Jews competed with Christian merchants.[91]

The textbooks present a reasonably reliable picture of the Christian Reformation, although two points might have been emphasized: (1) Luther's primary struggle was against the Catholic Church, with his anti-Jewish stance a by-product of this main struggle, i.e., when Luther became convinced that he could not recruit the Jews to this struggle, he came out against them. (2) Luther's views about Judaism, as articulated in his various writings, were not unusual for his period, which was characterized by the expulsion of Jews from all parts of Germany.[92]

Conclusions

Overall, the textbooks for the Jewish school system do not make use of stigmatic terminology or present Islam and Christianity stereotypically. They generally present these religions in a reasonably accurate and balanced fashion. With this, however, various biases are to be found, stemming from the presentation of inaccurate or insufficient information, which distorts the picture conveyed to the pupil.

Four main problems emerge from the descriptions of Islam in the textbook. First, there is insufficient emphasis on the complexity of the Jewish–Muslim relationship in the Islamic lands. Broad generalizations about the nature of Islam should have been avoided, as far as possible, and instead an analysis of the behavior of Muslim rulers in various places and periods should have been provided. This type of analysis would have led to the conclusion that in certain places "harmony, cooperation and understanding were evident in a given region, while at the same time degradation, repression and bitter hatred prevailed elsewhere."[93] Second, the textbooks avoid the use of a comparative view, i.e., the condition of the Jews under Christian rule. Such comparison is important because it could provide a broader historical perspective on the status of the Jews under gentile rule. Such a comparison could emphasize, as Bernard Lewis has noted, that "Jews and Christians under Muslim rule were normally called upon to suffer martyrdom for faith. They were not often obliged to make the choice, which confronted Muslims and Jews in re-conquered Spain, between exile, apostasy, and death."[94] Mark Cohen shares this view:

> . . . despite the theological intolerance that Islam shared with
> Christendom, the Jews of Islam experienced far greater security and far
> more integration with the majority society than with their brethren in
> Europe. During the first six centuries of Islam . . . the incidence of violent
> persecution, with great loss of life, was comparatively low. The discrimi-
> natory restrictions of the so-called Pact of 'Umar, most of them adopted
> from Byzantine-Christian-Jewish legislation, were more often than not
> observed in the breach. Such irrational concepts as the association of the
> Jews with the devil, a well-known feature of the medieval Christian atti-
> tude toward the Jews, has little place even in the popular Arab
> imagination. Blood libels – in Europe a by-product of the popular percep-
> tion of the diabolical Jew – were absent during these centuries. Expulsion
> did not occur. And we hear practically nothing during this period about
> persecution of Jewish converts to Islam for alleged unfaithfulness to the
> new religion.[95]

The third problem is that the textbooks tend to analyze past events through the prism of the present, thereby projecting ideas, values and norms from one historic period onto an earlier period. What is perceived as discrimination, repression and degradation in modern Western concepts is likely to have been perceived more as normative behavior in an earlier period. It should be emphasized that the Jews constituted an ethnic and religious minority within a Muslim majority; that this society was not egalitarian; and that Jews could not expect to become citizens with equal rights in that type of social system. As Ze'ev Hirschberg put it: "People in that period did not in the slightest perceive as degrading certain regulations that to us appear deeply humiliating. Those who imposed them and those who were subjected to them viewed them as a logical result of a factual situation that had evolved in the course of generations."[96] The presentation of such a nuanced view would have the chance of eliminating distortions still existing in the present Jewish textbooks.

Finally, it seems that the Jewish education system does not provide its students with enough information on Islam – a problem that is more acute in high school. According to the history curriculum, the subject is taught only in the seventh grade. In addition, those junior high school pupils who study Arabic as a second foreign language may also study the Arab culture in Israel.[97] In contrast, however, high school pupils may study the Arab minority in Israel (this subject is not mandatory)[98] and on certain aspects of the modern Arab–Israeli conflict, but they do not repeat what they had studied on Islam in seventh grade. It is no wonder, therefore, that the Jewish students are largely ignorant of Islam.

With regard to Christianity, the description of its attitude toward Judaism is replete with grim terminology (e.g., massacres, slaughter, edicts, etc.). This stems mainly from the charged nature of the Jewish–Christian encounter. The intensity of the contact between Jews and Christians, side by side with the ongoing theological and historic dispute over the origins of Christianity, made it difficult for textbook writers to treat these encounters with equanimity. Indeed, various biases are observable in the textbooks, although they stem primarily from the provision of incorrect or insufficient information, which distorts the picture conveyed to the pupil. More biases appear to be present in the textbook written for religious schools, which is not surprising in light of the emphasis on the Jewish perspective in this book.[99]

As in the presentation of Islam, the main problem in the presentation of Christianity is that the textbooks tend to analyze the events of the past from the point of view of the present, thereby assigning ideas, values and norms from one historic period to an earlier period. What is perceived as discrimination, repression and degradation in the conceptualization of modern Western civilization is likely to be perceived as normative behavior in an earlier period. Another problematic issue is the fact that most aspects of Christian history and religion are taught only in lower grades and in a superficial way. On balance, it seems that the Israeli pupil receives even less information on Christianity than on Islam.[100] Moreover, a broader treatment of the psychological aspects of hatred of the other is in place, along the lines of an appendix that appears in one of the textbooks for secular schools:

> The Jews resembled the Christians in every respect except in their religion. The Christians were uncomfortable with this resemblance. If they resemble us so much, if they live side by side with us, they thought, if they know us and our belief, they have no excuse for being different from us. The Christians felt that the Jews' stubbornness in adhering to their religion was illogical: either the Jews are foolish and do not understand what

every "logical" person (i.e., a person who thinks as we do) understands, or they are wicked and purposely refuse to practice and believe in the proper faith. The condition of the Jews did not improve when Christians made an effort to become familiar with their customs and writings. This effort was not made out of a desire to understand and learn, but as part of an attempt to "know the enemy." While there were things in the books of the Jews that were hurtful to a Christian, the Christians were not satisfied with [criticizing] these, but slandered the Jews in a series of libels. Preachers recounted that the Jews were plotting to eliminate Christian society, that they murder little children and drink their blood, and that they have a peculiar body odor and a tail. In other words, sometimes a group chooses to take someone slightly different from it and turn it in its imagination into something totally different – nearly inhuman. In this way, a small difference gives rise to deep hatred; not affinity but distance.[101]

Perhaps this sophisticated kind of approach would succeed in eliminating the biases that are still to be found in the Jewish textbooks. But beyond the presentation of factual data as objective as possible, the student should receive the message that in spite of the differences between the three religions, there are certain commonalities, such as the concept of Monotheism, the image of Abraham, the idea of divine revelation, the existence of a holy book, and the ethical orientation. As the new Bible curriculum in the Jewish education system encourages a comparison between the Jewish and Babylonian stories of the Creation and the Jewish and Mesopotamian (Gilgamesh) stories of the Flood,[102] so the future curriculum can advance a comparison between the roles of Abraham in the three monotheistic religions. Such a study, it may be surmised, would foster tolerance and empathy toward the Other.

Notes

1   On the various methods, see E. B. Johnsen, *Textbooks in the Kaleidoscope: A Critical Survey of Literature and Research on Educational Texts,* translated by L. Sivesind (Oslo: 1993), pp. 141–42. In his authoritative *UNESCO Guidebook,* Pingel classifies the hermeneutic analysis as part of the qualitative method. He also mentions linguistic and discourse investigation as possible modes of analysis, see F. Pimgel, *UNESCO Guidebook on Textbook Researcy and Textbook Revision* (Hannover: Verlag Hahmsche Buchhandlugn, 1999), pp. 45–47.

2   See in this connection, Elie Podeh, *The Arab–Israeli Conflict in Israeli History Textbooks, 1948–2000* (Westport, CT: Bergin and Garvey, 2002).

3   On the Israeli education system, see Haim Gaziel, *Politics and Policy-Making in Israel's Education System* (Brighton: Sussex Academic Press, 1996).

4   L. Sheleff, "The Stranger in our Midst: The Other in Jewish Tradition – From Biblical Times to Modern Israel," *Israel Studies Bulletin* (Spring, 1999), p. 7.

5   *Lessons in the Book of Deuteronomy.* Teacher's Guide, p. 111. The guide also cites commentaries on the verse from the Gemara.

6   *Ibid.*

7   *From the Sources on Conversion and Proselytizing.* Teacher's Guide, p. 6. Also

see p. 15 in the companion textbook.

8 According to the new Bible curriculum, the Book of Genesis and the Patriarchs stories are being studied in kindergarten, the second grade, the seventh grade and also certain thematic subjects (such as the Creation and the Flood) are studied in grades 11–12.

9 *From Generation to Generation*, II, p. 215. The story is taken from Y. Meyuhas, *Children of the Night* (Hebrew), p. 49.

10 For further commentary on the verses cited from Deuteronomy, see *Lessons in the Book of Deuteronomy*, Grade 6, Teacher's Guide, pp. 217–21. In this connection, Shlomo Dov Goitein argues that "the idea of war by commandment – *jihad* – is so characteristic of Islam that we tend to think of it as impressed in it from its beginnings, but this is not at all the case." See his article, "Muhammad," in H. Lazarus-Yaffe, *Chapters in the History of the Arabs and Islam* (Tel Aviv: Reshafim, 1981, Hebrew), p. 61. Similarly, Aviva Shussman has written "In the beginning, Muhammad's Islam was not a religion of wars, for he prophesied the end of the world and the Day of Judgment and other such prophecies. But with his arrival in Medina, his prophecies also included the announcement of a war of commandment. Apparently, Muhammad realized that he would not manage to attract believers by friendly persuasion." See "The Islamic Message," in H. Lazarus-Yaffe, *Islam* (Tel Aviv: Ministry of Defense Publishers, 1986, Hebrew), p. 25.

11 *From Generation to Generation*, II, pp. 200, 230.

12 *In the Days of the Crescent and the Cross*, p. 31.

13 *A Journey to the Past*, p. 21.

14 *From Generation to Generation*, II, p. 235.

15 Goitein uses the term "expulsion" for the *Qaynuqas* and the term "exile" for the *Nadirs*. See "Muhammad," pp. 65, 67.

16 *Ibid.*, p. 70. The author is referring to Deuteronomy 20:13–14, which says: "And when the Lord thy God delivereth it into thy hand, thou shalt smite every male thereof with the edge of the sword; but the women, and the little ones, and the cattle, and all that is in the city, even all the spoil thereof, shall thou take for a prey unto thyself; and thou shalt eat the spoil of thine enemies, which the Lord thy God hath given thee." Goitein adds that "in Judaism this tradition was annulled for tangential reasons, and in practice this rule was followed only in exceptional cases" (*ibid.*, pp. 70–71).

17 C. Cahen, *Islam From its Birth until the Beginning of the Ottoman Empire* (Tel Aviv: Dvir, 1995), p. 28 (translated from the French to Hebrew by I. Kopelevich).

18 Shussman, "The Message of Islam," p. 26.

19 See, e.g., H. Z. Hirschberg, *The Jews in the Lands of Islam*, p. 267.

20 *From Generation to Generation*, II, pp. 202, 208.

21 *A Journey to the Past*, p. 31.

22 H. Lazarus-Yaffe, "The Holiness of Jerusalem" in *Islam*, pp. 87–88.

23 *From Generation to Generation*, II, p. 232.

24 *Ibid.*, III, p. 42. Several examples of these laws are then presented, taken from B. Z. Dinur's book, *Israel in the Diaspora*, 1/A, p. 66. Here, too, the point is brought out that "the sultans tended to turn a blind eye in the matter of implementing many parts of Omar's laws" (*ibid.*, p. 43).

25 *In the Days of the Crescent and the Cross*, p. 31.

26 For an example of the Jewish perception, see H. Z. Hirschberg, "The Jews in the

Lands of Islam," in *Chapters in the History of the Arabs and Islam* (Jerusalem: 1957, Hebrew), pp. 270–71. The author treats the regulations as "The Conditions of Omar."

27 H. Lazarus-Yaffe (ed.), *Muslim Writers on Jews and Judaism* (Jerusalem: Shazar Center, 1998), p. 8.

28 *Ibid.*, p. 11.

29 This kind of approach is to be found in a special booklet published by the Ben-Zvi Institute for the Research of Jewish Communities in the East, in cooperation with the Ministry of Education and Culture's Society and Youth Authority, designed primarily for informal education. See H. Sa'adon, *Jews and Muslims in the Countries of Islam: Complexity and Variety* (Jerusalem, 1997, Hebrew). See especially pp. 19–20, which deal with the Covenant of Omar and its significance.

30 *In the Days of the Crescent and the Cross*, p. 36.

31 *Ibid.*, p. 47.

32 *A Journey to the Past*, p. 47. The student is asked in this context: "Jerusalem was conquered by the Muslims in the seventh century and by the Christians in the eleventh century. Compare the attitude of the Muslims to the inhabitants of Jerusalem and that of the Christians" (*ibid.*). For the Jews in Muslim Spain, see *In the Days of the Crescent and the Cross*, pp. 78–79; *A Journey to the Past*, p. 175.

33 *In the Days of the Crescent and the Cross* bid., p. 79.

34 *A Journey to the Past*, Teacher's Guide, p. 97.

35 *In the Days of the Crescent and the Cross*, p. 78.

36 Hirschberg, "The Jews in the Lands of Islam," p. 276.

37 *From Generation to Generation*, III, p. 19. Also see *A Journey to the Past*, pp. 208–9; *In the Days of the Crescent and the Cross*, p. 213.

38 *From Generation to Generation*, II, p. 362.

39 *From Generation to Generation*, III, p. 26.

40 *Ibid.* The description of the Jewish community in Eretz Yisrael takes up seven pages (26–33).

41 *Ibid.*, p. 28.

42 *Ibid.*, pp. 45–46.

43 *Ibid.*, pp. 46–47. For source segments, see p. 48.

44 Cf. with the descriptions in *ibid.*, pp. 42–47.

45 See *A Journey to the Past*, pp. 208–9; *In the Days of the Crescent and the Cross*, p. 213.

46 See, e.g., *The Jews Between Christianity and Islam* (1973) and *In the Days of the Crusaders* (1983), two textbooks published by the Ministry of Education and Culture in experimental editions only.

47 See, in particular, B. Ben-Baruch, *Greeks, Romans, Jews* (Tel Aviv: Tel Aviv Books, 1996), pp. 137–39.

48 *From Generation to Generation*, II, pp. 86–87.

49 *Ibid.*, p. 88.

50 *Ibid.*, p. 89.

51 *Greeks, Romans, Jews*, pp. 173–79.

52 *From Generation to Generation*, II, pp. 94–95.

53 *Ibid.*, p. 96.

54 *In the Days of the Crescent and the Cross*, pp. 76, 81–83. For a balanced account of some discriminatory laws, see *Greeks, Romans, Jews*, pp. 178–79.

55 *Jew Hatred From the Birth of Christianity to the Crusades*, Unit 3 (Tel Aviv: The Open University, 1985, Hebrew), p. 21.

56 *From Generation to Generation*, II, p. 22.

57 See also *Jew Hatred From the Birth of Christianity to the Crusades*, pp. 37–38.

58 *From Generation to Generation*, II, p. 404.

59 *Ibid.*, p. 405.

60 *Ibid.*

61 *Ibid.*, p. 408.

62 *Ibid.*, p. 411.

63 *In the Days of the Crescent and the Cross*, p. 89. For a similar description, see Tabibyan, *Journey to the Past*, pp. 140–41.

64 *In the Days of the Crescent and the Cross*, p. 90.

65 *Ibid.*

66 Tabibyan, *Journey to the Past*, p. 147.

67 *Ibid.*

68 *In the Days of the Crescent and the Cross*, p. 94.

69 *Ibid.*, pp. 102–6, *passim.*

70 Tabibyan, *Journey to the Past*, pp. 120–21.

71 *From Generation to Generation*, II, p. 442.

72 Tabibyan, *Journey to the Past*, p. 124. Also see *In the Days of the Crescent and the Cross*, p. 112.

73 Aviad Kleinberg, for example, explains that "the justification [in the past] for tolerance toward the Jews was the Christian belief that the Jews refused to change and that in punishment for rejecting Jesus they were frozen in time as a kind of historic fossil. However, since it turned out that the Jews . . . abused the educational role that they served in Christian society, and even worse, in their affinity for the Talmud they became as gentiles in relation to their our Torah, more and more Christians concluded that they no longer had a role in the West and that expelling them was permissible." See A. Kleinberg, *Christianity: From its Beginnings Until the Reformation* (Tel Aviv: Ministry of Defense Publishers, 1995, Hebrew), pp. 119–20.

74 Tabibyan, *Journey to the Past*, p. 267.

75 *From Generation to Generation*, II, p. 274

76 *Ibid.*, p, 457.

77 *Ibid.*, p. 450.

78 *In the Days of the Crescent and the Cross*, p. 126.

79 Tabibyan, *Journey to the Past*, p. 177.

80 *From Generation to Generation*, II, p. 462. A note explains that "Marranos means pigs. Some believe that this derogatory word was applied to the new Christians when their identity was exposed by their refusal to eat pork." *Ibid.*, p. 460.

81 *In the Days of the Crescent and the Cross*, p. 127.

82 *From Generation to Generation*, II, p. 465.

83 Tabibyan, *Journey to the Past*, p. 180.

84 *Ibid.*, Teacher's Guide, p. 97.

85 *From Generation to Generation*, III, p. 163.

86 *Ibid.*, p. 176.

87 *Ibid.*, p. 179. The book also emphasizes, both in the text and pictures, that while "in the history of our people Chmielnicki is called 'Chmiel the Wicked,' in

Unkraine he is considered a national hero." The pupil is asked: "Why is Chmielnicki considered a national hero in Ukraine?" *Ibid.*, p. 180.

88 *In the Days of the Crescent and the Cross*, p. 202.

89 See, e.g., *Jew Hatred and Anti-Semitism*, Unit 7, pp. 120–34.

90 *Ibid.*, p. 157.

91 Tabibyan, *Journey to the Past*, p. 267.

92 See in this context *Jew-Hatred and Anti-Semitism*, Unit 6, p. 29.

93 Sa'adon, *Jews and Muslims in the Lands of Islam*, p. 20. For this approach, see also B. Lewis, *Islam in History* (Tel Aviv: Zmora-Bitan, 1984, Hebrew), p. 125.

94 B. Lewis, *The Jews of Islam* (Princeton: Princeton University Press, 1984), p. 8.

95 *Ibid.*, pp. 126–27.

96 Hirschberg, "The Jews in the Lands of Islam," p. 275. See also Sa'adon, *Jews and Muslims in the Lands of Islam*, pp. 20, 45.

97 See, in particular, *In Five Voices: Young Arabs in Israel Tell about Their Lives and Culture* (Tel Aviv: The Center for Technological Education, 1994).

98 *The Arab Citizens of Israel: Mutual Relations between Jews and Arabs in Israel* (Jerusalem: The Ministry of Education, 1989).

99 Sara Vider, the history superintendent in the religious system, admitted that certain teachers in the religious education have reservations concerning teaching on Jesus "because we cannot ignore what Christianity had done to the Jews." See O. Kazin, *Ha'aretz*, December 23, 1999.

100 See in this connection the article, *ibid.* I should emphasize that this is a general observation, which is not based on any quantitative analysis.

101 *In the Days of the Crescent and the Cross*, p. 284.

102 *Tochnit ha-Limudim be-Mikra le-Ma'arechet Ha-Hinuch Ha-Mamlachtit* (Bible Curriculum to the State Educational System), (Jerusalem: Ministry of Education and Culture, 2003), p. 69.

Bibliography: Textbooks

A. Barnavi and A. Kleinberg, *Biyemei Hasahar Vehatslav: Yemei Habeinayim Vereishit Ha'et Hahadasha* (In the Days of the Crescent and the Cross: The Middle Ages and the Beginning of Modern Times). History for Grade 7. (Tel Aviv: Tel Aviv Books, 1997).

——, *ibid.*, Teacher's Guide.

B. Ben-Baruch, *Hame'ah Ha-19: Likrat Ha'olam Hamoderni* (The Nineteenth Century: Toward the Modern World). History for Grade 8. (Tel Aviv: Tel Aviv Books, 1998).

——, *Beimei Yavan VeRoma* (Greeks, Romans, Jews). History for Grade 6. (Tel Aviv: Tel Aviv Books, 1996).

Hayehudim Bein Natsrut Ve'islam (The Jews Between Christianity and Islam). (Jerusalem: Ministry of Education and Culture, 1973).

Midor Ledor (From Generation to Generation). Lessons in History for the State-Religious School. Part I. (Jerusalem: Ministry of Education and Culture, 1991).

——, *ibid.*, Part II, 1994.

——, *ibid.*, Part III, 1995.

Mikra (Bible): Curriculum for the State-Religious Schools (Jerusalem: Ministry of Education and Culture, 2003).

Min Hamekorot al Geirut Vegiyur (From the Sources on Conversion and Proselytizing). (Jerusalem: Ministry of Education and Culture, 1977).

——, *ibid.*, Teacher's Guide, Lessons in Oral Torah in the State School, 1978.

Mishamranut Lekidmah (From Conservatism to Progress). History for Grade 8. (Jerusalem: Ministry of Education and Culture, 1998).

Mizehut Ishit le-Zehut Le'umit: Sipurei Ha'avot ve-Zikatam le-Eretz-Israel (From Personal Identity to National Identity: the Patriarchs Stories and their Linkage to Eretz-Israel). Chapters from the Book of Genesis, for Junior High School. (Tel Aviv: The Center for Educational Technology, 2004).

E. Naveh, *Hame'ah Ha-19: Ha'olam Shel Etmol* (The Nineteenth Century: The World of Yesterday). History for Grade 8. Teacher's Guide. (Tel Aviv: Tel Aviv Books, 1998).

Shi'urim Besefer Devarim (Lessons in the Book of Deuteronomy), for Grade 6. Teacher's Guide. (Jerusalem: Ministry of Education and Culture, 1998).

K. Tabibyan, *Masah el Ha'avar: Miyemei Habeinayim ve'ad Ha'et Hahadasha* (Journey to the Past: From the Middle Ages to Modern Times). (Tel Aviv: Center for Educational Technology, 1997).

——, *ibid.*, Teacher's Guide.

Tochnit ha-Limudim be-Mikra le-Ma'arechet Ha-Hinuch Ha-Mamlachtit (Bible Curriculum to the State Educational System). (Jerusalem: Ministry of Education and Culture, 2003).

CHAPTER 11

Educating for Global Citizenship: Perspectives from the Abrahamic Traditions

ABDUL AZIZ SAID

Hassan Fathy (1899–1989) was an Egyptian architect who devoted himself to developing housing projects for the rural poor in Egypt by synthesizing traditional and modern building techniques. Fathy reminds our modern minds that, "The quality and values inherent to the traditional and human response to the environment might be preserved without a loss of the advances of science. Science can be applied to various aspects of our work, while it is at the same time subordinated to philosophy, faith and spirituality."

The work of Fathy represents the type of fusion between tradition, technology, and development that we should seek in educating for global citizenship.

Continuing Challenges

The modern world faces old trials in new appearances. The English poet William Blake captured the essence of crisis as he saw our inhumanity to one another. This is true of both our individual relationship and the social structures we build. I hear his voice reminding me of this pain:

> Cruelty has a Human Heart,
> And Jealousy a Human Face;
> Terror the Human Form Divine;
> And Secrecy the Human Dress.[1]

The world has reached a point of crisis that will require an ever-increasing social capacity for creative imagination and reason. We now find ourselves, as individuals, as states, and as a species, involved in a period of intense, and often bewildering change. The systems of government, production, culture, thought, and perception, to which we have become accustomed, are not working. Within the growing milieu of crisis, our perception of the world grows increasingly intertwined. At the same time, our experience of the world is fragmented and disjointed, constructed by the increasingly large gaps in access to knowledge, wealth, and political representation.

Our future depends upon conceiving an all-inclusive model of citizenship that reconciles these gaps in access. We need to find a way to synthesize the traditional and the modern to create new educational processes and institutions that will give individuals the material, intellectual, moral, and emotional skills necessary to transcend the crisis of our world.

One such source of traditional wisdom rests with the Abrahamic faiths. This is especially true in societies emerging from conflict and experiencing systemic, social, political, and economic change. Take the example of modern Iraq. Iraq is a 'nation of nations,' home to multiple ethnic and religious groups whose experience of history has often put them in conflict.

In order to emerge with a unified understanding of citizenship in light of such a diverse and at times contentious history, the new Iraqi should embrace an inclusive model for citizenship. Such a model moves beyond the limited national constructions of identity in order to transcend the hatreds of the past and present. This global model of citizenship can bind Iraqis together by first looking to their shared traditions in the Abrahamic faiths and how these sources of traditional wisdom find modern articulation through the work and principles of Hassan Fathy.

The world needs a model of education that is capable of conceiving a global model for citizenship. It must have the flexibility to discover new solutions to the world's increasingly complex and massive problems. Such a model can be reached by expanding the educational process to become more dialogical and open-ended and less paternalistic and past-oriented. Such a shift will require transcending the ideological, cultural, and spiritual caste system of education to engage in a genuine human dialogue based on the equal dignity of each individual.

In educating for global citizenship in the West and the Middle East, we must remember and honor our traditions. Specifically, we should look to the rich and vivid truths shared by the Abrahamic traditions and their conceptualization of the role of knowledge and education as a purposeful, ordered quest for meaning and beauty. These three traditions honor a God that seeks to be 'known.'

The path of the Divine is thus a path of knowledge; one that promises redemption, transformation, and salvation. Because God is whole and knowable, human beings should seek to know the Divine as truth and beauty. This divine path to meaning manifests itself socially as the process of education. In line with this guiding moral and epistemological order housed within the

Abrahamic traditions, institutions of education should concede that their purpose is to improve the human condition and serve the whole human community, not only understand it.

Education as an institution should acknowledge its inherent role as a catalyst for social change. More than the accumulation of knowledge, education represents a dialogic guidance mechanism of social development. In this respect, education is not just the system of preparing individuals to become 'citizens.' Rather, it is the space of integrating and creating a national, transnational, and individual (essential) consciousness founded in the pursuit of meaning. As such, education shapes social perception and thought in the construction of the boundaries of our knowledge. Whether these boundaries are elastic and open or inelastic and closed to new horizons of knowing is a function of our perception.

To manifest a dialogic character of social development, the essence of education must be the expansion of our repertoire of behavior. We don't just learn the 'right way' to do things, but teach the many paths to knowing as they reflect unique cultural, historical, and individual experiences. There are many ways of knowing. We think with reason, making tight sequential connections. We think with wonder, making connections of the random kind. We think with images, making connections of the visual kind. Each of these forms of thought and their expression as knowledge is part of the larger search for meaning that encompasses human existence in the Abrahamic traditions.

In the Abrahamic faiths, the divine is whole and as such is knowable. Since the divine is knowable, each individual has a responsibility to seek to know its essence through the search for meaning. Thus, in the moral tradition of the Abrahamic faiths and their articulation of this search as a guiding order, the global citizen should access 'knowing' as a mode of perspective consciousness. Education increases the boundaries of this perspective consciousness, thus opening new horizons to the individual in their search for truth, beauty, and order. Knowledge liberates us from our presumptions and illusions. This liberation is balanced in dignity.

In line with the belief in a just order guiding the Abrahamic traditions, the acquisition of knowledge should be predicated upon transforming the structural and relational basis of inequity and social polarization. Education is a public good whose effectiveness is predicated upon expanding the perceptual basis of any given society to exist simultaneously and harmoniously in a local and global context.

We should reconcile the process of observation and participation, creating educational institutions and processes that combine the roles of social participation and criticism. This is most readily achieved by liberating our creativity to interact with the magnificent diversity and vibrancy of the many ways of knowing developed by different civilizations.

The Abrahamic tradition of *the oneness of being* expresses itself in this liberation. Because the inelasticity in our traditional ways of seeing the world is precipitating a global crisis of identity, we are unable to conceive of new forms of knowledge, as social perception, and through it, inclusive models of citizenship. The Abrahamic principle of *oneness* can facilitate the conceptual framework for expressing a transnational versus a limited national consciousness.

In the new Iraq, what is achieved by liberating the population from Saddam Hussein if, we in turn, do not free minds to conceive of a global basis for citizenship? The movement from a national consciousness to a transnational consciousness is required to shift their understanding of citizenship from a local to a global context. Creating a basis for global citizenship first entails acknowledging the capacity for social change as transformation at the individual and group level. The process of transformation enables us to take a broader view of our world to integrate reason, feeling, sensing, and intuition.

Pluralism and Co-existence

We experience an enlargement of consciousness in a fundamental sense and thus are able to exist simultaneously with multiple religious, social, and national identities. The twentieth-century Lebanese universalist and mystic, Ameen Rihani, reminds us of the human experience of pluralism and co-existence as emerging from the individual:

> Nor Crescent Nor Cross we adore;
> Nor Buddha nor Christ we implore;
> Nor Muslim nor Jew we abhor:
>   We are free.[2]

The global citizen lives within the context of a world cultural system. The Abrahamic concept of unity implies that the global citizen exists in every polity, cultural, and social network. At the same time, this global citizen balances past and present, preserving the values and accomplishments of the past with the prospects of the future.

In both its spatial (global) and temporal (nonlinear) manifestation, the co-existence that global citizenship strives for is predicated upon pluralism. Cultural diversity creates intellectual possibility. The pluralism necessary to create global citizens should reflect the natural progression of humanistic ethics. Different linguistic, ethnic, cultural, and national entities are all valuable. They flower in unique spaces and manners whose richness is only understood in juxtaposition with the whole. To embrace difference with a critical eye and an open heart is to increase the variables underlying the mind's quantification of the heavens. The symphony of the spheres is heard when we take the time to listen to each and every voice.

Historically, whenever a conscious decision was undertaken to integrate the many forms of knowing, a cultural renaissance has emerged. A dark age for the Western world was ended by a golden age for the Islamic world. In

Andalusia, the co-existence of Muslim, Jew, and Christian made it the intellectual capital of the medieval world. The Abbasid capital of Baghdad in the tenth century comprised one of the most cosmopolitan cities ever known where Jewish, Muslim, and Christian scholars searched for truth in harmony.

The process of education involves learning to see the many faces of humanity, the essence unfolded in each person. The oppressor and oppressed are both people, experiencing life in all its vicissitudes. Reason and intuition are the two faces of truth. Planning and spontaneity are activities of one reality. Civilization and barbarism change into culture, propositional knowledge and anecdotal knowledge into the root of knowledge.

Harmony amid great cultural diversity is an exercise in awareness. This awareness reflects the progression of the individual's search to know the wholeness and oneness of the divine in the Abrahamic faiths. It comes from acknowledging basic differences in worldview among different peoples.

Acknowledgment of differences is appreciation, honoring the unique experience of each individual, citizen, believer, and civilization. This appreciation gains its wholeness through empathy. Once we are able, through education, to constantly shift subject and object, agent and structure in our dialogic analysis, we begin to experience the history of the other as our own, without judgment and without regret or hate. When we discover our individual authenticity – when we know who we are, we recognize the genuine uniqueness of others.

In addition to empathy, we should be conscious of the dual necessity of creativity and reason. If we do not interject reason in conjunction with creativity into the experience of knowing, we risk remembering only what has happened in our society rather than imagining what society is capable of becoming. The instability and negative social experience of years of protracted social conflict and weight of structural violence in post-conflict environments has a tendency to produce a social anxiety and expectation of perpetual violence. The individual, conditioned by their environment, experiences the world as singularly violent and hence produces all individual and social knowledge in a state of conflict.

The experience of violence becomes epistemic, reproducing ever greater monolithic claims and distancing itself from other forms of knowing in an attempt to isolate itself and the social pain upon which it is predicated. Over time, social and especially national consciousness becomes a function of the experience of pain.

You are a citizen to the extent to which you can claim a shared historical experience of exclusive deprivation and violence. To transcend this embedded cycle of experiencing and living violence will require that, in constructing educational models for the global citizen, we specifically acknowledge the necessity of a spiritual dimension.

By spirituality, the point of reference is not the traditional sense of a set of religious principles or doctrines. Rather the emphasis is placed upon the act of imagining oneself in relation to a larger whole. Self-reflection increases our capacity for synthesis in public dialogue.

The Capacity for Individual and Social Transformation

History is understood not just as a series of relationships or social structures, but within the context of the unfolding spirit and our place within the world. In looking inward, we gather the strength required to meet the many challenges of the world. This internal search reflects the just order of the Abrahamic faiths and their emphasis on the necessity of searching for meaning as a way of knowing the divine. Ibn ArabiMuhyiddin, a twelfth–thirteenth century Andalusian mystic and philosopher, helps us to know this sacred search for meaning from the comfort of our human heart:

> My heart has become capable of every form:
> it is a pasture for gazelles,
> and a convent for Christian monks, a temple for idols
> and the pilgrim's Ka'ba;
> the tables of the Tora and the book of the Koran.[3]

To forge a transnational consciousness in the Abrahamic traditions of the *oneness of being*, we are acknowledging certain normative goals. Especially in post-conflict and transforming societies, education institutions should work in their community to raise the issues untouchable by politicians desperate to pander to elite interest groups. Education is one of the key pillars of civil society where the discourse of social transformation is disseminated. Pragmatically, the education of the global citizen must avoid dictating the terms of good citizenship to individuals as often happens in transitional states.

In educating for global citizenship, we should be wary of the monolithic claims of any set of knowledge, whether religious, scientific or ideological, or based upon individual or communal prejudices. Such selectivity in meaning is a function of the need to maintain rigid group boundaries, and its exclusivity only serves to impinge upon the true nobility and nature of the mind and heart.

The Abrahamic traditions ground the social function of knowledge as constituting a just order in the sense that the knower is transformed through the search for meaning. In the tradition of the Abrahamic faiths, because God is whole and knowable, knowledge is seen as a virtue, a quality capable of saving the soul. A never-ending process of searching for meaning brings us closer to realizing the value of our individual soul.

All bodies of knowledge are subject to interpretation. In any tradition, this interpretation can be open or closed. We should continually be wary of any monolithic interpretation of the Abrahamic faiths and for that matter, any social ideology.

Monolithic epistemological (and even ontological) systems sustain themselves by decreasing the horizons for substantive questions. They are inelastic, unable to facilitate the social process of thinking (as accessing knowledge) to imagine other forms. They become increasingly rigid, requiring structural manifestations of intellectual discipline. You cannot go against the state, you cannot question the church, you cannot question capitalism or communism – the tale of the twentieth century is written in the violent consequences of this rigidity.

To transcend this legacy of monolithic knowledge will require engaging the natural diversity of our surroundings. This aspect of educating for global citizenship is especially important in societies emerging from social conflict and violent (whether manifest or structural) political transitions. In these societies, the social institutions, and particularly the educational sector, are in the process of *becoming*, reflecting the reordering of the social, political, and economic infrastructure of society. This means that there always exists a moment of normative determination in constructing the institutions of education in a society undergoing radical change.

This is a distinct window of time in which elite interests are often condensed and shaped into social institutions.

Pedagogy can become a function of reaffirming social stratification or a function of (re)discovering moral and philosophical orders through a spirit of inquiry at the heart of the Abrahamic spiritual traditions and their emphasis upon sacred knowledge. This rediscovery of Abrahamic tradition can be articulated in a modern (secular) space as 'ethical humanism', as a just and ethical guidance underwriting the search for meaning.

Education as Liberation & Transformation

In educating for global citizenship, we are seeking to endow individuals with the capacity to embrace the greater good of all humanity as an ethical goal. This goal must be embedded in every social activity. The twentieth-century poet and Kabbalah scholar, Gershom Scholem, speaks to the transformation of our mortal life.

In Scholem's poem, we find the essence of our quest into the Abrahamic faiths and their ability to provide the conceptual framework in which to educate the global citizen. The goal of education is to awaken each individual, especially those in poverty, to the highest order of existence, human dignity:

> You, who caused life itself to forget,
> in you, immortal, life now resurrects.
> Because you died in poverty and disgrace,
> to the Highest order you now awake.[4]

Creating global citizens will require conceiving of educational systems and institutions predicated upon freedom and guided by the Abrahamic traditions and their secular articulation as ethical humanism. To experience the search for truth and meaning unhindered, the global citizen requires freedom. In turn, open polities and democracies require an educated populace, one that is reflective upon their condition and believe in both development and progress.

If knowledge is built as an encounter between human beings, then its capacity for social change (freedom) is liberated as we embrace the cultural qualities of the many communities in which we coexist. Life is a path of learning where we are each constantly called upon to awaken ourselves and each other to search for freedom, truth, beauty, creativity, and above all, justice. In the end, one does not create a global citizen. Rather, we can create, restructure, and develop the realm of education so that each human being can see themselves in a global context. In turn, this global context of perception and citizenship is balanced by acknowledging the dignity of each individual and the presence of truth in every language.

Living in a pluralist cultural community, we stand before a thousand revolutions. These revolts are internal to the culture as it finds its essential voice. They also exist externally as the truths in each culture and community emerge to become intertwined. Together they destroy the sources of dehumanization that inhibit human development.

In the process of this social transformation, each global citizen becomes individually aware. In the Abrahamic tradition of *oneness*, each community finds its expression in an inclusive citizenship. Each community in Iraq finds its natural expression in this inclusive, global model of citizenship.

To help the new Iraqi realize the many benefits of global citizenship will require nothing short of a renaissance grounded in the traditions of the Abrahamic faiths. A renaissance is a revival, a remembrance of the past to produce new artistic and intellectual forms for the future. It represents a period of expanding horizons in which a vast increase in knowledge of the world and its inhabitants leads to a new understanding of the society and the individual.

The renaissance the modern world needs today is grounded in ethical humanism and its articulation of the social value of truth and knowledge as founded in the Abrabamic traditions. In Iraq, this means that the international community should strive to work with local scholars, artists, and historians to embrace the lessons of Andalusia and Abbasid Baghdad. Considering the problems posed by the legacy of Saddam Hussein's repressive political regime and the war of 2003, we should make every effort to establish a memory of co-existence. The way the new Iraqi thinks about their own identity will have a profound impact upon their ability to know and experience peace.

Global citizenship should call upon the traditions of the Abrahamic faiths to reclaim their local identities while living in the modern world. To create an inclusive open model of citizenship in modern Iraq will require a complete restructuring of the traditional liberal modernization approach to developing education systems in war-torn countries and zones of conflict.

Because of the sacred place of knowledge as the gateway to *oneness* and *wholeness* in the Abrahamic faiths, the education system in Iraq should enable a reconciliation of tradition and modernity. There is a precedent for such a shift in the life and work of Hassan Fathy. Fathy's work used **six general principles** to preserve the context of local cultural identity as well as their articulation as art and social forms in the environment.

At the most general level, the creation of a global model of citizenship and emergent renaissance will be dependent upon the ability of local Iraqis, international policy makers and aid workers to, at the minimum, embrace these principles to conceive of a new education policy in Iraq:

1. **Belief in the primacy of human values in designing social spaces:** Ground all education in a guiding, ethical order. This means ensuring that there is first and foremost no relative deprivation based upon class, gender, ethnicity, or religion in the classroom and opening up a public space for rediscovering the applicability of past experiences and values to the present.

2. **A universal rather than a limited approach to solving social problems:** Avoiding the arrogance of ideological dogma or the educational methodologies in the East (rote learning) and West (standardized testing) that limit open, process-oriented dialogue in the classroom.

3. **Utility of technology in enabling innovative solutions:** Iraq should realize its place in the Islamic world as one of the modern and historical centers of learning. We should work with Iraqis to bring this tradition to the forefront by embracing high standards of excellence in math and science-based education. At the same time, we should explore innovative ways to use technology to explore the liberal arts including literature, music, visual arts, and theatrical and traditional performance forms.

4. **The importance of community and socially-oriented education techniques:** Helping the new Iraqi to coexist in a 'nation of nations', a country with a diverse ethnic, religious, and historical context means engaging the whole of society, through the education system, in a dialogic process of searching for truth and meaning. It means acknowledging the many voices and truths of Iraq, including disenfranchised communities like the marsh Arabs, and enabling each community to exchange the best of its values and experiences.

5. **Importance of re-establishing pride and dignity through social development:** In constructing a new educational system for the Iraqi state, every effort should be made to acknowledge the importance of human dignity. This means acknowledging both the worth of every individual and their perspective in the classroom as well as taking the time to acknowledge that poverty is more than just material deprivation. It represents a condition in which your dignity has been removed, and traditional ways of knowing, like the Marsh Arabs, are considered antithetical to modern progress. Instead of defining society in opposition (modern vs. pre-modern), the new education system should seek to critically engage local as well as global traditions. Within this, an emphasis should be placed upon the function of dignity in creating social

cohesion. These educational activities therefore should not simply be targeted at K-12 or university level but take on a continuing system of liberal as well as science and technical-based education programs.

6. **Essential role that tradition plays in social development:** The fact is that the whole world needs the whole world. Each culture needs to exchange its richness and traditions with other cultures to continually expand its horizons. Each tradition has an inherent basis of knowledge that can be drawn upon to develop society.

William Blake reminds us . . .

> To see a World in a Grain of Sand
> And a Heaven in a Wild Flower,
> Hold Infinity in the palm of your hand
> And Eternity in an hour.[5]

Notes

This essay represents a revision of a keynote address presented February 12, 2004 at the "Principles of the Abrahamic Faiths: Traditions that Advance Education" sponsored by Creative Associates International and The Caux Round Table.

1   William Blake, "A Divine Image," *The Portable Blake* (New York: The Viking Press, 1946).
2   A. Rihani, "A Chant of Mystics," *A Chant of Mystics and Other Poems* (Beirut, Lebanon: The Rihani House, 1970).
3   M. Ibn Arabi, M. *Poem XI*, Tarjuman al-Ashwaq (London: Theosophical Publishing House, 1911).
4   G. Scholem, "Menashe Chayim," *The Fullness of Time* (Jerusalem: Ibis Editions, 2003).
5   William Blake, "Auguries of Innocence," *The Portable Blake* (New York: The Viking Press, 1946).

12

Lessons from the *Building Abrahamic Partnerships* Program at Hartford Seminary

YEHEZKEL LANDAU

I Professional Background and Institutional Context

Since June of 2004, Hartford Seminary has sponsored an interfaith training program for Jews, Christians, and Muslims called *Building Abrahamic Partnerships (BAP)*. An eight-day intensive course, aimed at developing basic concepts and skills, is offered every January and June as part of the Seminary's Winter and Summer terms. In addition, the first advanced-level leadership training for veterans of the basic course was conducted over five days this past July. I have served as *BAP* Program Director since its inception, as a Faculty Associate in Interfaith Relations at the Seminary. In this capacity I have designed, coordinated, and taught in both courses. My responsibility also includes financial and logistical administration, enlisting other members of the teaching staff, and recruiting participants.[1] In this essay I describe the two levels of this innovative program and offer a preliminary assessment of its effectiveness. It is still evolving, partly in response to participants' evaluations and accounts of their experiences.

Hartford Seminary is known nationally and internationally as a Christian institution for theological education with a highly regarded Macdonald Center for Islamic studies and Christian–Muslim relations. My appointment to the faculty in the fall of 2002 added a Jewish dimension to the communal life and academic program of the Seminary. The interfaith conversation was broadened from a bilateral dialogue to an Abrahamic trialogue, while retaining the specialized focus on Christian–Muslim relations. My role as *BAP* Director reflects the Seminary's commitment toward a more inclusive inter-religious agenda, as well as my own professional interests and commitments.

From 1978 until 2002, I lived in Jerusalem and was active, as a dual American–Israeli citizen, in various interreligious peacemaking efforts involving Jews and Palestinians. In the 1980s I directed the staff of the *Oz veShalom-Netivot Shalom* religious peace movement, and from 1991 until 2003 I co-founded and co-directed the *Open House* Center for Jewish–Arab Co-existence and Reconciliation in Ramle, Israel.[2] For over twenty years I also taught Jewish tradition and spirituality at several Christian institutes and ecumenical centers in Israel.

In Hartford, I continue my involvement in Jewish–Arab peacemaking through Open House and other grass-roots initiatives. My conviction remains that, without an explicit spiritual dimension, political agreements will fail to overcome the enmity and mistrust on all sides of the Israeli–Palestinian–Arab conflict. I have a 19-year-old son, Raphael, who is currently a soldier in the Israeli army. It is for the sake of his generation, and those following, that I am committed to the work of interfaith reconciliation. I am convinced that, if we fail to find spiritual remedies for our political ailments, we are condemning our children and grandchildren to even more hellish violence perpetrated by religious extremists and reprisals by governments. In both Judaism and Islam, saving one human life is tantamount to saving the whole of humanity. With so many innocent lives in the balance, I believe we are obligated by God to eliminate walls of separation, to overcome mutual misunderstanding and prejudice, and to work incessantly for inclusive justice, genuine peace, and the healing of wounded hearts.

Educational initiatives like *BAP*, while so urgently needed, are tragically stymied in the Middle East right now by political, cultural, and psychological obstacles. The success of *BAP* is partly due to its setting, the United States in general and Hartford Seminary in particular. The Seminary's history of sponsoring interreligious encounters, studies, and events is one conducive factor. Also, Hartford is situated in the heart of New England, making it accessible to students along the east coast, from Washington, D.C., to Maine. Some of the almost 190 participants in the eight *BAP* courses conducted so far have come from more distant places, including Alabama, Colorado, Wyoming, California, western Canada, the Netherlands, Israel, Syria, Turkey, Egypt, Nigeria, Indonesia, Singapore, Pakistan, and St. Thomas, Virgin Islands. Since there are sizable Jewish and Muslim communities in New England, we can draw students from all three traditions relatively easily. Equally important is the presence of Jewish, Christian, and Muslim communities in the greater Hartford area. This allows for visits to synagogues, mosques, and churches for the worship experiences built into *BAP*. The local congregations that have welcomed *BAP* students to their prayer services have been very gracious and accommodating. The ongoing relationships with local congregations are beneficial for the *BAP* participants who interact with them, for the congregations that are enriched by the curiosity and insights of the visiting students, and for Hartford Seminary in sustaining relationships with local communities of faith.

One last introductory point: using the term "Abrahamic" in the name of the program evokes the figure of Abraham/Ibrahim, a shared spiritual ancestor and role model for Jews, Christians, and Muslims. Such terminology is not unique to *BAP*. Many interfaith dialogues use "Abrahamic" as an alternative to "monotheistic." Aside from the symbolic and sentimental value of using Abraham in this way, the wisdom in this choice is debatable. In the compendium of supplemental readings for the basic *BAP* course, I include two articles that question whether Abraham is a unifying figure at all. Both articles are written by rabbis. Their reservations are motivated by different factors, but their conclusion is the same: each of the three traditions has "its own Abraham," and evoking the patriarch risks fostering division as readily as harmony.[3] Another problematic issue is raised by Prof. Ingrid Mattson, my Hartford Seminary colleague and the current president of the Islamic Society of North America (ISNA). She rightfully cautions that holding up Abraham/Ibrahim for veneration and emulation risks excluding Sarah and Hagar (and potentially all women) from the picture.

II Program Rationale and Goals

To my knowledge there is no Jewish–Christian–Muslim training program similar to *BAP* at any other seminary or religious studies department.[4] The lack of other such initiatives, more than six years after September 11, 2001, amazes me. By now it should be abundantly clear that all our faith communities need help to overcome mutual ignorance and estrangement. Because this is a painful process, we need trained clergy, educators, and facilitators to help us confront the exclusivism and triumphalism that have, at times, turned each of our sacred traditions into a weapon of unholy war.[5] In a US Institute of Peace *Special Report* issued in February, 2003, Rev. Dr. David Smock, who directs the USIP's Religion and Peacemaking Initiative, wrote:

> The overarching question is how to develop interfaith trust in the prevailing atmosphere of fear and mutual suspicion. In situations of trauma, as experienced continuously in the Middle East and as experienced in the West since 9/11, people are likely to turn inward. Accordingly, they have great difficulty in reaching out to the religious 'Other.' The prevailing attitude is often that no one's suffering can compare to our own suffering. In this climate of victimhood, the Other – whether nation, ethnic group, or religious community – is often labeled simplistically and unhelpfully as either good or evil.[6]

Overcoming ignorance is one challenge. Imparting information to enhance knowledge and understanding is standard fare for institutions of higher learning. This is certainly one of the aims of the *BAP* program. Three full days are devoted to presenting the basics of each tradition: historical development, beliefs and practices, denominational variety, and attitudes to other faiths. Yet there is another challenge that such a program has to address to be effective: helping participants overcome their fears and suspicions of one another.[7] Conditioned reflexes, including competing victim scripts, are very difficult to transform. Building trust takes time. It also takes a willingness to acknowledge and question one's own emotional investments: the need to be right, the assurance of being special if not superior, resistance to change, and loyalty to a faith community with its history and behavioral norms. For most Jews and Christians, the *BAP* program is their first opportunity to engage Muslims. For most of the Muslim participants, it is their first encounter with Jews. Such face-to-face meetings demand a level of openness and vulnerability which few people have the courage to risk. Those who rise to the challenge have to confront suspicions from co-religionists, even accusations of disloyalty. This is not an easy burden to carry. An interfaith activist soon learns that *inter*religious cooperation needs to be complemented by *intra*religious work in our respective communities. The latter keeps us grounded in our own traditions and communal loyalties. At the same time, it enables us to sensitize our co-religionists to the challenges and benefits of interfaith encounter.

How much can be accomplished in a one-week course? Surprisingly, a great deal – though everyone involved in *BAP* acknowledges that the January or June program is only the first step on a lifelong journey toward deeper understanding and, ultimately, spiritual fraternity and solidarity. The *BAP II* advanced training which we piloted in July deepens relationships forged in the basic course, and it strengthens interfaith leadership skills which participants can apply in their own communities.

The four goals of the *BAP* program reflect serious intellectual and emotional challenges: (1) *educating participants about the beliefs and practices of the three Abrahamic traditions*; (2) *creating a supportive learning community in which clergy, lay ministers, religious educators, and chaplains can forge mutually beneficial relationships across communal boundaries*; (3) *helping participants acquire pastoral skills useful in interfaith work*; and (4) *developing leadership strategies for promoting interfaith relations in increasingly heterogeneous societies*.

To achieve these goals, I assemble a teaching staff for each round of the basic course comprised of five Hartford Seminary faculty members and three "pastoral adjuncts," clergy from each of the traditions with experience leading local congregations. The Seminary professors other than me are present for designated segments of the program, while the rabbi, minister, and imam accompany the course with me from beginning to end. The three clergy adjuncts are expected to share their theoretical and practical expertise and to intervene when pastoral difficulties arise. Personal discomfort can provide a potentially rich learning opportunity for that individual and the whole group. Each *BAP* round has an appreciable number of such opportunities, and to address them we have evolved a two-pronged strategy:

(1) At the outset of the course, participants are told that their comfort zones

will be challenged during the week and that we need a consensual agreement to maintain fidelity to our overall goals. A list of ground rules for respectful dialogue (as opposed to debate) is read aloud and adopted. When necessary, these ground rules are reiterated to bring the group back to its agreed-upon norms for communicating;

(2) When someone hears a statement that irritates or offends, s/he is encouraged to say "ouch!" so that the group can address that person's feelings in real time. Often the "ouches" are sparked by one person speaking on behalf of an entire faith community, with co-religionists feeling misrepresented. Conversely, if someone experiences surprise and delight in learning something new, s/he is encouraged to say "wow!" Krister Stendahl, my Christian mentor and friend, calls this "holy envy," and he considers such an experience to be the ideal outcome of interreligious encounter. In *BAP*, there are usually more "ouches" than "wows," requiring sensitive and effective leadership to facilitate the group process productively.

III Content of BAP I

The content of the basic course is half academic and half experiential, in keeping with its intellectual and affective goals. Students taking the course for credit are required to submit two assignments: a 15–to–20-page research paper and a personal journal recording their insights and feelings during the week.[8] The academic element of the program consists of:

- the three days devoted to each of the three traditions, mixing frontal presentations and facilitated discussions; these include treatments of controversial topics, often the subjects of widespread misconceptions and prejudices – for example, what Israel and Zionism mean to Jews, or what the Trinity means to Christians, or what *jihad* means to Muslims;
- three evening sessions devoted to specific subjects, with resource persons from each of the traditions facilitating the discussion and offering input as a panel: one evening on "What Do We Mean by Spirituality?" (with interfaith triads exchanging accounts of religious experiences before the panel offers reflections); one on "Religion and the Media," featuring three professional journalists from the newspaper and television industries sharing examples and insights from their work; and a very practical session on "Sensitivities and Skills for Interfaith Partnerships," with the group generating its own list of successful strategies, frameworks, and interactive methods for establishing Jewish–Christian–Muslim relationships;
- and three half days of comparative text study, in four small groups and plenary discussions. The texts we choose for examination are of two kinds: passages that evoke inclusive justice, peace, and loving behavior; and others that are problematic, at least to outsiders, for they seem to

summon the faithful to exclusivist or belligerent behavior toward those who are different. In the first rounds of the course, the text study took place before the day-long introductions to the three faiths, but we found that it is more effective to have the overviews first and then the text-study, to make the passages more meaningful to those who are not familiar with their neighbors' scriptures.

The experiential dimension of the basic course includes:

- worship in a mosque on Friday, a synagogue on Saturday, and a church on Sunday, followed by group discussions of the respective prayers and practices;
- two to three artistic or symbolic exercises providing non-analytic ("right-brain") modes of self-expression;[9]
- and long lunch and dinner breaks to encourage fellowship and networking. Many participants have reported that these mealtimes are the best part of the course, allowing them to cross boundaries, overcome fears and prejudices, and forge new friendships.

Over seven rounds of the basic *BAP* course, some common denominators stand out in regard to content. On the day devoted to Jewish tradition, the brief introduction to the meaning of *Shabbat* and how it is observed by Jews invariably elicits "wows" from Christians and Muslims. Participants are generally intrigued by unfamiliar spiritual disciplines in each other's lives. Understandably, the discussion on how Jews view Israel and Zionism, and how Christians and Muslims respond, is emotionally charged. To minimize polarization and to illustrate religiously motivated peacemaking, I screen two video clips on the *Open House* peace center in Ramle, Israel. When Imam Yahya Hendi, a Palestinian-American and a Hartford Seminary graduate, is one of the pastoral adjuncts, he and I model respectful dialogue about the Middle East and sometimes embrace each other tearfully by the end of the session. The students can see, from our example, how Jews and Muslims, including Israelis and Palestinians, can be allies in religious peacemaking instead of adversaries.[10]

For Islam, it is the *hajj* pilgrimage and the five daily prayers that evoke "wows" of "holy envy" among Jews and Christians. Prof. Ingrid Mattson, in her presentation, counters misconceptions about Muslim women and helps the students understand the difference between the teachings of Islam and the different cultural manifestations (including distortions of the normative tradition) in nominally Muslim societies. Christians react in different ways upon learning that Muslims revere Jesus and Mary but do not accord them divine or superhuman status. Some Christians are pleased by this positive outlook toward their Lord and his mother. But others are disturbed, feeling threatened by another tradition that has its own view of Jesus, as prophet rather than savior. The Jewish participants, on the whole, are fascinated by this conversation but are outside it, since Judaism essentially ignores Jesus.

On the day allotted to Christianity, Prof. Ian Markham starts with a very effective exercise, evoking surprise and irony: On the blackboard he writes the word "God," followed by "Trinity," "Incarnation," "Bodily Resurrection of Jesus," "Virgin Birth of Jesus," "Hell, Demons, and Satan," "Substitutionary Atonement," "Historical Inerrancy of Scripture," and "The Incompatibility of Christianity with Evolution." He asks the Christians to raise their hands if they believe in God, and all the Christians do so. Then he goes down the list, and hands drop as the different doctrinal claims are considered, with the more liberal Protestants experiencing increasing discomfort, doubt, or outright disbelief. Ian then asks the Muslims in the group to do the same exercise. The Christians (and Jews) are amazed to discover that the Muslims affirm more of the classical Christian doctrines than do many of the Christians, since they are also taught in the Qur'an. This is a wonderful teaching moment, as Muslims and Christians, with Jews joining in, discuss the authority of sacred texts, the nature and meaning of revelation, and the place of subjectivity and rational criticism in the interpretation of scriptures. These concerns surface again when we study texts in all three traditions on Thursday and Friday.

IV Shared Worship

A few additional aspects of *BAP I* are worth highlighting. The formal worship in the mosque, synagogues, and churches toward the end of the course, as well as the devotions offered by participants at the start of the morning and afternoon sessions, are two complementary experiences that are spiritually and symbolically enriching. In the discussions over lunch that follow the public prayers on Friday, Saturday, and Sunday, participants ask clarifying questions and share "ouches" and "wows" that emerged for them during the worship. By the end of the week, Jews and Christians have generally overcome any initial apprehensions over entering a mosque, a new experience for almost all of them. The Christian and Jewish women feel solidarity with their Muslim sisters at the mosque, as they don headscarves (helped by the Muslim women) and share the same-gender piety in the women's section. Through their first-ever experience at a synagogue, whether modern Orthodox or Reform, Muslims develop a deeper appreciation of how Jewish tradition and the Hebrew language are so close to Islam and Arabic. At least one Catholic participant had what she called a "theophany" when the Torah scroll emerged from the Ark and was carried around the synagogue, with congregants singing and kissing the Torah as it passed.

On Sunday, the discussion over lunch following the Episcopal and U.C.C. church services helps to clarify denominational differences among Christians, and it allows Jews and Muslims to honestly share any discomfort they may experience in Christian worship. This emotional estrangement is particularly acute for Jews when a New Testament reading or sermon refers negatively to "scribes and Pharisees," or "the Jews" in the Gospel of John are castigated, or some other subject that has engendered Jewish–Christian and animosity over the centuries arises. These are the moments, holistically engaging head and heart and gut, where I believe *BAP* is most interpersonally genuine, spiritually and ethically concrete, and ultimately transformative in positive ways. For it is, above all, the hurt and the fear which we all carry that we are challenged to confront honestly and work through together. Theological discussions take us only part of the way toward reconciliation. Without the honest exchange of negative feelings and conditioned resistances, we are not being true to ourselves or to one another, and we are not living up to what this era of history demands of us. Instead, we are playing it safe by remaining superficial and abstract. It is necessary, but insufficient, for example, for Christians to examine, together with Muslims and Jews, the theological underpinnings of Christological prayers and hymns, or the meaning of a sacrament like the Eucharist. What Christians also need to know and understand is that most Jews and Muslims will react to these central aspects of Christianity with profound spiritual and emotional dissonance, sometimes even revulsion, engendering self-protective distance. This response is far deeper than cognitive disagreement. It is a kind of "spiritual allergy," a discomfort that touches the soul. And it is precisely this kind of reaction – by anyone in an Abrahamic trialogue – that needs careful and caring examination, once sufficient trust has been established within the group.

One Jewish psychologist shared her experience in the program with members of her Amherst, MA, synagogue during a *Shavuot* sermon in June 2005:

> Through my encounter with Muslim and Christian prayer, I understood more clearly our rabbis' entreaty that prayer be the vessel for the eternal fire of Divine love that burns away the separate self. . . . with a heart of humility, we need to listen to these and those voices, Muslim, Christian, Jewish so that the agony of splintered time will cease, so that we may find our way to *shleimut*, wholeness.

It is worth adding that there is a deliberate attempt in both the basic and advanced courses to include musical selections and artistic exercises, in order to add an aesthetic dimension that engages the heart and soul as well as the intellect. There is also a conscious attempt to make the several *kosher/halal* meals that are eaten together – supplementing the unprogrammed meals during the participants' free time – experiences of consecrated fellowship. Blessings from all three traditions are offered before the food is taken. All these exercises and experiences are ritualistic expressions of community across theological boundaries, and they create soulful bridges that allow for less inhibited exchanges in the classroom.

When people of different faiths share a prayer experience, the question that arises is: are they praying together as one fellowship, affirming a common set of religious truths, or are they spectators in each other's worship settings? Either mode of worshipping together is possible, and each has its own legitimacy and value depending on the desired outcome.[11] The last day of *BAP II*, the advanced course, is consciously designed to give participants experience with both kinds of liturgies: single-faith prayers and inclusive worship. Any of us may choose to opt out of a prayer experience because of conditioned resistances or sincere theological reservations. For example, in the very first *BAP I* course, some conservative participants (primarily Muslims) felt uncomfortable when the U.C.C. church we attended gave its blessing to same-sex relationships through some hymns. Over lunch afterwards, some of the participants shared their discomfort and said they would have preferred to watch the service from the balcony, establishing a clear distance from the congregation. In subsequent rounds of the course, this option was offered to the students in order to prevent such spiritual discomfort.

V A Theological Underpinning for BAP

As I work for mutual understanding and solidarity among Jews, Christians, and Muslims, my own theological assumptions are constantly challenged. A key question is whether one can develop a theology, or multiple theologies, of religious pluralism to undergird the building of Abrahamic partnerships. One theology, acceptable to all, that accounts for religious diversity within God's plan is inconceivable. The three traditions have disparate understandings of why the One God has allowed different, mutually irreconcilable theologies to coexist.

One can, of course, bracket the theological dimension entirely and promote interreligious encounter on the basis of practical necessity: Humanity as an endangered species requires collective effort in order to survive. No talk of redemption or reconciliation is necessary, according to this utilitarian perspective. But *BAP* has a deeper goal. It seeks to heal the historic wounds that have traumatized us and left us, as Abrahamic siblings, estranged from one another. It has a vision of interreligious reconciliation and cooperation that is hopeful – one might even say messianic – for it is rooted in our shared summons to emulate God by living lives of justice, peace, and love. To overcome our deep-seated fears and to bring us closer to the hoped-for Kingdom of God, we need new religious paradigms. One of the obstacles to such new, visionary thinking is the narrow way in which our traditions have formed our identities.

Redefining our particular identities in other than dualistic ways (us vs. them, saved vs. damned, righteous vs. sinful), requires humility and an appreciation for human diversity as a blessing rather than a threat. The *intellectual* challenge of dialectically affirming the Oneness of God and the multiplicity of theologies is compounded by the *emotional* challenge of transcending our victim scripts and demythologizing the adversarial relationship with our traditional "enemies." *BAP* encourages participants, in a relatively "safe" setting, to undertake both transformations, the intellectual and the emotional. The theological link between the two is the <u>symbolic transfiguration</u> *of God* (favoring more than one faith community), *of ourselves* (seeing ourselves as distinct but not superior or victorious over others), and *of our relationship with others* (as allies rather than adversaries).

Sadly, none of our traditions has adequately prepared us for this theological transfiguration, and that is why programs like *BAP* are needed. At this point in history, humanity is in dire need of more inclusive religious concepts and norms for what it means to be faithful – to God and to one another. One direction for my own theological thinking is exploring the implications of seeing the One God as a "multiple covenanter," inviting all of humanity (through Noah) and then different faith communities into complementary relationships of sacrificial service for the sake of God's Creation. We need to explore together new ways of doing theology, new ways of living together, and new ways of integrating the two. In this spirit, *BAP* participants are pioneers venturing onto unfamiliar terrain, where we are all equal in God's sight and where we all have unique insights to contribute toward a future of shared promise and blessing. Let us recall that in the Biblical account (Gen. 12:3), Abraham is promised: "in you all of the families of the earth shall be blessed." It does not say that all of humanity will merge into one family. The verse implies, instead, that distinct family and faith identities will remain, but that we will all share a common blessing.

VI Summary

As Jews, Christians, and Muslims sharing a fragile planet in a time of collective peril, we are called to face one another in repentance and humility. We all proclaim a messianic future unfolding and anticipated, but we have all failed to translate those proclamations into effective action. Instead, we have undermined our own beliefs and aspirations. We desecrate what we call holy, and we become our own worst enemies. Entrenched fears rooted in past or present traumas cripple our imaginations. Instead of envisioning a future in which we are all redeemed and blessed, we compensate ourselves for our insecurities by fantasies of unilateral victory and vindication.

We need new theologies of inclusiveness that affirm the oneness of God and a plurality of ways to worship and serve God. We need new models of religious and interreligious education. We need pedagogies that help us grow in faithfulness to the tradition of our forebears while we learn from the traditions of our neighbors, affirming them as valid and valuable. Above all we need new understandings of those neighbors. We must come to know them not only intellectually through increased factual knowledge – *yeda'* in Hebrew, a cognitive knowing based on new *in*formation. More critical are new heart-understandings of each other, grounded in mutual affection and appreciation. In Hebrew this is *da'at,* the kind of intimate knowledge and spiritual *trans*formation that Adam and Eve shared after leaving the Garden and its childlike innocence.[12] None of us is innocent of wrongdoing. At one time or another, each of our religious traditions has been complicit in domination and mass slaughter. If we are to write a new historical chapter that redeems our tragic past and present, we need collaborative initiatives in mutual re-education. We should be corrective mirrors for each other, so that we do not repeat our past mistakes. Many of those mistakes originate in the act of projecting evil onto others rather than acknowledging it in ourselves. If we can be helped to see our own limitations and moral lapses through the eyes of our Abrahamic siblings, we have a chance to truly experience the Kingdom of God on earth. The beginning of redemption is the humble recognition that we need one another to be redeemed. *BAP* is one modest effort to foster that recognition among Jews, Christians, and Muslims and to develop a praxis of partnership in that spirit.

Notes

1 Tuition income alone could not cover the costs of the program. I am profoundly grateful to the three foundations whose funding has made *BAP* possible: The Henry Luce Foundation, the William and Mary Greve Foundation, and the Alan B. Slifka Foundation.

2 For information on *Oz veShalom-Netivot Shalom,* see <www.netivot-shalom. org.il>; for information on *Open House,* see <www.friendsofopenhouse.org>. See, also, my research report "Healing the Holy Land: Interreligious Peacebuilding in Israel/Palestine," Washington, D.C.: United States Institute of Peace, *Peaceworks* No. 51, September 2003.

3 Alon Goshen-Gottstein, "Abraham and 'Abrahamic Religions' in Contemporary Interreligious Discourse," in *Studies in Interreligious Dialogue,* Volume 12, Issue 2, 2002, pp. 165–83; and Rabbi Avi Safran, "Avraham Avinu – the 'interfaith superstar,'" in the *Connecticut Jewish Ledger,* October 11, 2002, p. 11.

4 A US Institute of Peace *Special Report,* written by Rev. Dr. David Smock and entitled "Teaching about the Religious Other" (Washington, D.C., July 2005), summarizes presentations by 16 participants in a two-day workshop on programs and curricula for teaching about the Abrahamic Other, in America and abroad. I took part in that workshop, sharing information about the *BAP* program (p. 4).

5 For examinations of how our understandings of the sacred can be used to justify violence, see R. Scott Appleby, *The Ambivalence of the Sacred: Religion, Violence, and Reconciliation* (Lanham, MD: Rowman & Littlefield Publishers, 2000); Charles Kimball, *When Religion Becomes Evil* (New York: HarperCollins Publishers, 2002); Oliver McTernan, *Violence in God's Name: Religion in an Age of Conflict* (Maryknoll, N.Y.: Orbis Books, 2003); Mark Juergensmeyer, *Terror in the Mind of God: The Global Rise of Religious Violence* (Berkeley: University of California Press, 2001); and Ian Markham and Ibrahim M. Abu-Rabi, editors, *September 11: Religious Perspectives on the Causes and Consequences* (Oxford: Oneworld Publications, 2002). For an analysis of how Abrahamic religions (Judaism and Islam especially) can be forces for both conflict and reconciliation,

see Marc Gopin, *Holy War, Holy Peace: How Religion Can Bring Peace to the Middle East* (New York: Oxford University Press, 2002).

6   David Smock, "Building Interreligious Trust in a Climate of Fear: An Abrahamic Trialogue," *Special Report 99*, Washington, D.C.: United States Institute of Peace, February 2003, p. 3.

7   For a Jewish approach to these challenges, see Jonathan Magonet, *Talking to the Other: Jewish Interfaith Dialogue with Christians and Muslims* (London: I. B. Tauris & Co., 2003), especially chapter two, "The Challenge to Judaism of Interfaith Dialogue" (pp. 11–22), and chapter 8, "Risk-taking in Religious Dialogue" (pp. 90–106).

8   I have the privilege of reading and grading the materials submitted. The journals, in particular, have taught me a great deal about how the course, including the interactions outside the classroom, impacts the students.

9   At the opening dinner one of two exercises is used for self-introductions and initial group bonding:
(1) three condiment containers (clear salt and pepper shakers plus an opaque bottle of soy sauce) are presented as representing Judaism, Christianity, and Islam. Participants are asked to group them so that two traditions (represented by the salt and pepper shakers) are deemed closer in nature than either is to the third (the soy bottle), and to explain this choice in their self-introduction. Three alternatives are possible, and each is valid according to its own criteria for relating the faith traditions. Many Jews and Christians use the soy bottle to represent Islam, which is "opaque" to them. Often Muslims and Jews see Christianity as the "opaque" and distant Other, finding more affinities between Islam and Judaism as ways of life centered on normative behaviors like dietary rules. A few students resist the premise of the exercise, and they either refuse to do it or they change the rules, e.g., by suggesting that the ingredients of all three containers be poured into one vessel; or (2) an 8" × 11" piece of paper with a serrated border, representing a postage stamp, is given to each student. Everyone is asked to draw his or her own religious stamp, serving as an "ambassador" image to adherents of other religions. Colored markers are provided, and each person gets a chance to share her/his stamp and explain its symbolism.

On the last day of the course, before the closing dinner, large A3 sheets of paper are disseminated, each with a blank circle surrounded by the words *shalom* (in Hebrew), *Salaam* (in Arabic), and *peace*. Participants use colored markers to draw their visions of interreligious peace. Then they share the results in turn, while sitting in a circle, after which the group walks around the circle in silence, looking closely at each of the drawings placed on the chairs. This exercise helps participants see how the week has affected them intellectually and emotionally, and it provides successful closure to the course.

10   See our co-authored article, "Jews, Muslims, and Peace," in *Current Dialogue*, Vol. 41, June–July 2003, Geneva: World Council of Churches, pp. 12–13. In the *BAP I* course this past June (2006), an unfortunate, but educationally significant, incident occurred in my modern Orthodox synagogue on *Shabbat*, following the morning prayers. The rabbi conducted a question-and-answer session for the *BAP* students and some members of the congregation, as he had done several times before. This time the Middle East situation became the focus for intense, and increasingly bitter, exchanges. A few Jewish congregants got defensive and made some bellicose statements which hurt the Muslim students (including four women

from Damascus, Syria) and undermined for all of us the "safe" environment we had created over the week. Later that afternoon the whole group re-convened at the Seminary to process what had happened. Many tissues were consumed as students and teachers shared their pain over the verbal assault, along with mutual affection and care. Despite the shock and pain caused by this experience, it proved beneficial in taking the group to a deeper level of empathy and solidarity with one another. It did leave me thinking, however, about how to better prepare the members of my synagogue for the challenge of hosting non-Jewish visitors for interreligious conversation.

11 For an example of a Christian participant observer analyzing Jewish prayers and customs, see Harvey Cox, *Common Prayers: Faith, Family, and a Christian's Journey Through the Jewish Year* (Boston: Houghton Mifflin Company, 2001); and for a chronicle of a Jew's journey through Christian and Muslim devotional rites, see Yossi Klein Halevi, *At the Entrance to the Garden of Eden: A Jew's Search for God with Christians and Muslims in the Holy Land* (New York: William Morrow, 2001).

12 For examples of such transformation of the heart, see Yossi Klein Halevi, *At the Entrance to the Garden of Eden, op. cit.*, and Donald Nicholl, *The Testing of Hearts: A Pilgrim's Journey* (London: Darton, Longman and Todd, 1998).

PART
IV

Contemporary Relations and Challenges

CHAPTER 13

Peacemaking among the Religions of Abraham: Overcoming Obstacles to Co-existence

NATHAN C. FUNK AND MEENA SHARIFY-FUNK

In harmonious relationships, dialogue is often taken for granted; sometimes it is not even noticed. In delicate or troubled relationships, dialogue is commonly regarded as a dangerous compromise – at best an expression of naïveté, and at worst an act of betrayal or disloyalty.

As a few minutes of internet research can reveal, contemporary Christian–Muslim, Muslim–Jewish, and Christian-Jewish relations clearly fall into the "delicate" category.[1] In many cases the quality of discourse is deeply unsettling. Calls for racial and religious cleansing are disturbingly commonplace in blogs and in weblogs of reader commentary that follow stories on respectable news sites, and information sources purporting to convey the "bitter truth" about the Abrahamic "other" are far from marginal. Utilizing a medium that is conducive to unedited, knee-jerk expressions of hostility and selective representation of reality, protagonists of conflict are finding the internet useful for disseminating messages of exclusion. Radicalized Muslims are accusing Christians and Jews of grave moral sins – arguing in effect that political offences committed by Christians and Jews are symptomatic of a more profound deviation from the original truths of their traditions, as understood by Muslims. Polemical thinkers within the Christian and Jewish traditions, in turn, are representing Islam as a completely alien and hostile phenomenon, and proclaiming that co-existence with Muslims is impossible. Too often, theological disputations mirror contemporary political disputes, and project a future dominated by mythic images of struggle and confrontation.

Ironically, the dynamics of our post-modern era seem to be reinforcing divisions within the Abrahamic family rather than effacing them. The Abrahamic faiths stand divided not only by the geopolitics of nation-states, but also by their common heritage. This heritage ensures not only deep resonance among faith traditions, but also more points for disputation than are to be found among religions that share fewer common sources and spiritual affinities. As F. E. Peters notes,

> [H]ostility among Abraham's heirs seems often to have masked a common fear of each other's allure. Polemic among the three communities has in fact been produced mostly for home consumption, written to reassure its own believers that they, not their obviously (if we look closely) attractive rivals, were the Chosen People.[2]

Sadly, polemic among the three communities contributed to a number of negative historical encounters. The accumulated residues of traumatic historical experiences – from medieval confrontations to the Holocaust, colonialism, the Arab–Israeli conflict, and the contemporary "war on terrorism" – have been reactivated and reinforced by the events of recent years, bequeathing heavy burden of identity conflict on children who will be born in the early 21st century.

Nonetheless, it is to be hoped – and we do not have the luxury of giving up on hope – that the children of Abraham may now be on the threshold of finding within themselves the magnanimity required to appreciate one another on deeper levels. The fact that they have not achieved this in the past may have much less to do with inherent deficiencies within the faiths than with the psychology of fear and adversarialism that has developed in the shadow of political conflict. Overcoming this psychology will require the active cultivation of (1) a clear understanding of how selective perception and geopolitics are driving the Abrahamic faiths apart, (2) deeper appreciation and mutual knowledge of each tradition's resources for transforming conflict, and (3) a much stronger and more substantive sense of Abrahamic solidarity – unity in diversity. To change the way the children of Abraham are relating to one another and set in motion new dynamics, there is a need for initiatives that disentangle political and religious dimensions of the current impasse, while drawing attention to religious resources for change and deep resonances among the traditions.

Disentangling Precepts and Political Psychology

In the present climate of recrimination and insecurity, it is not difficult to understand why many Muslims, Christians, and Jews choose to frame contemporary conflicts in relation to religious categories, as theologically driven rivalries between competing claimants to truth and cultural enlightenment. After all, the religions of Abraham may share a common source, but their intertwined histories provide precedents for conflict. Religious adherents are willing to sacrifice to maintain the integrity of their beliefs, and political leaders are eager to gain legitimacy by appealing to religious values and narratives. Making sense of these realities without reductionistic oversimplification is one of the most important challenges facing conflict analysts in the post-9/11 era.

Notions of irreconcilable conflict among the spiritual heirs of Abraham are both damaging and disempowering. In our current context, the human cost of believing in inevitable rivalry has become starkly apparent. Such a conviction not only obscures secular sources of tension, but also impoverishes spiritual traditions by turning believers away from their most compelling and universally appealing moral inheritances. The resultant accentuation of religious differences and other markers of group distinctiveness clears the way for entrepreneurs of confrontation, and impoverishes the human moral imagination.[3]

Because exaggerating religion's role in conflict can reinforce negative trends or lead to paralysis, many analysts have been tempted to "explain away" the religious dimension of conflict by pointing exclusively to secular factors such as group identification and competition for power, status, and resources. This reaction has its roots in the visceral reaction of many modern intellectuals to "populist" narratives that exaggerate historical clashes while ignoring obvious spiritual affinities. While useful insofar as it demystifies worldly motives that are obscured by exclusively religious narratives, denial of the role religion can play in conflict can do as much to marginalize religious peace efforts as overstated claims about religion as the monocausal source of antagonism.

To deal constructively with the religious dimension of contemporary tensions, an integrated approach to conflict analysis is necessary. Analysts and conflict resolution practitioners need to cultivate the habit of examining "religious" conflicts with two eyes, one religious and one secular. Concepts from the social and behavioural sciences need to be "partnered" with genuinely religious insights, as a basis for exploring both theological and political dimensions of conflict. When religious and social scientific insights are paired, it becomes possible to take the interpretive (cultural and religious) aspects of conflict more seriously,[4] and to discover ways in which religious and material dimensions of conflict interact and, at times, camouflage or discolour each other. It also becomes possible to discover, within the contested realm of religious belief and symbolism, natural affinities between deeply religious understandings of peace and more secular bases for affirming human dignity (for example, contemporary international discourse about peace, human development, ecological sustainability, and human rights).

There are many ways in which a well-informed understanding of religious traditions can sharpen political analysis. A clear distillation of similarities and differences between the precepts of two traditions, for example, can illuminate ways in which observers as well as participants in conflict err when they mistake modern political psychology for "ancient hatred." At the same time, careful efforts to explore similarities and differences between the traditions can prevent trivialization of the theological and religious-identity dimensions of conflict, and make new ways of relating to one's own and another's tradition possible.

A fair-minded overview of similarities and differences among the religions of Abraham leads quite naturally to the conclusion that theological incompatibilities offer only a partial explanation for current troubles. Differences in precepts cannot fully account for many of the more egregious instances of historical antagonism. Serious and disciplined inquiry naturally tends to lead toward the conclusions that the Abrahamic faiths share strong affinities, despite the presence of clauses in religious texts that have been interpreted in ways that permitted offences against the religious "other." The resultant breaches in intercommunal relations have been far from trivial in importance, but differences in religious precepts only made these offences possible. Actual instances of intercommunal conflict owe much to power-political distortions of religion, polarization of collective religious identities, and impoverishment of historical narratives about interreligious relations. Carefully mapping out these historical and political factors and then "putting them on the table" can be one of the most helpful impetuses for reclaiming religious traditions for peace. Because interpretation of traditions takes place within political contexts, reflection on these past and present contexts can have a purifying and restorative function, while also helping to prevent cooptation of faith traditions by contemporary entrepreneurs of conflict.

By initiating deliberations with theological and historical deliberations, the "Children of Abraham" conference enabled participants to reflect on the interdependent development of the three principal Abrahamic traditions, and on instances of co-existence as well as competition. The deliberations invited constructive self-criticism and proactive exploration of possibilities for new beginnings – together with a realization that excluding religious frameworks from peacemaking processes will prevent an adequate response to present tensions.

Current political and economic conditions privilege adversarial approaches to Abrahamic relations, for a variety of reasons. First, the Abrahamic religions exist not only in texts that speak of past human encounters with the transcendent, but also in a world of large-scale social relationships. The religions, therefore, play a powerful role in the construction of cultural and national identities, and religious interpretation thereby becomes vulnerable to pressures arising from geopolitical competition and the efforts of political leaders to imbue their actions with religious legitimacy. Second, as an element of collective identity and a reservoir of cultural symbols, religious elements are frequently used in the definition of "enemy images" and the telling of conflict narratives. Third, the existence of adversarial relations between communities defined wholly or in part in religious terms can present serious challenges to religious peacemaking, particularly when religious warrants for peacemaking under conditions of insecurity have received little attention from political and clerical leaders.

(1) Geopolitical Cooptation

With respect to the first point, the social nature of religious identity can make it difficult for communities to insulate interpretations of religious precepts from historical and political processes. A survey of every major world religion reveals that, insofar as religion is a constitutive element of cultural and national identities, patterns of realistic geopolitical conflict have a way of influencing the interpretation and application of religious values. Although religious values have provided "brakes" on some conflict behaviours and barriers to others, geopolitical conflict has its own power political logic, and "selects" less peaceable and pluralistic interpretive options within a faith tradition. Religion can therefore become a mobilization and legitimacy tool and a coopted adjunct to nationalism and ethnicity – fuel for fire rather than water. In our present world historical context, leading protagonists of Western-Islamic as well as Middle Eastern conflict draw at least some of their passion from conflict-saturated Abrahamic religious commitments, rein- forcing divisions that also have "realistic" bases linked to land, resources, economics, and perceived strategic imperatives. Among these leading protag- onists of confrontation, religious and political considerations reinforce each other; religion adds to the intensity of conflict, without unilaterally directing it.

(2) Religiously Coloured Enemy Images

The second dynamic, the use of religious vocabulary in inter-Abrahamic enemy images, is a particularly tragic correlate of the geopolitical cooptation process. While many of the ways in which these enemy images are constructed reflect real religious history and actual negative encounters among traditions, the application of concepts from social psychology – including the funda- mental attribution error and selective perception – can lead to richer insights into conflict narratives within present-day Abrahamic communities.

Bias in attributing motives can be seen quite clearly in the manner in which protagonists from each of the Abrahamic religions steadfastly assert the intrinsically peaceful character of their own tradition – attributing deviations to extenuating circumstances and the need for "defense" – while refusing to grant the same charitable judgment about intentions to their counterpart faiths. With respect to the "other," breaches of the peace reflect innate dispo- sition, not circumstances and external pressures. Collective self-esteem is further reinforced by perpetuating unfavourable "us–them" contrasts and engaging in competitive theological discourse. A result is the oft-heard refrain,

"We are peaceful, but what about them?" Group solidarity and existential security are both served by such habits of thought and perception, albeit at a price of lingering ignorance and misinformation.

Sadly, religious symbolism is all too common in North American and Middle Eastern conflict narratives. In the United States, for example, 9/11 has become a shared trauma in a narrative of religious nationalism that connects present-day concerns about terrorism to such distant events as Arab-Islamic conquests, the Crusades, and clashes with the Barbary pirates, as well as to imagined millenarian futures centered around events in Israel/Palestine. Radical Muslim framings of history are similar to their Western counterparts, as Osama bin Laden's designation of adversaries as "Jews and Crusaders" indicates. In the Middle Eastern context, the eclipse of memory about shared Jewish–Muslim–Christian glories and the projection of the earliest Abrahamic rivalries onto the present Israeli–Palestinian conflict is one of the great tragedies of our time. The gradual disappearance of a generation of Arab Muslims and Middle Eastern Jews who could remember better (or at least tolerable) times – together with the increased emigration of Middle Eastern Christians – should evoke a sense of urgency among historical researchers keen to discover "unstoried experiences" about everyday Abrahamic co-existence.

Although this-worldly stakes of contemporary conflicts should never be ignored in a way that grants exclusive privilege to psychological analysis, the perceptive observer of Abrahamic relations cannot help but notice a deep reluctance among many of Abraham's children to face their tradition's collective shadow. This hesitance is facilitated by projection – preoccupation with faults of the other that are also one's own – and by a perception that admitting wrongdoings committed in the name of religion will cause the faithful to lose faith. The need for a positive sense of self-identity impedes the difficult work of self-criticism and – just as importantly – seeing the other in oneself and oneself in the other. At a more mundane and concrete level, this means inability to see the self as others see it and unfair religious apologetics perpetuated within isolated and sheltered in-group conversations.

Intriguingly, this inability to face the shadow-side of one's communal identity is also apparent in Western secular culture, with its unbalanced tendency to associate religion (or at least the religions of *others*) with irrationality and conflict. Best-sellers about religion's deficits, for example, almost completely neglect the great harms committed during recent centuries in the name of non-religious ideologies, including nationalism, "command" communism, and fascism. Although these secular excesses are familiar to narrators of the popular "end of history" story of Western neoliberal triumphalism, efforts to assert the "finality" or unique merit of contemporary Western values are experienced by contemporary Muslims as arrogant, humiliating, and rife with double standards.

(3) Neglect of Religious Peace Resources

Given contemporary geopolitics and the role that the "religious other" plays in enemy images, it should come as no surprise that religious peace resources have been neglected, and that many members of Abrahamic religious communities associate feelings of vulnerability and inauthenticity with interpretations centered around peacemaking. How, one might ask, can "letting down the defences" in the face of threats and genuinely traumatic encounters be religiously legitimate? Is not reaching out to the other without preconditions a prelude to surrender? Such questions are implicit in much contemporary religious and political discourse, which adopts a far more liberal approach to the reinterpretation of religious "conflict texts" than to morally creative responses to "peace texts," which are restricted to their original historical contexts. Religiously based paradigms for pluralism, appreciation, and mutuality are rejected as inauthentic or relativistic, leaving the task of fostering pluralism to secular authorities who rely on pragmatic rather than symbolic, passionate, and scripturally enriched arguments.

In a situation of escalated conflict, religious peace discourse tends to find itself at a competitive disadvantage. Psychologically, appeals to embrace the other appear to lack a proper concern for fused (some might say "confused" or conflated) national and religious loyalties and allegiances. Intellectually, they may also appear to lack the rigor, focus, and zeal associated with more exclusive forms of religious identification. Given what is known about the "other" and the "self" from inherited narratives and present experiences, casual religious arguments about peacemaking appear to presuppose moral relativism and an inability to discriminate between truth and falsehood. Maintaining boundaries becomes a pre-eminent virtue.

Trends toward conflict escalation create conditions that help to select for adversarial forms of religious expression and leadership. As *Table 1* suggests, the pressures created by contemporary conflicts activate religious cultures of interpretation that accelerate rather than decelerate conflict. Each of the three Abrahamic religions bears within itself sub-traditions within which the imprint of past conflicts with communal outsiders is keenly felt and remembered, and these sub-traditions can come to the fore in situations of social tension, particularly when exponents of alternative perspectives are passive or disorganized. Nonetheless, each religion also bears within itself exemplars and memories of peacemaking – sub-traditions that can and must be taken into account for a proper appreciation of Abrahamic faith's deeper significance and possibilities. Activating these pacific understandings or faith is one of the key challenges of religiously based conflict transformation, as is working to create conditions "on the ground" that give life-affirming and peaceful expressions of religious identity credibility and persuasive power.

Table 13.1   *Religion in Conflict and Peacemaking*[5]

WAYS RELIGION ENTERS POLITICS	WAYS RELIGION CAN ACCELERATE CONFLICT	WAYS RELIGION CAN CONTRIBUTE TO PEACEMAKING
Religiously engaged actors (individuals and groups)	Actors using religion as "power tool," "force multiplier," or barrier	Actors using religion as a bridge or as a source of empowerment for peaceful change
Religious symbols, identities, and narratives	Competitive polarization of identities and narratives of rivalry/victimization ("us" vs. "them")	Open religious identities and narratives with positive role for the "stranger"
Religious cultures and values	Exclusive understandings of goodness and virtue; strong in-group/out-group biases	Inclusive understanding of spiritual values; commitment to social justice, nonviolence, and reconciliation
Religious texts and interpretations	Cutting off dialogue about interpretation; authoritarianism; emphasis on righteous or purifying violence	Affirmation of transcendent divine mystery, of immanent human responsibilities, and of open-ended quest for understanding

Rediscovering Abrahamic Traditions through Dialogue

In the present context of war and political violence, conventional modernist prescriptions for transcending interreligious conflict are inadequate. Opposing secularism to religious culture or "universalism" to "particularism" cannot solve the problems posed by escalated identity conflict, and actually heightens the sense of identity threat experienced by partisans of beleaguered Abrahamic traditions. It also, one might add, distracts attention from material sources of contemporary problems, including unequal power relations between world regions and competition for privileged access to petroleum resources. While a broadly shared consensus on key norms and standards would be of great value, such a framework cannot be imposed (the ostensible purpose of the present War on Terrorism). A much more vigorous approach to dialogue is needed.

Destructive encounters can bring out the worst among adherents of the Abrahamic religious traditions, but carefully constructed positive encounters can significantly aid efforts to rediscover resources for peace. Sincere dialogue among Jews, Christians, and Muslims has become one of the most vital tasks for ensuring that religious expression remains life-affirming and life-enhancing in our present global era. Though not a substitute for intra-religious dialogue, interreligious encounters have unique potential not only for cultivating appreciative understanding of the "other," but also for arriving at deeper self-knowledge.

To transcend past legacies and come to know one another better, representatives of Abrahamic traditions need to negotiate the very content and conduct of the "dialogue" that must emerge among them. There is no ideological or theological prerequisite for this dialogue. What is required, however, is a shared conviction that co-existence in preferable to the moral incoherence that arises when in-group/out-group distinctions become absolute and solipsistic thinking prevails (*"mirror, mirror on the wall . . . "*). Both genuine and manipulated interreligious hostility call for authentically religious responses, and for justifications for co-existence with the "other" that emerge from within the heart of each tradition, and from experiences of forging relationships across boundaries.

Dialogue is not a panacea and (fortunately) does not erase differences. Moreover, each religion is a "particular universalism," with diverse possibilities of interpretation and expression. There are no guarantees of positive outcomes. But there are many benefits:

(1) Seeing the "Religious Other" in Social, Cultural, and Political Context

It is helpful to situate *interreligious* dialogue in the larger context of *human* dialogue among people with different beliefs, social identities, value priorities, and material interests. Dialogue enables people to sort through the many factors that shape their own behaviors and those of their counterparts. In an interreligious context, dialogue supports recognition that, while some of the reasons for actions related to peace and conflict are profoundly religious, others reflect the contexts through which beliefs are filtered and inflected. Having first-hand experience of how people in different religions struggle to translate precept into practice can be vital for discerning how deeply "religious" a given action may be. Awareness of context can also raise awareness of diversity within religions and religious experiences. Muslims in the West, Christians in the East, and Sephardic Jews may have unique experiences that can enrich Abrahamic encounters.

(2) Developing an Experiential Basis for Making "Fair" Contrasts between Belief Systems, and between Practices

All too often, judgments about the "religious other" are predicated on self-serving contrasts, through which one's own *essential doctrines and values* receive reinforcement through comparison to the *most extreme interpretations and problematic practices* of the other. Whereas unfair contrasts juxtapose "our" precepts with "their" most deviant practices and most "unusual" beliefs (effectively using the misrepresented "other" as a foil for the idealized "self"), fair contrasts compare a "full package" of precepts with another "full package" of precepts, and contrast "our" full range of practices with "their" full range of practices. Developing the habit of making fair comparisons can arguably create a basis for seeing oneself in the other and the other in oneself, without erasing distinctiveness.

(3) Finding Points of Commonality and Complementarity in the Domain of Religious Values

It is not an exaggeration to state that most of the religious values held by Muslims, Christians, and Jews are shared. Followers of the Abrahamic religions differ, however, in the *priority* they give to different values (e.g., justice and mercy, orthodoxy and orthopraxis, accountability and forgiveness, love and law), and in the ways they formulate and practice the same values (e.g., forgiveness, faithfulness). With respect to the value of forgiveness, Christians idealize (but do not always practice) unilateral, preemptive (i.e., unconditional) forgiveness as a means of breaking the cycles of violence or the bondage of sin, while Muslims and Jews place greater emphasis on the virtues of conditional forgiveness, based on acceptance of responsibility and moral accountability by the wrongdoer. Yet Muslims and Jews have also been known to practice unilateral forgiveness, and conditional forgiveness is built into contemporary Christian approaches to restorative justice (perpetrators, after all, are encouraged to accept responsibility, in a manner that facilitates healing of victims and of the community). Discussing similarities and differences in understandings as well as applications of values can create opportunities for revitalized practices and for insights that support peacemaking. It can also shed light on the interface between culture and religion – different subcultures within a single religion, for example, can differ more profoundly than members of different religions in the resolutions they propose for various value polarities (e.g., individual and community, "modest dress" and "self-expression," reason and revelation, equality and authority, human relationship and economic efficiency, "freedom to do" and "freedom to be").

(4) Developing a More Realistic Understanding of the Self

It has been said that "s/he who knows but one language/culture knows no language/culture." This may be an exaggeration, yet dialogue in any context offers an escape from self-referential thinking and a pathway to growth. To become more truly ourselves, we need to be able to see ourselves as others see us. Through dialogue, we might even discover profound meaning in our common membership in the "Abrahamic family." It is a truism that the worst fights are fights within the family; choosing to value our relatedness can provide a basis for conflict transformation and self-knowledge. Rather than a threat to authenticity, encounter with others is actually an opportunity to rediscover a tradition, to relocate the essential and redefine authenticity even as greater respect develops for others. Many participants in interreligious dialogue have found themselves drawn towards deeper exploration of their own tradition, through personal investigation and intrareligious conversations.

Interreligious dialogues that focus on peace can prompt efforts to reclaim precisely those elements of one's own tradition that have been marginalized by contemporary conflict. They can lead to new insights about how conflict – past as well as present – has affected religious consciousness. Such introspection can lead to a cleansing or purification of collective memory – to a critical self-awareness of political manipulations and distortions of faith – that need not dampen commitment to essential precepts, particularly if critical reappraisal is accompanied by efforts to reappropriate past "peace leaders," rediscover examples of nonviolent resistance to provocation, and renew outreach efforts intended to mend relationships and confront the "burdens of history."[6] Conscientious effort to understand ways in which a tradition may have "gone astray" can create new possibilities in the present, expanding awareness of positive precedents as well as exclusionary temptations.[7] Thus can encounters with the "other" broaden the peacemaking repertoire and potential of each participating tradition.

(5) Fostering the Emergence of "New Stories"

While it is true that participation in interfaith dialogue is not always without costs – particularly in zones of violent conflict – those who commit to sustained interaction with the religious "other" often find that their world changes in remarkable ways. They discover (to borrow a phrase from Patrice Brodeur) that Christian, Muslim, and Jewish extremists are "codependent."[8] They revisit their "shared history," and find experiences and testimonies that need to be revived.[9] "Old stories" about the "other" lose their appeal, and new experiences call for new narratives that support the objective of *getting religion out of the conflict and into the peace.*[10]

Given the dramatic rise in structured interaction among representatives of the religions of Abraham, it could be argued that the children of Abraham are "between stories." The old stories of confrontation are tired and deeply constraining. Their problematic assumptions have become all too apparent. Many are seeking to rededicate themselves to fostering the emergence of new stories about Abrahamic solidarity.

Moving Toward Abrahamic Solidarity

Through formal dialogue as well as through informal habits of "living in relationship" with one another, Christian, Muslim, and Jewish peacemakers have an opportunity to embrace their interdependence, and to acknowledge those aspects of their spiritual and cultural heritages that are shared. Formulating these new narratives of Abrahamic solidarity will require sustained communication at a deep level, willingness to grow, and acceptance of risk.

Given the extent to which Abrahamic religions have been coopted by religious nationalism and drawn into contemporary geopolitical conflict, building Abrahamic solidarity will require sustained efforts to challenge the legitimacy of religious as well as secular militancy, and to transform the role of religion in conflict by providing positive options. The following principles are already being applied in dynamic religious peacebuilding initiatives, and provide hope for our common future.

(1) Educate for Religious Literacy and Respectful Co-existence

Jonathan Swift famously remarked that it only takes a little religion to provoke antipathy between human beings, and much more to foster loving relationships. "At little religion," it would appear, can be a dangerous thing. In many zones of intercommunal conflict, adversaries' conversance with the depth and intricacies of their traditions is profoundly limited; the atrocities in Bosnia, for example, were perpetrated by religious neophytes emerging from the collapse of a communist order. Other conflicts display a similar pattern, with religion functioning as a categorical identity equivalent to "nation" or "tribe" more than as a source of spirituality and transformation.

Pointing to such examples, R. Scott Appleby has argued that a key basis for ameliorating religiously justified conflict is broad-based religious literacy.[11] This need not presuppose "religious indoctrination of the masses" – though deeper study among the religiously committed is something to be desired – but does mean taking religions seriously in public as well as confessional education.

In a secular educational system, taking religion seriously can mean learning about world religions and the dynamic roles they have played in history. Particular attention can be given not only to historically "emergent" meanings of religious values such as human dignity and ecological stewardship, but also to the complex and mutually constitutive interactions among religious traditions. Secondary school and university curricula should also draw attention to "high points" in religiously defined civilizations – moments characterized by openness to others, conversation across confessional boundaries, and cooperation in the advancement of human knowledge.[12]

Genuinely religious education can go farther in exploring the unique dynamics of particular religious traditions, sensitizing the laity to the constant interplay between text and context, and to the struggle to bring out the peace teachings of religious traditions under adverse historical circumstances. Such education can convey knowledge of precedents for peacemaking, as well as familiarity with the disciplines of hermeneutics.

Interreligious dialogue meetings have a vital role to play in religious literacy, not only for immediate participants but also for broader religious communities. Whenever religious leaders meet to engage in dialogue about peace and co-existence, there is a powerful demonstration effect. When religious leaders as well as religious laypersons temper apologetics and engage in genuine dialogue, they "give religion a good name" and set a positive example. They move to the forefront of leadership in efforts to apply their own most essential values – which, fortuitously, are also the values that have the most universal appeal. While it is true that religion has too often gotten a "bad rap" from hard-line secularists who discount the largely *non-religious* nature of modern wars and postmodern economic exploitation, religious leadership in the cause of peace is one of the best ways to ensure popular appreciation for the role of spiritual values in modern life. Acts of dialogical engagement should not stop with symbolism, however; interreligious study and dialogue can lead to enhanced knowledge and collaboratively produced study documents for broader dissemination.

Education for religious literacy need not gloss over enduring differences between understandings of religious truth. It is sufficient that religious education resist the psychological temptations noted earlier in this essay, and affirm that appreciation and respect *do* not require agreement.[13] In addition, care needs to be taken to encourage *respectful* disagreement with those who find it difficult to embrace contemporary forms of religious pluralism and critical hermeneutics. Humiliating *those* who adhere to non-pluralistic religious syntheses only exacerbates conflict by creating a "siege" mentality among traditional and revivalist communities.

(2) Explore Linkages between the Journey toward Peace and the Journey toward God in Abrahamic Faith traditions

According to the dominant narrative in the theory and practice of international relations, religion is a distorting factor in international diplomacy that is best constrained to the domain of domestic politics or personal belief. Contemporary international relations theory identifies the Peace of Westphalia in 1648 - settling the Thirty Years War – as the decisive break between a religiously inflamed medieval political order and the modern world of nation-states. The result is a lack or preparedness to consider potential religious contributions to peacemaking, and a predominance of secular peace constructs that exclude the traditional spiritual overtones of the peace ideal. Not only are potential contributions to peacemaking lost; actual conflicts are exacerbated. When religion is viewed solely as a distorting factor in global politics, the religious impulse is forced into narrower channels marked by defensiveness and negation of the existing order.

In light of Raimon Panikkar's observation that peace is a shared myth and symbol that holds positive meaning for virtually the whole of humanity, making space for sacralized conceptions of peace in public discourse can become a constructive response to over-politicized or "defensive" forms of religious expression.[14] Religious peace traditions emphasizing spirituality, connectedness, and reverence for life provide not only a compelling response to religious war discourse, but also a valid critique of secular modernity and the inequities of globalization.

(3) Affirm that Peacemaking Requires as Much Struggle and Courage as War Making

To counteract perceptions that "this-worldly" peace means surrender to secular modernity, passivity in the face of wrongdoing, or acceptance of injustices, Abrahamic leaders seeking to galvanize religious peace discourse would do well to heed the advice given by William James in his essay, "The Moral Equivalent of War." Both religious texts and historical experiences have granted all three Abrahamic traditions ready access to narratives of struggle and martial metaphors; only by asserting the priority of the inner struggle and disciplined non-violent activism can religious leaders transform these themes through spiritual and social disciplines. From Gandhi to Chaiwat Satha-Anand and the Christian Peacemaker Teams, there are many religious leaders who have demonstrated the power of interiorization and non-violent discipline to redirect religious enthusiasm towards constructive programs of social change that require courage, risk, and sacrifice for a greater whole.[15] Rereading the mystical traditions of the Abrahamic religions can also provide impetus for shifting the relative weight given to internal/moral and external/martial struggle, promoting new syntheses linking spiritual development to non-violent engagement with social justice issues.

(4) Encourage Prospective Thinking about Alternative Interfaith Futures

Recent controversies surrounding Danish cartoons, Pope Benedict's Regensburg address, the grave situation in Iraq, and the future of multiculturalism in Western societies suggest a need for prospective thinking about the future of Abrahamic relations. Particular attention needs to be given to the requisites of co-existence and the prevention of interfaith crises.

Honest people can differ in their reading of Pope Benedict's intentions as expressed in the 2006 Regensburg address, and all people of goodwill should reject the actions of those who used his remarks as an excuse for deeds that deepened the Christian–Muslim divide. Nonetheless, there are good reasons to suspect that the more provocative passages in his speech were not altogether accidental, and that they reflected inexperience in interfaith relations, particularly Muslim-Christian relations, and a prospective, self-justifying approach to interreligious discourse. His subsequent visit to Turkey, in contrast, was far more skilful and compatible with lessons learned about Catholic-Muslim relations since Vatican II. It reflected the contributions of interfaith dialogue to experientially grounded knowledge of how others respond to one's own discourse, as well as a prospective concern for future relationships.

Whatever our evaluation of Pope Benedict's theology of interreligious (and indeed, intrareligious) relations, one point that he has raised should be taken up by Christians, Muslims, and Jews in interfaith forums: the issue of *reciprocity*. Pope Benedict has focused on reciprocity primarily as it relates to freedom of religious practice and expression, in the West and in the Islamic world. This is a valid concern. Let us not stop with this issue, however; let us also consider the many other *reciprocities* that might be cultivated in interfaith and intercultural relations: reciprocities of respect, of spiritual recognition, of acknowledging relatedness, of political co-operation, and of commitment to conflict resolution, justice, and human rights. Reciprocity should not be a narrow demand from one side to another; rather, it should be a framework for ongoing dialogue, a basis for improving relations in many spheres, and for building greater consensus about shared values. Only through open ended dialogue about the terms of Abrahamic co-existence can we learn to address the needs and fears of the other, and arrive at a point of genuine security and harmony with one another. Such an ideal may seem far off, but we would do well to consider a dream articulated by Kenneth Cragg, a life-long protagonist of Christian–Muslim and Abrahamic understanding: "How self-conscious we still are about our identities! . . . Can we not hope that some-time, somewhere, we might somehow be so aware of God . . . that we might forget we are partisans of His theologies?"[16]

(5) Begin Telling New Stories Now

The rapid ascendance of "clash of civilizations" thinking in the aftermath of 9/11 reflects not only the increasing politicization of religious and cultural identities, but also the impoverished nature of Abrahamic historical narratives. If past conflicts continue to dominate present relations and conceptions of the other, the "Crusaders" will always be sallying forth from behind the walls of their Levantine fortresses and the "Mohammedans" will always be at the gates of Vienna. We need new stories, and we need to start telling them now.

Particularly vital at the present juncture in history is the demonstration value of interfaith co-existence and peacebuilding initiatives. Positive examples of Abrahamic solidarity need to receive far greater "air time," as do the justifications used by those who are pioneering them. Abrahamic solidarity movements offer our greatest hope for revitalizing the spiritual content of Abrahamic identities at a time of great polarization.

Notes

1 While Christian–Muslim and Jewish–Muslim tensions are more pronounced in our current era, residues of past wrongs and polemics still cast a shadow over Christian–Jewish relations.

2 F. E. Peters, *The Monotheists: Jews, Christians, and Muslims in Conflict and Competition: Volume II: The Words and Will of God* (Princeton, NJ: Princeton University Press, 2003), p. 383.

3 Freud's observations concerning the "narcissism of minor differences" (national or ethnic as well as religious) may fail to capture the import of religious distinctions for those whose lives are defined by a powerful desire to live in communion with the divine, the persistence of adversarial relations among the religions of Abraham through misdirected and manipulated communal sentiment has done much to tarnish the reputation of religion itself. This is evident not only in the rising popularity of anti-theistic literature (Christopher Hitchens and Sam Harris, among others), but also in a more longstanding tendency among social scientists to overcompensate for exaggerated notions of primordial religious rivalry by "explaining away" the religious dimension of conflict.

4 Marc Howard Ross, *The Management of Conflict: Interpretations and Interests in Comparative Perspective* (New Haven, CT: Yale University Press, 1993).

5 Previously published in Nathan C. Funk, "Transforming Islamic–Western Identity Conflict: A Framework for Strategic Engagement," *International Journal of Peace Studies*, Vol. 12, No. 1 (Spring/Summer 2007), pp. 23–51.

6 Joseph Montville, "Justice and the Burdens of History," in Mohammed Abu Nimer (ed.), *Reconciliation, Coexistence, and Justice in Interethnic Conflict: Theory and Practice* (Lexington Books, 2001), pp. 129–43.

7 Joseph Montville and Heidi Winder, "Creative Coexistence in Muslim Spain," in *Posive Approaches to Peacebuilding*, ed. Sampson, Abu-Nimer, Liebler & Whitney (Washington, DC: PACT Publications, 2003); Maria Rosa Menocal, *The Ornament of the World: How Muslims, Jews, and Christians Created a Culture of Tolerance in Medieval Spain* (Boston: Little, Brown and Company, 2002); *Waging Peace: A Two-Part Discussion of Religion-Based Peacemaking* (Washington National Cathedral and USIP); David A. Smock (ed.), *Interfaith Dialogue and Peacebuilding* (Washington, DC: United States Institute of Peace, 2002).

8 (Date of presentation in Ottawa.)

9 Paul Peachey, George F. McLean, and John Kromkowski, *Abrahamic Faiths, Ethnicity and Ethnic Conflicts* (Washington, DC: The Council for Research in Values and Philosophy, 1997); Jonathan Sacks, *The Dignity of Difference: How to Avoid the Clash of Civilizations* (New York: Continuum, 2002); Bradford E. Hinze and Irfan A. Omar, *Heirs of Abraham: The Future of Muslim, Jewish, and Christian Relations* (Maryknoll, NY: Orbis Books, 2005); James L. Heft (ed.), *Beyond Violence: Religious Sources of Social Transformation in Judaism, Christianity, and Islam* (New York: Fordham University Press, 2004).

10 Harold Coward and Gordon Smith (eds.), *Religion and Peacebuilding* (Albany,

NY: SUNY, 2004), Marc Gopin, *Holy War, Holy Peace: How Religion Can Bring Peace to the Middle East* (New York: Oxford University Press, 2002); Gerrie Ter Harr and James J. Busuttil (eds.), *Bridge or Barrier: Religion, Violence, and Visions for Peace* (Leiden, The Netherlands: Brill Academic Publishers, 2004).

11 R. Scott Appleby, *The Ambivalence of the Sacred: Religion, Violence, and Reconciliation* (Lanham, MD: Rowman & Littlefield, 2000).

12 Menocal; Richard E. Rubenstein, *Aristotle's Children: How Christians, Muslims, and Jews Rediscovered Ancient Wisdom and Illuminated the Middle Ages* (New York: Harcourt, Inc., 2003).

13 Joseph Liechty, "Mitigation in Northern Ireland," in David Smock (ed.), *Interfaith Dialogue and Peacebuilding* (Washington, DC: United States Institute of Peace, 2002); Miroslav Volf, *Exclusion and Embrace: A Theological Exploration of Otherness, Identity, and Reconciliation* (Abingdon Press, 1996).

14 Raimon Panikkar, *Cutlural Disarmament: The Way to Peace* (Westminster/John Knox: 1995).

15 Monika K. Hellwig, "Peacefulness, a Personal Discipline," in *A Case for Peace in Reason and Faith* (Collegeville, MN: The Liturgical Press, 1992), pp. 77–89.

16 Kenneth Cragg, "Preface," in *We Believe in One God: The Experience of God in Christianity and Islam*, ed. Annemarie Schimmel and Abdoldjavad Falaturi (London: Burns & Oates, 1979), p. ix.

14

Trialogue of Abrahamic Faiths: Towards an Alliance of Civilizations

AZYUMARDI AZRA

Seen from an Islamic perspective, the three religions – Judaism, Christianity and Islam – have their shared origin in the personage of Abraham (Arabic, Ibrahim). The original religion of Abraham was called in the Qur'an *millah Ibrahim*, Abrahamic 'way of life,' or rather, religion. According to the teaching of Islam, Muslims should recognize not only the prophecy of Abraham, but also the relations of Islam with Judaism and Christianity, the followers of which were called *ahl al-kitab*, people of the [revealed] Books.

The three religions have a great deal of similarities and affinities as well as shared histories in the land now known as the Middle East. Those shared histories could be sweet to remember, but also could be bitter to recollect. But in the last few years harsh encounters in the course of history among the children of Abraham tend to be more prominent in the discourse and relations; and at the same time forgetting long periods of peaceful co-existence among them in various parts of the globe.

The three religions could be appropriately regarded as siblings in that each of them is unique in itself; each has its own nature and character that is distinctive from the other. Therefore, they are different in their own ways that in the end brought them into misunderstanding and conflict. Even worse, they could be involved in bitter jealousy and rivalries not only to gain followings, but also to control power and hegemony as reflected during the heyday of European colonialism in the three G's (**G**olden, **G**lory, **G**ospel); all of these in the end could bring them into violence and wars.

Despite all differences and conflict, there is no question that the followers of the three religions are all the children of Abraham who are part and parcel of one single humanity, coming from one single parents, Adam and Eve. Despite all differences in races, religions, cultures, economic well-being, political systems and the like, the children of Abraham are all brothers and sisters.

So that they, and human beings as a whole, should make the best efforts in order to be able to live in harmony and peaceful co-existence that will bring a great benefit to civilizations.

Furthermore, living in harmony and peace makes it possible for groups of people, including the adherents of Abrahamic religions, to forge an alliance of civilizations. As far as the children of Abraham are concerned, Bulliet (2004) has suggested use of the term 'Islamo-Judeo-Christian Civilization' to indicate that the overall relations among them had produced a distinctive civilization. In fact, as Bulliet further maintains, the relations of the three religions is more simply scriptural, but also includes civilizations. In fact, there has been prolonged intertwining of these sibling societies that created profound intellectual and cultural cross-fertilization not only in the Middle East, but also in Europe and beyond that in the end produced 'Judeo-Christian-Islamo' civilization.

But the fact is that, besides intellectual and cultural cross-enrichment and cross-fertilization, the history of Children of Abraham had also been colored by tension, conflicts, and wars that were destructive not only of human life, but also for human civilization as a whole. That is why now it is the duty of all of us to recreate a new narrative of an alliance of civilizations, both among Children of Abraham and the rest of humanity.

Conflict and Accommodation

Looking at the totality of relations among the followers of the three Abrahamic faiths, again it is clear that the picture is not always encouraging. Recent events in the aftermath of September 11, 2001 have resulted in a worsening of relations among them; in fact in certain ways it could be worse now than when Islam first became known to the Judeo-Christian world – or more precisely in Europe – with the establishment of the first contacts and encounters between them, on the one hand, and the Muslims, on the other, as early as the seventh century. In the first one hundred years of Islam, the extent of Islam's territorial expansion continued to gain momentum. Byzantium and Spain confronted the Muslims across the battlefields of Eastern and Western Europe respectively to no avail; and Muslims in the end held sway in these areas.

There is no doubt that the expansion of Islam was painful for Europe because much of European territory was lost to Muslim forces. The "Crusade" between 1095 and 1250 was the most significant of various European responses to the spread of Islam. Beginning in the eleventh century, the crusaders under the Frankist knights made serious and concerted attempts to arrest the development of "Muhammadanism" in Europe. The Crusade, as the word implies, was believed as a struggle to save Christian Europe by warding off the "barbaric" Muslims. The series of bloody encounters, which took place in the numerous Crusades that followed, constituted a major part of European history. Even though the Europeans in the end successfully re-conquered the Iberian Peninsula from the Muslims in 1492, they faced a new strong force of Muslims, the Ottomans, who had made their way into Southeastern Europe.

Despite these harsh encounters and even bloody wars, and despite the Muslims allowing the European Christians and Jews to remain in territory conquered and controlled by Muslims, European understanding of Islam by and large was basically minimal. In fact, the Europeans launched continued propaganda to tarnish the image of Islam; this religion was held in contempt, it was condemned as false, and the Prophet Muhammad was depicted as "anti-Christ" or infidel, the scourge of God. This attitude went on for centuries. It was only from the second half of the twentieth century onwards that this kind of perception of Islam and the Prophet Muhammad was some-what corrected. Other than this, misperceptions and distortions of the image of Islam and the Muslims remain strong among much of the Western public.

Thus, throughout the history of its relationship with Islam and the Muslims, Europe's understanding and appreciation of Islam and Muslims were generally negative; hostility remained the basic feature of attitude among Europeans towards Islam and Muslims. There had been in the course of history, however, some Christian notables who tried to learn about Islam and to change the attitude of the Christians for the better towards Islam and Muslims. One of the most prominent among them was Peter the Venerable, the Abbot of Cluny, who initiated the first Latin translation of the Qur'an, Muslim legends, history and an explanation of Islamic teachings. These works contributed significantly to a better understanding of Islam and Muslims in Europe. Other works soon followed the suit.

During the Renaissance, a number of prominent Europeans further tried to acquire a better understanding of Islam. After the Turkish defeat of Byzantium, John of Segovia pointed to the need to deal with Islam and the Muslims in other ways besides wars and conversion. He initiated a new trans-lation of the Qur'an in cooperation with Muslim jurists. He also proposed an international conference to exchange opinions between Muslims and Christians. All of these were conducted in order to have a better grasp of Islam and Muslims.

In addition, during the Renaissance, Arabic and Islamic studies were initi-ated in many institutions, which led to a more balanced and accurate view of Islam and the Muslims; this is the origin of a field of study known as "Orientalism." Unfortunately, Orientalism was developed and practiced not only for academic purposes, but also for the interests of colonialism and evan-gelization in the Muslim lands. Since the early 1970s, Orientalism has been severely criticized for retaining certain biases and distorted images of Islam and Muslims (cf. Said, 1978). As a result, a new approach to Islamic and Muslim studies has evolved, and the terms Orientalism and "Orientalists" have tended to become "dirty" words; the term "Islamic studies" and "Islamicists" have been increasingly adopted instead.

Despite conflicts between Muslims and Europe in medieval times, it is also now widely recognized that various aspects of Islamic civilization have contributed greatly to the rise of Europe and the West as a whole. There is an abundance of literature devoted to these subjects and there is no need to dwell on it.

But it is important to recall that in the period of Muslim rule in Spain, Jewish and Muslim thinkers and scientists worked together to produce what might be called a 'Judeo-Muslim civilization.' This 'alliance of civilizations' continued in North Africa and Arabia after the rest of Muslims and Jews, escaping inquisition, were driven out from Spain by the victorious Christians. In fact, Jewish civilization was said to have experienced a kind of revival under Muslim rule in North Africa, Arabia and Ottoman Turkey.

The Muslims during the heyday of Islamic civilization not only preserved Greek learning, but also made a considerable original contribution to the increased knowledge of nature with their research and experiments. Various kinds of knowledge and sciences that had been developed by Muslim scientists were later transmitted to Europe. The Muslims, therefore, with their intellectual supremacy in scientific discovery, and in the physical and natural sciences, prepared the ground for the European Renaissance. All of these in turn produced what might be called 'Islamo-Christian civilization.'

Therefore, it is now increasingly recognized by the historian of human civilizations that Western civilization owed its origins not only to the Greek, but also to the Judeo-Christian–Muslim traditions that had mutually interacted through centuries. That is why it is not really appropriate to talk about the 'clash of civilizations,' particularly among the Children of Abraham.

In this context, it is relevant to quote *Alliance of Civilization* (2006) on this particular point that, notwithstanding historical period of tension and confrontation between adherents of the three monotheistic [Abrahamic] religions – conflicts which themselves were often more political than religious in nature – it is important to note that peaceful co-existence, beneficial trade and reciprocal learning have been hallmarks of relations between the adherents of Judaism, Christianity and Islam from their earliest period until today. As has been said earlier, during medieval times, Islamic civilization was a major source of innovation, knowledge acquisition, and scientific advancement that contributed to the emergence of the Renaissance and the Enlightenment of Europe.

Peace and Trialogue

What is the role of the three Abrahamic religions in conflict and peace, particularly among their adherents? There is no easy answer to this question; to answer it one needs to look not only at religion as such, but also at other factors surrounding religion, such is political and economic factors that drive the adherents of religions to wage violence and war.

One might argue that religions have an ambiguous character related to the matter of conflict and peace. Arguably there are certain verses in each and every Holy Book that could contain or incite conflict even war among them, but they must not be taken as the fundamental teachings of the three Abrahamic religions, for there is not doubt that the essence of religions is peace on earth. Or, there could be individuals in the name of a certain Abrahamic religion who wage conflict, violence, terrorism, and even war; but, again, they are not representatives of that particular religion. In fact they are misled people and are on the fringe of that religion. The bulk majority of adherents of Abrahamic religions are peace-loving people who respect diversity and pluralism and love to live in harmony and peace.

Therefore, I would suggest that the idea that any of the Abrahamic religions plays an important role in creating conflict is misleading. One should try not to associate any particular religion with conflict and violence, let alone to perceive it as the source of conflict and violence. Conflict and violence conducted in the name of religion by certain adherents of a particular religion in most cases are the result of various factors, particularly politics and economics working in the environment of the faithful, that have nothing to do with religion and God.

Therefore, we may suggest that religions are one of the sources of harmony and peace; but we have to admit that at the same time the Abrahamic religions, as any other religion, have been and could be used by certain individuals or groups of believers as a justification of conflict, violence and even war. In recent times, the use and abuse of religions for political purposes steadily increased; the tendency is even stronger when, in the midst of political uncertainties, economic deprivation, and cultural alienation, more and more people look to religion as *the* only solace they can get. Combined with a literal understanding of religion and a search for 'authenticity,' the tendency of radicalism and violence in the name of religion is, no doubt, gaining a greater ground.

Confronting these tendencies, mainstream religious organizations and institutions have a crucial role to play; they should enhance their capacity to explicate and disseminate the true peaceful nature of religions. It is now high time for mainstream religious organizations and institutions to raise their voices and to intensify their activities against the use and abuse of religions; and work together to create lasting harmony and peace for peoples and nations.

There are many other factors or root-causes that contribute to the failure of followers of the three religions, or human beings as a whole, to live in harmony and peace. Underlying these factors or root-causes is the existence of various kinds of structural violence. Most structural violence is the result of uncontrolled lust on the part of individual and groups of people. Therefore, these root-causes of tension, conflicts, and wars should be first resolved by abolishing structural violence in order for all of us to be able to talk about peace, harmony and peaceful co-existence. So long as we fail to resolve those root-causes, we will continue to fail to live in harmony and peace.

In order to create peace and harmony, there must be concerted efforts of all of us to bring about a more balanced economy and resources. It is no secret that most of the economic resources are in the hands of only a few countries; while a large number of human beings continue to live under the poverty line and in miserable conditions. It is clear that it would be difficult to talk about peace and harmony while economic disparity continues to hold sway in many parts of the globe; the poor and the deprived are to some extent more prone to being the victims of violence. But, it is now even more unfortunate that the discrepancy in economic well-being and welfare is increasing steadily because of the seemingly unstoppable economic globalization that in effect gives the privileged few greater economic power and domination over the poor and the deprived.

Harmony and peace is clearly very difficult to create when 'cultural imperialism' is also a dominant feature of life today; due to the continued increase of globalization, as many human beings are on the receiving end of cultural hegemony and imperialism. There are many indications that radicalism and violence among some people is, to some extent, the result of looking for cultural identity or cultural and religious authenticity in the midst of cultural disorientation and dislocation resulting from cultural hegemony and imperialism.

To create harmony and peace in this kind of sorry situation, we all should adopt the paradigm of multiculturalism. Through this paradigm of multiculturalism, people will recognize the rights of cultures of other peoples to exist. Only through the politics of cultural recognition can we all prevent the globe from being involved in the so-called 'conflict of cultures,' or even worse 'conflict of civilizations.'.

Our time has also seen the rise of violence and in fact terrorism in the name of religion that involves children of Abraham. In such a situation how could they create an alliance of civilization? To answer this complex question, one needs to go beyond the surface of conflict, violence and terrorism.

It is again clear that root-causes of conflict, violence or terrorism in the name of religion are very complex; in fact there are combinations of various factors including politics, economics, and to some extent also certain teachings or interpretation of religions. In most cases, politics seems to be the most important factor (cf. Azra 2005a). To take the most recent cases of terrorism in Indonesia such the Bali I (2002), Jakarta Marriot (2003), Kuningan Jakarta (2004), and Bali II (2005) bombings, it is apparent that politics, both domestic and international, is the main cause of terrorism. At the domestic level, the perpetrators of the bombings have been motivated by their anger and hatred of the Indonesian political system that they regard as being 'un-Islamic.' This is particularly true when Megawati Soekarnoputri was president of the Republic of Indonesia; for some Indonesians it is unlawful for woman to become the leader (*imam*) of state whose bulk majority of population is Muslim.

As for international politics, it is clear that even before the tragic events of September 11 in the United States, the Muslim perpetrators of terrorism condemned certain injustices in international politics and relations. For them the US and other Western countries are the enemies of Islam and Muslims. Western countries, particularly the US, are basically hostile to Islam and the Muslim world. In fact, they believe, the US and other Western countries have conspired to destroy Islam and Muslims. A number of international cases such as the US continued support of Israel at the expense of the Palestinian, are the US military campaign in Afghanistan and Iraq, have only added fuel to their anger and hatred of the US and its allies.

One of the most important root-causes is the continued existence of structural violence that in turn produces a great deal of political, economic, technological and cultural injustices at virtually all levels of life, from local, national to international levels. At the international level – where we would love to imagine the existence of 'one single humanity' and alliance of civilizations – political injustices and violence continue to take place. Look at what happens in Iraq, where the international powers and international institutions such as the United Nations failed to halt the US military invasion and occupation. In fact the UN continues to be dominated by the US and its allies in order to justify their injustices and in effect maintain the structural violence.

Those who possess hard power and military might continue to impose their will upon other peoples. Cornered harshly by these seemingly invincible forces, these people respond by any means necessary or take up arms; indeed some of them become suicide bombers, blowing up other people and themselves. Again, all of these violences and injustices are taking place despite the efforts of international agencies, particularly the UN. Circles of violence among warring groups of peoples continue to sacrifice innocent human beings and the civilized world. These are some of the very blatant forms of structural violence that continue to hold sway among human beings and their civilizations.

This kind of violence cannot be resolved unless we are able to put an end to political structural violence at the international level. Towards that end, international institutions such as the UN must be reformed and restructured. There is no secret that the UN, particularly the Security Council, has been and is still dominated by the Great Powers; the UN has continued to succumb to the wishes of those who vote against the resolutions that aim to create peace and harmony among peoples and nations. Concerned nations and peoples, therefore, must continue to fight for reforms of the UN.

That is also the case with other international institutions such as the Organization of Islamic Conference (OIC), expected among others to protect Muslim nations and communities from political and economic structural violence. In the midst of increased problems faced by Muslims following the unfortunate events such as September 11, 2001, Bali bombing I (2002) and II (2005), Madrid bombing (March 10, 2004), London bombing (July 7, 2005), OIC should be able to play a better role in the mediation of the conflict. It is unfortunate that OIC has been afflicted by continued rivalries and quarrels among its members so that, in the end, it fails to play its role in the creation of peace and harmony. Therefore, the OIC members should try to put aside their differences and work for harmony and peace for the peoples and nations.

Alliance of Civilizations

The relations between the children of Abraham, particularly in the Middle East, no doubt have had a significant impact throughout the world. The continued Israeli–Palestinian conflict is a major factor in the widening rift between the Muslim and Judeo-Christian worlds. As stated in *Alliance of Civilizations* (2004: 17), the Israeli–Palestinian conflict has taken a symbolic value that colors cross-cultural and political relations among adherents of the three major monotheistic faiths [Judaism, Christianity and Islam] well beyond its geographic scope.

Therefore, it is necessary to resolve the conflict by achieving just and sustainable solutions; and this requires courage and bold vision and action in the future on the part of Israelis, Palestinians and all countries capable of exerting influence, particularly the US and other great Western powers. The progress on this front rests on the recognition of both the Palestinian and Jewish national aspirations and on the establishment of two fully sovereign and independent states living side by side in peace and security. Some constructive agreements have been actually reached between those concerned parties such as the Madrid Conference (1991), the President Clinton Peace Initiative (2000), and the Arab League Peace Proposal (2002). What is needed now is the bravery and boldness among these children of Abraham to bring these accords further.

Looking at the whole history of the children of Abraham which produced an alliance of civilizations in the past, and the initiatives taken recently to create peace in the Middle East, it is not really appropriate to talk about the 'clash of civilizations'. In fact, this 'theory' has unfortunately distorted the history of relations between cultures and civilizations. It has been shown that the relations between the children of Abraham are not only tension, conflict and war; but rather are full of constructive exchanges, cross-fertilization and peaceful co-existence throughout centuries. If there are conflicts now among children of Abraham and others, what we need is not theory of clash of civilizations, but a theory of alliance of civilizations.

In this respect, the initiative taken by the then Secretary General of the United Nations (UN) to launch the *Alliance of Civilizations* in 2005 should be applauded. Co-sponsored by the Prime Ministers of Spain and Turkey, the Alliance of Civilizations affirms a broad consensus across nations, cultures and religions that all societies are bound together in their humanity and interdependent in their quest for stability, prosperity, and peaceful co-existence. Furthermore, the Alliance of Civilizations is based on a multi-polar perspective that promotes a culture of dialogue and respect among all nations and cultures.

The Alliance of Civilizations put a special focus on relations between Western and Muslim societies that to certain extent are Judeo-Christian–Muslim societies. In the context of an alliance of civilizations among the children of Abraham, there is an urgent need to find an acceptable solution to the Israeli–Palestinian conflict. As suggested earlier, the only acceptable and viable solution is the establishment and recognition of two fully independent states: Israel and Palestine. Without such a solution, it is not only very difficult to create peace in the Middle East, but also to forge an alliance of civilizations among the children of Abraham.

For that purpose, religious leaders of the children of Abraham have a special part to play. They should be more resolute in promoting the teaching of Abrahamic religions on peace, harmony and peaceful co-existence. There also should be more dialogues and exchanges among these religious leaders, not only at the top level of leadership, but more importantly also at the mid- and lower levels of leadership that are in direct contact with people at the grass-roots. Only with these we can be optimistic of the peaceful future of the children of Abraham.

Bibliography

Alliance of Civilizations: Report of the High Level Group November 13, 2006, New York: United Nations.

Azra, Azyumardi, *Indonesia, Islam, and Democracy: Dynamics in a Global Context* (Jakarta & Singapore: ICIP & Equinox, 2006)..

——, 2005a, "Terrorism: Religious Factor," paper presented at International Summit on Democracy, Terrorism, and Security, [in conjunction with one year commemoration of Madrid bombing], Madrid, Spain, March 8–11, 2005.

——, *The Origins of Islamic Reformism in Southeast Asia: Networks of Middle Eastern and Malay-Indonesian 'Ulama' in the 17th and 18th Centuries* (Crows Nest, Australia; Honolulu; and Leiden: AAAS and Allen-Unwin; University of Hawaii Press; KITLV Press, 2004).

——, "Bali and Southeast Asian Islam: Debunking the Myths," in Kumar Ramakrishna & See Seng Tan (eds), *After Bali: The Threat of Terrorism in Southeast Asia* (Singapore & London: IDSS & World Scientific, 2003).

Bohnstedt, John W., *The Infidel Scourge of God: The Turkish Menace as Seen by German Pamphleteers of the Reformation Era* (Transactions of the American Philosophical Society, N.S. LVIII/9, 1968).

Bulliet, Richard, *The Case for Islamo-Christian Civilization* (New York: Columbia University Press, 2004).

James, Helen (ed.), *Civil Society, Religion and Global Governance: Paradigm of Power and Persuasion* (London & New York: Routledge).

Lewis, Bernard, *From Babel to Dragoman: Interpreting the Middle East* (London: Weidenfeld and Nicolson, 2004).

Lewis, Bernard, *What Went Wrong? Western Impact and Middle Eastern Response* (Oxford: Oxford University Press, 2002).

Nathan, K. S., *Religious Pluralism in Democratic Societies: Challenges and Prospects for Southeast Asia, Europe, and the United States in the New Millennium* (Kuala Lumpur: KAS Singapore and Malaysian Association for American Studies (MAAS), 2007).

Said, Edward, *Orientalism* (New York, Pantheon, 1978).

Toynbee, Arnold, *The Western Question in Greece and Turkey: A Study in the Contact of Civilizations* (Boston: Houghton Mifflin, 1923).

The Children of Abraham at a Time of Crisis: Challenges and Opportunities

RABBI DAVID SAPERSTEIN

The Model of Christian–Jewish Relations

From the sweeping changes in Jewish–Christian relations in the past 60 years, there is much that can be learned about relations among the three Abrahamic faiths. By any objective standard, the millennial legacy of hatred, mistrust, and abuse between Christians and Jews should have made Christian-Jewish reconciliation in our day nigh unto impossible.

As slavery and racism have been the moral cancer in the soul of America, so anti-Semitism and oppression of Jews have been a central moral cancer of Western Civilization and Christian Europe. Yet, the history is far more complex than commonly held by many, particularly in my Jewish community. Many of the images held by Jews of unremitting Christian hatred fail to reflect the multi-textured relations of the communities and that some of the more ferociously egregious actions and ideas were all along formally repudiated by the Church. Yet too frequently, in different times and places, Jews did indeed face state sanctioned, academic sanctioned, church sanctioned anti-Semitism; accusations of deicide and blood libels (murdering Christian children to use their blood in baking *matzo*, accusations made even as recently as the mid-'90s in an astonishing controversy at Uppsala University, Sweden's Harvard); persecution and discrimination, pervasive legal and financial restrictions, pogroms and massacres; bigoted myths and caricatures of the Jew – of hooked noses and international conspiracies; pseudo-scientific racialism; and ultimately the Holocaust. Even though the pseudo-scientific roots of Nazism were not grounded in Christian dogma or theology, too many Christians held a religious world-view justifying abusive treatment of one human being by another; one people by another that facilitated the rise of Nazi anti-Semitism.

In contrast, the history of Muslim–Jewish relations over the centuries was not so hostile. While there was ongoing conflict on the borders between Christendom and Islamic dominance, within Muslim countries Jews often enjoyed the freedom to live as Jews, and had opportunities to participate in the broader society – a freedom that was rare in Christian lands. While technically (and in some ways functionally) second-class citizens, Islam's Abrahamic cousins were tolerated in a way quite different than in many Christian lands.

Yet despite two millennia of difficult Christian–Jewish relations, out of the moral cataclysm of the Holocaust, *just one single generation later*, we witnessed the shattering of many institutional structures of anti-Semitism in Christian life, the purging of anti-Semitism from the formal institutions and teachings of Christianity, the expansion of teaching about Christianity (and other faiths) in Jewish religious school curricula, and the forging of a level of Christian-Jewish dialogue, understanding and cooperation never before seen in our histories.

Yet clearly the struggle is not yet over. Irrational anti-Semitic canards that underlie much of the hatred continue. Some tens of millions of Americans still hold such anti-Semitic attitudes. Many of the national Protestant denominations are still unprepared to understand the role that the Land and the State of Israel play in the consciousness and identification of the Jewish people. And one cannot understand the Jewish community on Israel without understanding the basic postulates with which most Jews (and many of Israel's non-Jewish supporters) begin, among them: Israel is the historic homeland of the Jewish people to which we have returned. Israel's security is indispensable to the future of the security of the Jewish people. If the Arab nations believed that they could militarily destroy Israel today, they would not hesitate to do so; only Israel's strength, enhanced by American support stands in the way of that happening. This is not the place to argue the merits of those postulates and certainly not to suggest that other narratives lack validity, but to submit that if you do not understand these postulates, you cannot understand the Jewish people's attitude to Israel.

Across the globe, the resurgence of anti-Semitism in forms Jews thought we would never see again, has sent shockwaves through the Jewish community. And we are witnessing the rise of anti-Semitism in the Muslim world in many forms never witnessed before in history – including, ironically, those heretofore associated only with Christian and other forms of Western anti-Semitism: the cartoonish images with exaggerated so-called Semitic features, assertions of the blood libel, the widespread popularizing of conspiracy theories such as the Elders of Zion, and the arrogation and adaptation of Nazi images. Propelled quickly across the globe by new technologies, these dehumanizing images and messages become linked with the use of violence for political and ideological and religious causes.

Conversely, the post-9/11 images of Muslims, with widely accepted images reducing Muslims and all of Islam to the most extreme and violent expressions of Islam and of Muslims, pose an equally compelling and urgent moral challenge to those who want to build stronger relations between the Abrahamic faiths. No true dialogue or cooperation is possible unless we address each other's fears and our respective sense of vulnerability as well as our respective (and sometimes common) dreams and aspirations.

What made the changes that took place between Jews and Christians work? Let me suggest seven lessons for a broader Abrahamic agenda:

First, each of the Abrahamic faiths cherishes the *Tanach*, the Hebrew Scriptures, the Christian Old Testament, and a patrimony, physical or spiritual, in Abraham.

These common roots, with all the similarities and differences with which we view them, provide a starting point for dialogue and cooperation.

Second, local activity and local visionary leaders who call for improvement in our relations, while indispensable, are not sufficient.

This will work only when there is ownership of such process at a national/institutional denominational, organizational, and institutional level with the imprimatur of key leaders and organizations and their constant engaged activity over many years. Conversely, without local support and engagement, national and international efforts will come to naught.

Third, developing dialogue and cooperative programs often can best be accomplished via the mosques, the churches, and the synagogues.

These institutions share a common role in American society and serve to make such cooperation feel more natural and less awkward. In fact, overwhelmingly, the dialogue and cooperation that goes on at the local levels of our varied communities happens out of these institutions. With the Muslim community, however, it is made somewhat more complex because the Muslim community does not have structured denominations; and the complex concept of "clergy" has made it harder to find partners and to understand exactly who our partners are.

Fourth, only a willingness to deal effectively with the extremism in our own midst can allow us to avoid being distracted from our ultimate goals.

On the one hand, if we devolve into endless discussions about those extremists, that debate crowds out other discussions and hands to the extremists control of our agenda, curtailing hope for cooperation and understanding. On the other, the issue cannot be skirted. When mainstream/mainline religious leaders fail to act clearly and assertively to delegitimize the extremists in our communities, it breeds distrust and suspicion that poisons efforts at cooperation. Striking this balance remains a difficult challenge. Achieving this balance can be difficult because we know comparatively little about the Muslim community. Again, on all sides, there are concerns about how to know with confidence with whom to work and whom to trust. And for that we need the guidance of trusted friends in our respective communities.

Fifth, dialogue alone is not enough, cooperative undertakings are vital.
It is our willingness to engage in cooperative endeavor addressing common concerns that allows us to build the bridges of trust and understanding that can withstand the inevitable strains and crises that plague relations whenever varied communities try to come together.

Sixth, regrettably, too few of us have the kind of social and personal inter-actions with each other that build true friendships , trust, and understanding.
Creating such opportunities is vital to success in developing good relations.

And seventh, only through the willingness to expunge from our own psyches, literature, and culture the stereotypes that we hold of each other can we hope to change the patterns of distrust and misperception that have emerged.
This means that we will be able to address crises that arise only if we are prepared to engage in the kind of honest soul-searching and sharing that this ongoing dialogue represents. No coalitional relationship can work if it is built on misperception or inequality. How was this accomplished in Christian and Jewish relations?

The Christian world came to grips with the existence of the evil of anti-Semitism manifested in its teachings, its policies, its indifference; it formally repudiated that anti-Semitism; and it committed itself to changing the future by entering first into dialogue, and then into cooperative endeavor, with the Jewish community. It began with Vatican II's repudiation of the anti-histor-ical myth of deicide and its affirmation that the Covenant of God with the Jewish people had never ended. The World Council of Churches acknowl-edged in 1968, "the guilt of Christians who have all too often stood on the side of the persecutors instead of the persecuted." In 1982, the WCC Executive Committee concluded: "Teachings of contempt for Jews and Judaism in certain Christian traditions proved a spawning ground for the evil of the Nazi Holocaust." Similarly, the Prague meeting of Catholics and Jews in 1992 also formally asserted the Catholic Church's acceptance of the role of Catholic anti-Semitism in relation to the Holocaust. This trend led to the recognition of Israel by the Church of Rome and the extraordinary Yom HaShoah events in 1994, when the Pope and the Chief Rabbi of Rome sat as equals.
The Jewish community, for its part, has had to overcome its disappoint-ments and distrust, to address the present strands of Jewish cultural disparagement and mistrust of the "*goyim*," to enter in good faith into these dialogues and cooperative endeavors, to understand the tradition of love, tolerance and acceptance that represents normative Christianity, a tradition

that must be balanced against the history of anti-Semitism in the Christian community.

Jews and Christians still have a way to go, but we have come far. In our relations with Muslims and theirs with us, however, this journey, for all of us, is just beginning. And serious efforts to learn about each other, as we did with Christians and Jews, must be embraced by the institutions and leaders of our communities.

As Rabbi Eric Yoffie, President of the Union for Reform Judaism (URJ), observed in his address to the Islamic Society of North America convention this summer in announcing a national effort of the URJ and the Islamic Society of North American (ISNA), the largest umbrella Muslim group in North America, to strengthen Muslim–Jewish dialogue and cooperation (to which Dr. Siddiqi alluded in his contribution):

> One reason that all of this happens is the profound ignorance to which I referred. We know nothing of Islam – nothing. That is why we must educate our members, and we need your help. And we hope in doing so we will set an example for all Americans.
>
> Because the time has come to put aside what the media says is wrong with Islam and to hear from Muslims themselves what is right with Islam. The time has come to listen to our Muslim neighbors speak, from their heart and in their own words, about the spiritual power of Islam and their love for their religion.
>
> The time has come for Americans to learn how far removed Islam is from the perverse distortions of the terrorists who too often dominate the media, subverting Islam's image by professing to speak in its name.

We must recognize as well that you can postpone but you cannot ignore issues of core principle that divide us – that our interests will *not* always be congruent, that sometimes we will have to agree respectfully to disagree, and that central to the success of our endeavor is developing *modus operandi* to handle such differences.

And if relations are to be deeply rooted in our communities, then we must strive to clarify our respective beliefs, our respective pain, and our respective hopes.

Against that backdrop, what might a common agenda be for today that can bring the three faiths together, particularly on a global level?

Confronting Fundamentalism

Today as we look at the world scene, for almost all major religious faiths, including the Abrahamic faiths, we face a common struggle against fundamentalist extremism and extremists – those who are so sure of the exclusive rightness of their religious beliefs and of God's call to them that they are willing to impose their religious, political, and moral views on others, using force if necessary. This is a struggle that everyone knows well, and I need not expand upon it.

Let me focus instead on one of the most vexing challenges to finding a common response. I submit that the battle against fundamentalism cannot be won by forces from without but only from within each of the respective faith groups. The fascinating challenge as partners is: how then <u>can</u> we help each other and how can we work together?

For here is the paradox: whenever one faith group (or for that matter, a government such as a Western democratic government) tries to shape another, the very act of giving its stamp of approval (for example, giving support to open, tolerant, and moderate expressions of religious thinking) risks undermining those it seeks to help with the very people we would like them to win over. Since so much attention has been given in international affairs to Islam in this regard, let me use that as an example – although a similar analysis can be made to each of our faith communities. In the struggle between moderate and fundamentalist Islam when Christians or Jews offer support it is often perceived as support that is tied to Western colonialism and Western cultural, political and economic imperialism that many around the globe feel is represented by the worst aspects of globalism. This allows those whom we seek to support to be discredited and their influence on their public undermined. This is a difficult challenge, particularly when many of these struggles sit atop the crossroads of the clash of civilizations among political, economic, and cultural powers in which religion is often seen as a surrogate for these other struggles for influence and legitimacy.

Neither we in the religious communities nor democratic political leaders have been very sophisticated in our approach to seeking ways to help legitimize more moderate forms of religious expression. While we should all be respectful of the advice from the mainstream groups within other faith communities as to how much public support they want from other faith groups, there are things we can do beyond – and more effectively than – just publicly embracing more moderate voices with all the risks that creates.

First, we can fight against a cultural bias against moderate religious expression in the general culture. In contrast to the mid-century generations of Reinhold Neibuhr, John Courtney Murray, Stephen Wise, Abraham Joshua Heschel, and Martin Luther King, Jr. – a period when, from Morocco to Turkey and from Pakistan to Indonesia, moderate Muslim thinkers and politicians dominated religious and cultural discourse – there has evolved in our culture a bias that asserts that the more fundamentalist one is, the more religiously authentic and legitimate he or she is. This is asserted by fundamentalists, too often affirmed both by the media and through cultural representations, and too often acquiesced in by the theologically liberal segments of our respective religious communities.

Two generations ago that was not the case, and it need not be so in the next. This is an arena in which mapping out common strategies in a broad campaign to be far more assertive and confident in putting forth the richness, vibrancy, creativity, and legitimacy of the moderate streams of our traditions can benefit from thorough cooperation. I feel the keen irony that even as many of the more theologically conservative streams of our communities have recently rediscovered the core social justice agenda that has never been lost in our more moderate streams, there has been little shift in this equation of fundamentalism and authenticity. (Take the Jewish community. This is a particular paradox, since over the past 50 years, the Reform Jewish Movement, the most theologically (as well as politically and culturally) liberal stream of the community has been the fastest growing segment of the community, growing by leaps and bounds for a confluence of reasons. It is indeed the fastest growing theologically liberal denomination in America. Yet, this cultural defensiveness still permeates much of our own view of the Jewish community.) It is in our common interests to lift up to our communities, to the broader public, and to the media our influential liberal theologians and their ideas; we have to tell others of the successes of our moderate and liberal mosques, churches, and synagogues in meeting the educational, spiritual, and social justice questing of our members, and explain the richness of our religious lives that ensue.

Second, internationally, this mix of religion and geopolitics makes the stakes even higher and the challenge more difficult. But we do know a number of factors that can make a difference in strengthening moderate religious leaders and institutions. Among them: consistently calling extremism what it is; putting a human face on the violence done in the name of religion; ensuring the existence of non-violent effective political options to achieve the political goals of religious communities (the Israel-Palestinian conflict leaps to mind and economic and social programs needed to meet the needs of the community generally and of the younger generation more particularly); encouraging allies and intermediaries not directly associated with other religions to expand financial support for moderate religious voices, theologians, and civic leaders; providing technological training and internet infrastructure; promoting best practices; and strengthening civil society structures (independent courts, newspapers, labor unions, and so forth).

I would observe that the same is true for democratic governments. As one example, consider what would have been the impact seven years later if, immediately after 9/11, moderate Muslim nations had led an international effort to provide, with oversight and care, massive amounts of funding to develop a school system in Pakistan to compete with the *madrassas*?

We need strategies that seek to split factions within the fundamentalist communities. And we must never lose faith that true dialogue can change people, even religious ideologues. The goal of course is to aid moderate religious voices by helping them to promomte their ideas to the public at length. If the extremist elements in our society are the only ones developing civil society institutions then moderate voices have no chance of being heard. If terrorist organizations are the only institutions creating economic opportunities in Muslim nations then the youth have no alternative to these radical Islamic organizations. As stated in the United States Institute of Peace's August 2007 report entitled *Engaging Islamists and Promoting Democracy*, the success and appeal of Islamists worldwide is because they are brimming with energy and ideas and have "vast and easily mobilized grassroots networks through charitable organizations and mosques." Moderate voices therefore need to not only speak out with their voices, but with their hands as well; they must replicate the model used by Islamists worldwide.

Finally, when leaders engaged in such struggles do decide to reach publicly across religious lines for cooperation and dialogue, the other two communities must respond as vigorously as possible. Let me focus on four examples involving the Muslim community: each a success and failure. When the leaders of the Abrahamic faiths from the Middle East joined in 2002 in the Alexandria Declaration for Peace – a process facilitated by the Anglican Church – we all missed the opportunity to raise it up, build on it, and move the cooperative endeavor forward. We should have challenged every mosque, synagogue, and church across the globe to read the document from their pulpits, to study the document, and to use it as a basis of dialogue and discussion among us. We should have used that enterprise as a model of the ability of local clergy to produce similar statements on a range of issues. Instead we let this significant accomplishment languish.

So, too, recently when the Council of Religious Institutions of the Holy Land (comprised of the Israeli Chief Rabbi, the Patriarchs of the Christian Churches in the Holy Land, and key Muslim leaders including the head of the *Sharia* courts) established a series of goals for the Council to preempt conflict, work through differences, and promote mutual understanding (<http://www.elca.org/advocacy/issues/middleeast/07-11-07-communique. html>). In the context of the impending Annapolis talks (which took place November 2007), it conveyed a powerful religious message and common ground at a crucial time. It too provided a valuable framework that should have been used by Jewish, Christian, and Muslim institutions everywhere as the basis for dialogue and as a common voice on crucial issues.

The third is the letter to the Christian world released in Fall 2007 by 138 prominent Muslim leaders (<http://www.acommonword.com/lib/downloads/CW-Total-Final-v-12g-Eng-9-10-07.pdf>). It is a document that the entire world should read, and we all should have moved immediately to ensure it was distributed widely, that media reported on it, and that it was responded to with seriousness by a range of Christian and Jewish leaders and groups. There have been some thoughtful Christian responses, but that is a process that has only just begun. And while addressed to Christians primarily, the ISNA document is more replete with references to Jewish sacred texts than to the Christian New Testament, affording an opportunity for Jews to enter the conversation as well. (A similar letter, this one addressing the Jewish community, was released in February 2008.)

The fourth is the recent *Fatwa* repudiating and condemning without qualification that terrorism and religious extremism are antithetical to Islam (<http://www.isna.net/index.php?id=316>). This *Fatwa*, which uses sacred Muslim texts as its foundation, was published by the Fiqh Council of North America, a group of Islamic scholars affiliated with the Islamic Society of North America. Despite this important religious ruling by a religious body affiliated with the largest Islamic group in America, there was not one question asked about it when it was released at a recent event at the National Press Club, and few media outlets reported it. This was a remarkable missed opportunity. (This event occurred after the conference at which this essay was presented but while the print version was being edited.)

Over and again we hear: why can't prominent Muslim leadership publicly state the things they say privately? Here are such public affirmations, and we have not moved to take advantage of what they offer. It is not too late, but we must move to maximize the impact of this document.

I have focused on confronting Muslim extremism because it is a topic of immense interest in international efforts, but the Abrahamic communities can develop joint strategies to confront extremism in religious communities more broadly along similar lines.

Let me cite more briefly other areas in which we can map out common ground.

Secularism

We all have a common stake in responding to the challenge posed by secularism. The array of recent atheist attacks on religion is but a symbol of a broader challenge posed by powerful secular elements of Western culture.

Religious Freedom in the US

In 1990, the US Supreme Court came down with one of the worst decisions in American history for religious freedom. In *Oregon v. Smith*, the Court held that the strict test the Court had established for justifying government restrictions on religious freedom and on other first amendment rights would no longer be used for religious liberty claims. For the first time, Muslim groups joined other religious groups in a legislative campaign working to restore the strict test legislatively. When the Court struck that law down, it led to a patchwork quilt of advocacy efforts to enact laws and executive actions protecting religious freedom. This agenda will continue to provide fertile ground not only for legislative cooperation but as an agenda requiring that we learn each other's practices and beliefs.

Religious Persecution Around the Globe

In 1998, by a unanimous act of Congress, the International Religious Freedom Act (IRFA) was enacted, aimed at leveraging US influence to assist those who are victims of religious persecution across the globe. In the first decade, the mechanisms created by the legislation (the US Ambassador for Religious Freedom, the US Commission on International Religious Freedom, and the State Department's Annual Report on Religious Freedom) have all functioned to assist Muslims, Christians, and Falun Gong practitioners in China; Christians in Saudi Arabia and North Korea' Bahais and Jews in Iran; Buddhists in Burma: among scores of manifestations of efforts on behalf of religious freedom documented and responded to by this process. This provides a significant arena of cooperative endeavors for the Abrahamic faiths.

Strange Bedfellows – International Human Rights and Justice Issues

Each of the Abrahamic traditions holds positions supportive of human rights and social justice based on the notion that we are all created in the image of the Divine. In the US this took forceful political shape when a remarkable religious coalition made up of organizations that may seem to be strange bedfellows was built in part around the IRFA. This coalition of fundamentalist Evangelical Christian communities, the Catholic church, and the Reform Jewish community, with more occasional participation by mainline Protestant churches, Muslim groups, and the broader Jewish community provides a model for broader Abrahamic engagement on international human rights and justice issues. Over the past decade, these groups have worked together with remarkable effect on issues such as human trafficking, the passage of the Sudan Peace Act, Darfur, HIV-AIDS funding, North Korean human rights, and debt relief as well as on domestic issues such as prison rape laws. As a result of this advocacy, laws were passed, executive orders implemented, and funding levels skyrocketed.

Some of this required powerful international cooperation among the Abrahamic community and beyond. For anyone who wonders whether the religious communities of the world can still make a difference and work together effectively, no issue so dramatizes the impact of the religious community than the struggle for debt relief for the poorest nations of the world. For nearly two decades, academics identified the debt burden on the poorest nations as one of the greatest moral and practical dilemmas of the contemporary international order. But nothing happened. Then, as the turn of the millennium approached, the religious communities of Europe and North America, joined by others across the globe, began the Jubilee Campaign. Drawing on the biblical imagery of the restitution of property and the elimination of debt as the Jubilee's means of proclaiming liberty to all the inhabitants of the land, they mobilized a major international campaign that captured the attention of the media and politicians. The religious community's distinct approach was to put a human face on this catastrophe and convey that this debt is a form of bondage – impoverishing nations, diverting resources from nutrition, health care, education and sustainable development – depriving children and families of the most basic of human needs. Yet, it is an especially bitter bondage, for today's heavy chains of debt were yesterday's supposed ladders of development. Made in good faith, often with noble intentions, these debts were supposed to help these nations build infrastructure, develop financial resources, and get a leg up in international trade. But, politics, recession, and – in many cases – corruption intervened. These tools of development became the shackles of endless unpayable debt.

The religious communities' response was to say to policy makers: do as Moses demanded of Pharaoh and let these nations go. All these efforts helped lead to the historic 2000 agreement in Cologne in which developed nations committed $100 billion in debt relief to the world's poorest and most debt-ridden communities.

Global Climate Change

Perhaps the most intuitively religious of these great social issues of our day is the challenge to the environment. The National Religious Partnership for the Environment, a Christian–Jewish effort to forge a powerful religious voice on environmental issues, has spearheaded the effort. The potential of this undertaking is staggering, and the Muslim community shares our passion to protect God's creation. Think of it: in much of the world there are more houses of worship than any other public institution often more than libraries, hospitals, schools, and firehouses combined. In the US there are some 300–400,000 houses of worship. If every one of them engaged in a serious effort to conserve energy to recycle goods and purchase recycled goods to help clean up their neighborhoods and plant trees to speak out on environmental policy for their 140 million congregants, what a transformation of the environmental issue we would see!

As religious leaders, we know why we must be involved. As the Hebrew Scriptures asserted: *La'adonai ha'aretz um'loah* – "The Earth is the Eternal's and the Fullness thereof." What we own, we own in a trust relationship with God, requiring that we protect the corpus the body of the trust, that is, God's creation.

But the unprecedented urgency of today's crisis challenges our ability to apply our stewardship and conservation to those values and traditions to the world in which we dwell, a crisis whose complexities we only now are beginning to see.

Just at the very moment in human history when technology allows us to see with clarity, wonder, and awe how precious is God's creation, we are suddenly confronted by startling evidence of its peril. And of damage already being wrought by our own hands, by our ignorance, and by our indifference, affecting all of us, indiscriminately: global warming, ozone depletion, the escalating eradication of entire species of life, destruction of our rainforests, runaway world population. The population of the world doubled between the year 1 and the year 1200. Today, it is doubling once every 40 years.

The *Midrash* (Jewish commentaries on Scripture) recounts: In the hour when God created the first human, God brought the human before all the trees of the Garden of Eden and said, "See my works, how fine and excellent they are! Now all that I have created, for you have I created it. Think about this and do not corrupt and desolate my world – for if you destroy it, there will be no one after you to set it right again" (*Eccles. Rabbah*).

The task of our religious faiths is to ensure that God's mandate is heard today by all humanity. For this Earth is our garden, and this time we face not expulsion, but devastation. And that we cannot – we dare not – allow, neither for our children's sake, nor for God's.

These are just a few of the array of moral issues confronting the world on which cooperation could flow easily. Hate crimes, prison reform, primary and secondary school education reform, efforts to stamp out diseases, and struggles against racism, all represent a sampling of other areas where ongoing cooperation between our faith groups is making a significant positive impact.

Summary

Dr. King said in his remarkable Riverside Church speech on Vietnam:

> We are now faced with the fact, my friends, that tomorrow is today. We are confronted with the fierce urgency of now. . . . Procrastination is still the thief of time. Life often leaves us standing bare, naked, and dejected with a lost opportunity. . . . Over the bleached bones and jumbled residues of numerous civilizations are written the pathetic words, "Too late."

This sense of urgency should animate the theme of this volume on the meeting of civilizations – Muslim, Christian, and Jewish. Never before has our world needed to hear more clearly the values of human dignity, charity, societal justice, and peace that are common to the three Abrahamic faiths more than it does today. And never before has the potential for our cooperative enterprise been more compelling than it is today. Out of this conference one theme should resound: We are not the prisoners of a bitter and unremitting past but, rather, together we can be the shapers of a better and more hopeful future for all God's children. And that – Muslim, Christian, and Jew alike – we can all embrace and affirm.

16

Health and Science: Win–Win Modalities Towards Brotherhood

RICHARD J. DECKELBAUM

According to *Webster's* dictionary, health can be defined as "the condition of an organism, or one of its parts, in which it performs its vital functions normally or properly," and science is defined as "a possession of knowledge as distinguished from ignorance or misunderstanding." "An hour's study of nature is better than a year's prayer," declared the Prophet as quoted in a commentary by Ziauddin Sardar in the July 12, 2007 issue of *Nature*. Thus, science and health, along with parallel studies in science and health, have historically been associated with improvements in the intellectual, as well as, physical, aspects of being.

Scholars from Islam, Judaism, and Christianity have long interacted closely and favorably in improving human health, mutual understanding, and advancement of society. When Galen, 129–216 was born in Pergamum, Mysia (now Bergama, Turkey) the Children of Abraham were not established as such. However, Galen's, impressive body of works, when translated, are viewed as a template for Islamic medicine and he is revered in the Middle East as "Jalinos." Both Avicenna and Vesalius (see below) were not only heavily influenced by Galen's writings, form, methods, and outlook; they were also spurred on to test his theories and conclusions following his very dictates on identification and curing of illness, on detailed investigations of the body, and on experimentation. This led to further developments in medicine and science. Galen was truly the forefather of the great physicians, scientists, and thinkers of the Children of Abraham. Just as his contributions influenced the rise and spread of Islamic medicine in the Arab empire, so did the Muslim contributions mingle with those of the Jewish physicians, philosophers, and scientists, which in turn impacted the later developments in western, or Christian, medicine and science.

Many examples exist of contributions from individuals from each religion.

Abd Allah Ibn Sina, or Avicenna (980–1037), may be regarded as the father of modern medicine. Avicenna was a physician, philosopher, polymath, astronomer, chemist, scientist, poet, soldier, theologian, and statesman. He wrote over 450 works, the most famous being *The Canon of Medicine*, which was the standard university medical text both for eastern and western civilizations until the 18th century. As an example of just one of his contributions, he discovered the contagious nature of infectious diseases, and introduced quarantining. He introduced clinical trials and wrote the first description of bacteria and viruses. According to Sarton, he is "one of the greatest thinkers and medical scholars in history . . . the most famous scientist of Islam and one of the most famous of all races, places, and times." About the same time, Abu al-Qasim ibn Al-Zahrawi (936–1013), also known as Abulcasis, emerged as the "father of modern surgery" and was regarded as Islam's greatest medieval *surgeon*. He wrote a thirty-volume encyclopedia of medical practices, *Kitab al-Tasrif*, which served as the primary source of European medical knowledge for 500 years. He emphasized treating patients regardless of their social status and he invented surgical devices. He was the first to describe how to ligate blood vessels.

Moshe ben Maimon or "Maimonides" (1135–1204) was a rabbi, philosopher, and physician. Author of the *Mishneh Torah* written in Hebrew, Maimonides also penned medical texts and treatises in Arabic. He was head of the Egyptian Jewish community and an early advocate of preventative medicine. To my knowledge, he was the first to promote the healing power of chicken soup and used his poultry broth primarily to treat respiratory illnesses and inflammation as well as to treat other conditions including hemorrhoids, constipation, and leprosy! Christian scholars contributed somewhat later as exemplified by Andreas Vesalius, "the Humanist" (1514–1564), who was an author, an anatomist, and a physician. He is considered the founder of modern human anatomy and was the author of *On the Workings of the Human Body*. This included many of the first and numerous detailed anatomical drawings. Vesalius regarded humanism as the rebirth of truth and perfection.

Health nutrition programs are not only human-effective but also cost-effective. For example, it has been estimated in terms of benefit/cost ratios (in dollar terms) that breast feeding promotion in hospitals and integrated child-care programs show benefit/cost of 5/67 and 9/16, respectively. Iodine supplementation in women has a benefit/cost ratio of 15/520, and iron fortification, 176/200.

In terms of populations of the children of Abraham, we can consider a number of barriers that currently exist to scientific and medical advancements. These include inequalities of infrastructure, trained personnel, scientific research support, access to health service and unequal health budgets in different religious and cultural geographic settings. Political restrictions also exist which bar free scientific thinking and even collaborations between investigators, scientists, physicians, and health professionals from different religions within the same geographic location. There are security and safety concerns for some of the individuals who participate in collaborative programs during times of political and security conflict. Mistrust among the different religions transfers as well into science and medicine.

Nevertheless, there are strong examples of success in health and science programs in the Middle East. Arab scientists and physicians have collaborated with Israeli counterparts closely over the last two decades following a period of prolonged separation as a result of the 1948 war involving multiple parties in the Middle East. Numerous collaborative projects resulted after the Israel–Egypt peace agreement initiated by President Anwar Sadat's visit to Prime Minister Menachem Begin in Israel. I was personally involved in collaborative projects between physicians and scientists from Egypt, Israel, and the West Bank and Gaza relating to malnutrition, persistent diarrhea, intestinal parasites, as well as studies on the impact of various hepatitis viruses in the different populations. These programs led to health interventions, which improved the status of the populations in all population groups. The Medical School for International Health was established as a collaboration between Ben-Gurion University of the Negev and Columbia University Medical Center as a distinct medical program aiming to educate medical students to become physicians in the classic sense, i.e., being able to treat pneumonia, sore throats, and other common medical conditions, but also to be able to obtain the skills, attitude, and knowledge necessary for improving the health of whole populations whether in developed or developing country settings. This school is open to students of all religions, and indeed, the cohorts' different classes have brought all religions together as they pursue the study of global health in medicine. A recent RAND report on strengthening the Palestinian health care system stressed not only Palestinian health, but how this can be improved upon by interaction with neighboring populations of different religious backgrounds. Programs now are being planned for improving health conditions for all people in the Middle East region involving institutions from Arab, Jewish, and Christian backgrounds.

What are the immediate and future needs for improving interactions in health and science? These include building equality in the areas of scientific discovery and health. It will be necessary to maintain open doors and trust during times of mistrust and conflict. Indeed, throughout history in general and the history of science and medicine, conflict and mistrust have never been absent. Maimonides was forced to flee Cordova because of persecution against the Jewish population. The Inquisition tortured, killed and exiled philosophers, scientists, and physicians, among thousands of others. Muslims have long been considered "infidels" and their culture, history and scientific achievements ignored.

There is a major need to address emerging health and education problems in terms of both physical as well as mental health. Increased funding for training, services, research, and infrastructure for science and health are required for areas populated by the children of Abraham. As we move forward, we need to consider what the costs of doing nothing are. In addition, we need to realize that "human life is much more than the sum total of all our mistakes" (Sari Nusseibah, *Once Upon a Country*, 2007).

One needs to consider that populations will rapidly feel and appreciate the benefits of improved health and access to health services. These can be achieved in a relatively short period. Periods of a few months or even within a year or two will allow the children of Abraham to realize that cooperation and interaction offer much more positive outcomes than conflict, battles, and wars. Moving ahead, the Children of Abraham need to think of things that can go right, and actually do them.

Acknowledgment

The contributions of Ms. Mary Lou Westberg for her researching, editing, and providing material for this essay are greatly appreciated.

The Contributors

Mustafa Abu Sway is Associate Professor of Philosophy and Islamic Studies, and Director, Islamic Research Center at Al-Quds University in Jerusalem/Palestine. He graduated from Bethlehem University (BA, 1984), Boston College (MA, 1985 and Ph.D., 1993). Dr. Abu Sway taught at the International Islamic University–Malaysia (1993–96), and has been at Al-Quds University since 1996. He was also a visiting Fulbright Scholar-in-Residence at Wilkes Honors College/Florida Atlantic University (2003–4). He is one of the winners, along with Dr. Khaled Salem from Al-Quds University, of the Science and Religion Course Award, 2001, The Center for Theology and the Natural Sciences, Berkeley, CA. He has published two books: *Islamic Epistemology: The Case of Al-Ghazzali* (Dewan Bahasa dan Pustaka, 1995), and *Fatawa Al-Ghazzali* (International Institute of Islamic Thought and Civilization, 1996). He also co-authored the *Islamic Education Textbook* (7th Grade) (2001), and the *Islamic Education Textbook* (11th Grade, vol. 1) (2005) for the Palestinian Ministry of Education. Dr. Abu Sway has been active in interfaith dialogue for many years. He contributed a paper, "Ibrahim in the Islamic Scriptures," to *Abraham in the Three Monotheistic Faiths* (PASSIA, 1998), and "Prophet Moses: The Islamic Narrative" to *Moses in the Three Monotheistic Faiths* (PASSIA, 2003).

Azyumardi Azra is Professor of History and Director of Graduate School Syarif Hidayatullah State Islamic University, Jakarta, Indonesia. He was rector of this university for two terms (1998–2002 and 2002–2006). He earned his MA and Ph.D. degree in history from Columbia University (1992) with the dissertation "The Transmission of Islamic Reformism to Indonesia: Networks of Middle Eastern and Malay-Indonesian 'Ulama' in the 17th and 18th Centuries." In May 2005 he was awarded Doctoral Degree *Honoris Causa* in *Humane Letters* from Carroll College, Montana, USA. He is a Honorary Professorial Fellow, University of Melbourne, Australia (2004–9); and a member of Board of Trustees, International Islamic University, Islamabad, Pakistan (2004–9). He is also a member of Indonesia Academy of Sciences (2006–on); and Indonesian Council of National Research (2006–on).

Prof. Azra is a member of advisory board of a number of international institutions such as the Multi-Faith Centre, Griffith University, Brisbane, Australia (2005–9); the US Institute of Global Ethics (2004–on); Center for the Study of Contemporary Islam, University of Melbourne (2005–9); the UN Democracy Fund (UNDEF, New York, 2006–8); LibforAll (2006–on); and

Asian Muslim Acton Network (AMAN, Bangkok 2004–present); International Institute for Democracy and Electoral Assistance (IDEA, Stockholm 2007–2009). He is also member of the Tripartite Forum [governments, UN offices and Civil Society organizations] for Interfaith Cooperation for Peace, Development and Human Dignity, launched at the UN in New York on March 24, 2006; External Evaluator of the Institute for the Study of Muslim Culture (ISMC, London, 2006–9); and head of Indonesian members in United Kingdom–Indonesian Islamic Advisory Group, formed by Indonesian President Susilo Bambang Yudhoyono and British Prime Minister Tony Blair in March 2006.

In addition, he is editor-in-chief of *Studia Islamika: Indonesian Journal for Islamic Studies* (1994–present); advisory board of *Journal of Qur'anic Studies* (SOAS, London), and *Journal of Usuluddin* (Universiti Malaya, Kuala Lumpur).

He has been an international visiting fellow at Oxford University, University of Philippines, New York University, Columbia University, University of Melbourne and many other universities. He regularly presents papers on various topics at national and international conferences.

He has published 19 books and numerous chapters in internationally edited books; his latest books are *The Origins of Islamic Reformism in Southeast Asia*, Crows Nest (Australia: Asian Studies Association of Australia and Allen & Unwin; Honolulu: University of Hawaii Press); Leiden: KITLV Press, 2004; *Dari Harvard hingga Makkah* [From Harvard to Mecca] (Jakarta: Republika, 2004); *Indonesia, Islam and Democracy* (Jakarta & Singapore: ICIP & Equinox, 2006); *Indonesian Islam: An Account of Institutional Development* (Bandung: Mizan, 2007); and *Jejak-jejak Jaringan Kaum Muslim* [Traces of Muslim Networks] (Jakarta: Hikmah, 2007).

In 2005 he was awarded The Asia Foundation Award in conjunction with its 50th anniversary for his significant contribution to the reforms of Islamic education. And in conjunction with the anniversary of Indonesian independence, on August 15, 2005, he was awarded the Bintang Mahaputra Utama – the highest star awarded to a civilian – by the President of the Republic of Indonesia, Susilo Bambang Yudhoyono, for his contribution to the promotion of moderate and peaceful Islam.

Benjamin Braude is Associate Professor of History and Co-director of the Program in Middle Eastern and Islamic Studies at Boston College. His BA, MA and Ph.D. are from Harvard. As a visiting professor he has taught at the École des hautes études en sciences sociales (EHSS) in Paris, Universidad Complutensa de Madrid, Smith College, and Harvard University. He has also been a visiting fellow at Princeton University and the Institute for Advanced Studies, Hebrew University, Jerusalem. The co-edited *Christians and Jews in the Ottoman Empire, The Functioning of a Plural Society* and *Essays on Aggadah and Judaica*, are two of his works. His articles on the relations between Jews, Christians, and Muslims and ethnic identities have appeared in *Annales,* the *William and Mary Quarterly,* and the UNESCO *History of Humanity Scientific and Cultural Development,* among other publications. Now he is completing two related works on Noah in the Abrahamic tradition, Sex in the Sistine Chapel: the Mysteries of Michelangelo's Noah, and Sex, Slavery and Racism: The Secret History of the Sons of Noah.

Mark R. Cohen, the well-known historian of the Jews in Arab lands in the Middle Ages, is Professor of Near Eastern Studies at Princeton University. His books include: *Jewish Self-Government in Medieval Egypt; Al-mujtama' al-yahudi fi Misr al-islamiyya fi al-'usur al-wusta; The Autobiography of a Seventeenth-Century Venetian Rabbi; Leon Modena's Life of Judah; Under Crescent and Cross: The Jews in the Middle Ages,* which has been translated into Hebrew, Turkish, German, and Arabic; *Poverty and Charity in the Jewish Community of Medieval Europe;* and *The Voice of the Poor in the Middle Ages: An Anthology of Documents from the Cairo Geniza.* Cohen has held Fellowships or has taught as a visiting professor at the Hebrew University of Jerusalem; its Institute for Advanced Studies; Ain Shams University in Cairo; the Free University in Berlin; the Guggenheim Foundation; the Central European University in Budapest; the Wissenschaftskolleg in Berlin; and the National Endowment for the Humanities. He has lectured widely in the US, Europe, Israel, Japan, Qatar, and Egypt, before both scholarly and general audiences

Harvey Cox, Hollis Professor of Divinity, has been teaching in the Faculty of Arts and Sciences and the Divinity School at Harvard since 1965. Author of *The Secular City* and other books, he specializes in the interaction of religion, politics and culture. For several years he has taught a course on Jerusalem (where he has lectured at Christian, Jewish and interfaith institutions), as a test case of inter-religious conflict and cooperation. He now teaches a course on "Religion and Politics in Current 'Fundamentalist' Movements."

Diane E. Davis is Professor of Political Sociology in the Department of Urban Studies and, until July 2007, was associate dean of the School of Architecture and Planning at MIT. Editor of the research annual *Political Power and Social Theory,* Davis is also co-director the DUSP–MIT Project called *Just Jerusalem: Visions for a Place of Peace.* She is the author of *Urban Leviathan: Mexico City in the Twentieth Century* (Temple University Press 1994; Spanish translation 1999), and *Discipline and Development: Middle Classes and Prosperity in East Asia and Latin America* (Cambridge University Press, 2004) as well as co-editor of *Irregular Armed Forces and their Role in Politics and State Formation* (Cambridge University Press, 2003). Her research interests include local governance in the developing world, leftist mayors, urban political economy, and the politics of urban policy in cities in conflict. Current research focuses on the social, spatial, and political transformations of cities of the developing world as a consequence of globalization, police impunity, and illegal commerce and trade. She is completing a manuscript titled *Policing Transitions* that examines the tensions between public and private police in the developing world.

Richard Deckelbaum received a B.Sc. and M.D. from McGill University. He directs the Institute of Human Nutrition at Columbia University. In addition to a long professional involvement with basic research in the cell biology of lipids and issues of human nutrition, he has also been active in translating basic science findings to practical application in different populations. He has chaired taskforces for the American Heart Association, the March of Dimes, and has served advisory committees of the National Institutes of Health, the RAND Corporation, and the Institute of Medicine of the National Academy of Sciences. Early in his medical career he helped establish the first children's hospital in the West Bank of Jordan and then continued later to organize research programs among Egyptian, Palestinian, and Israeli populations – projects funded by the United States Agency for International Development and the National Institutes of Health. He founded the Medical School for International Health, a collaborative distinct medical school of Ben-Gurion University of the Negev and Columbia University. Currently, he continues in projects related to health and science as a bridge between different populations in the Mideast.

Reuven Firestone is Professor of Medieval Judaism and Islam at Hebrew Union College in Los Angeles. His books include *Journeys in Holy Lands: The Evolution of the Abraham–Ishmael Legends in Islamic Exegesis* (SUNY Press), *Jihad: The Origin of Holy War in Islam* (Oxford University Press), *Children of Abraham: An Introduction to Judaism for Muslims* (Ktav), *Jews, Christians, Muslims in Dialogue: A Practical Handbook*, with Leonard Swidler and Khalid Duran (New London, CT: Twenty-Third Publications, 2007), *An Introduction to Islam for Jews* (JPS, forthcoming), and is currently writing *The Revival of Holy War in Modern Judaism* (forthcoming). His articles appear in *The Journal of Semitic Studies, The Journal of Near Eastern Studies, The Journal of Religious Ethics, The Journal of the American Academy of Religion, The Journal of Jewish Studies, Jewish Quarterly Review, Judaism, Studia Islamica, The Muslim World, The Journal of Ecumenical Studies, The Encyclopaedia of Islam, The Encyclopaedia of the Qur'an*, and the *Encyclopedia of Religion*.

Nathan C. Funk (Ph.D., American University, 2000) is Assistant Professor of Peace and Conflict Studies at the University of Waterloo's Conrad Grebel University College, with previous appointments at American University and George Washington University. His writings on international conflict resolution and the role of cultural and religious factors in peacemaking include two co-edited volumes, *Peace and Conflict Resolution in Islam* (2001) and *Ameen*

Rihani: Bridging East and West (2004), and the forthcoming book, *Making Peace with Islam* (2008). His doctoral dissertation focused on the role of unofficial dialogue in Middle East peacemaking efforts. He has lived in the Middle East and South Asia, designed internet courses on peace and conflict resolution, and contributed to research and training projects at the United States Institute of Peace.

Mohamed Hawary is a faculty member at Ain Shams University, Cairo, where he completed his dissertation in 1983 on *The Divinity Among the Children of Israel from the Period of Moses until the Exile of Babylon.* He is Director of the Center for Study of Contemporary Civilizations (CSCC), Ain Shams University, and Professor of Religious Jewish Thought and Comparative Religions, Department of Hebrew Studies, Faculty of Arts, Ain Shams University, Cairo, Egypt. Among his publications are: *Circumcision in Judaism, Christianity and Islam, Comparative Religions* (in Arabic), (Cairo, 1987); *Sabbath and Friday in Judaism and Islam, Comparative Religions* (in Arabic), (Cairo, 1988); *Fasting in Judaism, Comparative Study* (in Arabic), (Cairo, 1988); *Commentary on the Ten Commandments in the Judaeo-Arabic Manuscripts* (in Arabic), (Cairo, 1993); *The Differences Between the Karaites and the Rabbanites in Light of the Cairo Genizah* (in Arabic), (Cairo, 1994); *Jewish Polemics Against Christianity in Light of the Cairo Genizah* (in Arabic), (Cairo, 1994); *Medical Vocabulary for the Cairo Genizah* (in Arabic), 1994.

Yehezkel Landau is Faculty Associate in Interfaith Relations at Hartford Seminary, a position underwritten by the Henry Luce Foundation. After earning an A.B. from Harvard University (1971) and an M.T.S. from Harvard Divinity School (1976), Landau made *aliyah* (immigrated) to Israel in 1978. A dual Israeli–American citizen, his work has been in the fields of interfaith education and Jewish–Arab peacemaking. He directed the Oz veShalom-Netivot Shalom religious Zionist peace movement in Israel during the 1980s. From 1991 to 2003, he was co-founder and co-director of the Open House Center for Jewish–Arab Co-existence in Ramle, Israel. (See the website <www.friendsofopenhouse.org>). He lectures internationally on Jewish–Christian–Muslim relations and Middle East peace issues, has authored numerous journal articles, co-edited the book *Voices from Jerusalem: Jews and Christians Reflect on the Holy Land* (Paulist Press, 1992), wrote a Jewish appraisal of Pope John Paul II's trip to Israel and Palestine in 2000 for the book *John Paul in the Holy Land: In His Own Words* (Paulist Press, 2005), and authored a research report entitled "Healing the Holy Land: Interreligious Peacebuilding in Israel/Palestine" (United States Institute of Peace, Sept. 2003, accessible at <www.usip.org/reports>). At Hartford Seminary, Prof. Landau coordinates an interfaith training program for Jews, Christians, and Muslims called "Building Abrahamic Partnerships" (see <www.hartsem.edu or e-mail ylandau@hartsem.edu>).

Moshe Ma'oz is Professor Emeritus of Islamic and Middle Eastern Studies at Hebrew University, Jerusalem; Visiting Scholar at WCFIA, Harvard University. His BA and MA are from Hebrew University and D.Phil. from Oxford University. He was a visiting professor and fellow at many universities and research institutes. Prof. Ma'oz has published widely on political and social history of the modern Middle East, notably Syria, Palestine, Arab–Israeli relations, as well as religious and ethnic communities. He has participated in many Israeli–Palestinian dialogues and, for many years, headed the Truman Institute for the Advancement of Peace, Hebrew University. He now works on Muslim attitudes to Jews and Israel.

Elie Podeh is an Associate Professor, Head of the Department of Islam and Middle East Studies, the Hebrew University of Jerusalem; editor of *The New East* (Hamizrah Hehadash) – the Hebrew journal of the Middle East and Islamic Studies Association of Israel (MEISAI); and senior research fellow at the Harry S. Truman Institute for the Advancement of Peace. He has published several books and articles on inter-Arab relations, the Arab–Israeli conflict and education. Among his publications: *The Quest for Hegemony in the Arab World: The Struggle Over the 8aghdad Pact* (1995); *The Decline of Arab Unity: The Rise and Fall of the United Arab Republic* (1999); *The Arab–Israeli Conflict in Israeli History Textbooks, 1948–2000* (2002; Arabic version, 2006); *Rethinking Nasserism: Revolution and Historical Memory in Modern Egypt* (edited with Onn Winckler, 2004); *Arab–Jewish Relations: From Conflict to Resolution? Essays in Honor of Professor Moshe Ma'oz* (edited with Asher Kaufman, 2006); and *Britain and the Middle East: From Imperial Power to Junior Partner* (edited with Zach Levey). His current research deals with the ways in which the Arab states celebrate and commemorate their national holidays.

Abdul Aziz Said is the senior ranking professor at the American University, Washington DC, and the current occupant of the Mohammed Said Farsi Chair of Islamic Peace. He founded the International Peace and Conflict Resolution Program at American University, currently directs the American University Center for Global Peace, and serves on the board of directors of Global Education Associates, International Center for Religion and Diplomacy, IREX, Jones International University–University of the Web, and Search for Common Ground. Professor Said is a frequent lecturer and participant in national and international peace conferences. He has been a consultant to the US Department of State, the Department of Defense, the United Nations, and the White House Committee on the Islamic World. Dr. Said has written, co-authored, and edited eighteen books, most recently, *Making Peace with Islam* (Lynne Rienner Publishers) and *Contemporary Islam: Dynamic, Not Static* (Routledge, August 2006).

Rabbi David Saperstein, the Director of the Religious Action Center of

Reform Judaism, heads the social justice and public policy arm of the largest segment of American Jewry, the national Reform Jewish Movement. Currently the longest serving representative to Congress and the administration of a national faith group or denomination in Washington, during his 33 years as director of the Center he has headed several national religious coalitions and serves on the boards of numerous national organizations including the NAACP, People for the American Way, Leadership Conference on Civil Rights, and the National Religious Partnership on the Environment. In 1999, Rabbi Saperstein was elected as the first Chair of the US Commission on International Religious Freedom, created by a unanimous vote of Congress.

Also an attorney, Rabbi Saperstein teaches seminars in both First Amendment Church–State Law and in Jewish Law at Georgetown University Law School. A prolific writer and speaker, Rabbi Saperstein has appeared on most major television and radio news and talk shows. His articles have appeared in the *Washington Post, The New York Times,* and the *Harvard Law Review.* His latest book is *Jewish Dimensions of Social Justice: Tough Moral Choices of Our Time.*

Rabbi Saperstein is married to Ellen Weiss, Vice President for News of National Public Radio. They have two sons, Daniel and Ari.

Muhammad Shafiq is a visiting professor of Islamic and Religious Studies in the Department of Religion, Nazareth College, Rochester, NY. He is Executive Director and a founding member of the Center for Interfaith Studies and Dialogue (CISD), <www.naz.edu/dept/cisd>. He is a member of the Rochester Interfaith Forum and a founding member and current chair of the Muslim–Catholic Alliance of Rochester. He is also Executive Director/Imam of the Islamic Center of Rochester. Born in Karak, Pakistan, he received an Islamic as well as Western education. He graduated from Peshawar University with an MA in Islamic Studies (1394/1974). He was awarded the Presidential Gold Medal Award, and in (1396/1976) Pakistan's Quaid-i-Azam merit scholarship for higher studies. Shafiq studied at Temple University under Isma'il Raji al Faruqi. He completed his MA and Ph.D. in Religion at Temple. He was awarded a Fulbright post-doctoral fellowship in (1408/1988) to conduct research on Isma'il al Faruqi's thought. Afterward, he served as professor and chair of the Islamic studies department at Peshawar University until 1997. Shafiq has published over forty articles and several books, among them: *Interfaith Dialogue: A Guide for Muslims* (co-author); *Islamic Concept of Modern State: A Case Study of Pakistan*; *Growth of Islamic Thought in North America*; *Islamic Da' wa* (The Call).

Index